TRANSNATIONAL FEMINIST ITINERARIES

NEXT WAVE NEW DIRECTIONS IN WOMEN'S STUDIES *A series edited by* Inderpal Grewal, Caren Kaplan, *and* Robyn Wiegman

TRANSNATIONAL

Situating Theory **FEMINIST**

ITINERARIES

and Activist Practice

Edited by ASHWINI TAMBE and MILLIE THAYER

DUKE UNIVERSITY PRESS DURHAM AND LONDON 2021

© 2021 DUKE UNIVERSITY PRESS
All rights reserved
Printed in the United States of America on acid-free paper ∞
Project editor: Lisa Lawley
Designed by Aimee C. Harrison
Typeset in Minion Pro and ITC Franklin Gothic
by Westchester Publishing Services

Library of Congress Cataloging-in-Publication Data
Names: Tambe, Ashwini, editor. | Thayer, Millie, editor.
Title: Transnational feminist itineraries : situating theory and
activist practice / Ashwini Tambe and Millie Thayer, eds.
Other titles: Next wave (Duke University Press)
Description: Durham : Duke University Press, 2021. | Series:
Next wave | Includes bibliographical references and index.
Identifiers: LCCN 2020051607 (print)
LCCN 2020051608 (ebook)
ISBN 9781478013549 (hardcover)
ISBN 9781478014430 (paperback)
ISBN 9781478021735 (ebook)
Subjects: LCSH: Feminist theory. | Transnationalism. | National-
ism and feminism. | Intersectionality (Sociology)
Classification: LCC HQ1190 .T739 2021 (print) | LCC HQ1190
(ebook) | DDC 305.42—dc23
LC record available at https://lccn.loc.gov/2020051607
LC ebook record available at https://lccn.loc.gov/2020051608

Cover art: Péju Alatise, *The Rapture of Olurombi's
Daughter*, 2013. Mixed media textile. © Péju Alatise.
Courtesy Sulger-Buel Gallery.

TO CLAIRE MOSES, who brought us together
and whose work has built lasting solidarities across feminist fields

EDITED VOLUMES are an underappreciated form of scholarship. They are enormously time-consuming and require tact, patience, and stamina, but they also spark deeply meaningful intellectual collaboration. Mysteriously, they don't get the credit they deserve in current academic hierarchies. Some of the most influential texts shaping our feminist academic formation have been edited volumes, and we are humbled and delighted to be in a position to continue the genre.

Many people helped us in bringing out this volume. First, we offer profound thanks to all the participants in the "Whither Transnational Feminisms?" panels at the 2017 Women's Worlds Conference in Florianópolis for their contributions to our enormously generative conversations, as well as for the hard work and creativity of the conference organizers who brought together so many feminist scholars and activists from around the world.

The process of putting together the book required many hands and minds. Our authors' enthusiasm and consistent attention were indispensable to the project and to keeping our spirits high. They responded with promptness and good humor to several rounds of queries, and most importantly, their ideas sparked wonderful conversations among us. We give deepest thanks to our research assistants for their behind-the-scenes labor: Anna Storti for her help leading up to the initial submission in the fall of 2018; Cara Snyder for her efforts in putting together the revised manuscript in the fall of 2019, as well as for her earlier translations of conference abstracts into Portuguese; and Clara Montague for her work from 2020 to 2021 on the often-maddening details of a final manuscript, including configuring image files, checking footnotes, assembling the bibliography, and creating an index. To have the assistance of such sharp and experienced minds was our privilege.

Staff at *Feminist Studies* made valuable contributions as well. Thanks to Brittany Fremaux for her help at various stages in imagining the relationship between the journal and this edited volume and to Karla Mantilla for being such an expert at keeping things humming at the journal. The journals *Feminist Studies* and *International Journal of Politics, Culture, and Society* both deserve our thanks for their permission to reprint segments of previously published articles. The articles are Christine Keating and Amy Lind, "Plural Sovereignty and the Diverse Family in Ecuador's 2008 Constitution," *Feminist Studies* 43, no. 2 (2017): 291–313; Kathryn Moeller, "Searching for Adolescent Girls in Brazil: The Transnational Politics of Poverty in 'The Girl Effect,'" *Feminist Studies* 40, no. 3 (2014): 575–601; and Srila Roy, "Women's Movements in the Global South: Towards a Scalar Analysis," *International Journal of Politics, Culture, and Society* 29, no. 3 (2016): 289–306.

We also acknowledge the generosity of Sonia Alvarez and Claudia de Lima Costa, who served as discussants at the Florianópolis conference, and we appreciate the provocative participation of audience members such as Clare Hemmings and Manisha Desai. We'd especially like to thank the anonymous Duke University Press reviewers for their discerning critiques and extraordinarily useful suggestions. Thanks also to Duke's senior executive editor, Ken Wissoker, for being so perceptive, encouraging, and gracious throughout. Ryan Kendall, Joshua Tranen, Lisa Lawley, Aimee Harrison, the other staff at the press, and our copyeditor, Kim Miller, have provided outstanding support. Finally, profuse thanks to Péju Alatise for granting permission to use her inspirational work on the cover of the book.

Ashwini Tambe would like to thank Millie Thayer for being an incredible coauthor and coeditor. Every moment of their collaboration felt to her like a gift and a joy, from that hot summer day in 2016 when they wondered over the phone whether they could convene a gathering of transnational feminist scholars in Florianópolis, Brazil, to the subsequent juggling of time zones in order to speak and write together across continents to the many miles of tracked comments and email exchanges about words and sentences they wanted to get just right. She would like to also thank her University of Maryland writing group colleagues Holly Brewer, Jessica Enoch, Kristy Maddux, and Laura Rosenthal for their astute comments on the ideas in chapter 1 and suggestions for its structure. She also appreciated discussing chapter 1 with students in her University of Maryland graduate seminar on feminist theory and social movements. She thanks staff members Catalina Toala, Wendy Hall, and Jacqueline Adams for facilitating the hiring of graduate research assistants. Finally, she feels lucky to have benefited from Claire Moses's savvy mentorship and Priti Ramamurthy's modeling of how to stay sharp and grounded at all times.

Millie Thayer feels deeply grateful for the chance to work with Ashwini Tambe on this project, which brought together so many of their shared intellectual and activist commitments. Writing with Ashwini felt like a guilty pleasure, something to look forward to, and their many exchanges expanded her understanding of both transnational feminism and enduring friendship. Her thanks also go to those who have helped shape her conceptions of transnationalism and social movements over the years: colleagues Isabel Casimiro and Carla Braga at Universidade Eduardo Mondlane in Mozambique; Evelina Dagnino and Luciana Tatagiba at the Universidade Estadual de Campinas in Brazil; and Sonia Alvarez, Kiran Asher, Rebecca Dingo, Agustin Lao-Montes, and Joya Misra, among many others, at the University of Massachusetts, Amherst. Most especially, she is indebted to the many feminist and women's rights activists in Brazil and Mozambique who have shared their hopes and struggles with her. During 2018, as she worked on the book from Mozambique, her work was supported by a grant from the Fulbright Foundation; in spring 2019, a Research Development Award from the School of Social and Behavioral Sciences at the University of Massachusetts Amherst allowed her to dedicate some of her time to completing the book.

Introduction

ASHWINI TAMBE & MILLIE THAYER

WE PUT THE FINISHING TOUCHES on this book during a moment of re-markable civil protest against anti-Black violence. The unprecedented scale of multiracial public demonstrations across large cities and rural areas in the United States revealed a swell in support for dismantling systemic racism. Quite rapidly, it became clear that this was not solely a national-level reckoning; around the globe, across six continents, hundreds of thousands gathered in public rallies against racism.[1] Many of the solidarity practices reminded us of a mode of cross-border connection that transnational feminists have long upheld: one that forges alliances based on common analytic goals rather than similarity of identities. These protests beyond the United States were not a simple mimicry of the US cause, even though many protesters held up "Black Lives Matter" signs. They were self-reflexive in nature, turning the spotlight on very local problems: in Auckland, New Zealand, protesters focused on the brutal policing of Maori and Pacific islanders (Perrigo 2020); protesters in Jalisco, Mexico, focused on the police killing of bricklayer Giovanni Lopez Ramirez (McDonnell and Linthicum 2020); French protesters in Paris focused on the 2016 death of Malian immigrant Adama Traore in police custody (Godin and Douah 2020); and a statement by FeministsIndia (2020), a 750-strong online collective, highlighted the Indian state's violence against Dalits and Muslims. They exemplified for us a transnational solidarity that presumes differences between varied locations rather than claiming sameness.

These protests also took place amid the raging COVID-19 pandemic, an experience that has underscored a sense of connectedness across hierarchies of geopolitics: no part of the world is immune to this virus. Indeed, the health and economic ravages of the pandemic have exposed cracks in the myth of US invincibility. Analyzing this moment calls for understanding asymmetric linkages across disparate social locations as well as a commitment to unsettling US dominance and global inequalities—both signature features of transnational feminist approaches. Transnational feminist understandings of race, gender, and sexuality as mutually constitutive categories also align with the way protesters have framed their agendas. Although the killing of George Floyd in Minneapolis sparked a wave of demonstrations in many cities, Black cis and trans women victims such as Breonna Taylor in Louisville and Dominique Fells in Philadelphia were also the focus of attention in numerous locations; compared to previous demonstrations against US police brutality, protesters were more engaged with the specific articulation of racism, gender, and sexuality.[2] This historic moment, in other words, underscored for us the analytic and political fruitfulness of an approach we have held dear.

What came to be known in US academic circles as *transnational feminism* emerged during another period of worldwide social upheaval in the 1990s: a period of restructuring of industrial production, globalization of financial capital, and liberalization of markets and media. The human costs of these massive shifts were borne disproportionately by women and marginalized, often racialized, populations. Movements soon emerged in the Global South to challenge the commodification, impoverishment, and violence they wrought. At the same time, UN initiatives brought feminists from flourishing movements in Asia, Africa, and Latin America face to face with their northern counterparts, now populating government agencies, development institutions, academic circles, and nongovernmental organizations (NGOs). The often-uneasy alliances that emerged built on decades of earlier efforts by activists and researchers to forge connections across national boundaries to address problems affecting women.

The scholarship in US settings that came to define transnational feminist approaches engaged insightfully with these changing historical conditions shaping cross-border feminist practice. In 1994 Inderpal Grewal and Caren Kaplan's landmark work *Scattered Hegemonies* turned an evaluative lens on such North-South (or East-West) collaborations, criticizing a hegemonic feminism that presumed universalist understandings of womanhood; they presented it as complicit with modernist national agendas and oblivious to the "multiple, overlapping and discrete oppressions" among women in distinctive locations (17). At the same time, it challenged a culturalist and masculinist postmodernism inattentive to the economic forces further entrenching inequality around the world. M. Jacqui Alexander and Chandra Talpade Mohanty's *Feminist Genealogies, Colonial Legacies, Democratic Futures* (1997), appearing a few years later, built on their own important earlier work decentering the implicit subject of Western feminism. They articulated how solidarity between feminists critical of racial capitalism could look across geographic locations and they also merged important currents of US women-of-color feminism with critical development studies. Such books broke new ground by seeking out the voices of those outside Euro-American centers of power and advocating a transnational feminist politics of coalition among differently situated subjects. At the same time, like all harbingers of the new, their work was suggestive rather than exhaustive. It was left to those who followed to flesh out the contours of a new conceptualization of feminist practice.

Over the past two decades, the work of others, such as Richa Nagar, Valentine Moghadam, Wendy Harcourt, and Janet Conway, has been richly generative on topics such as ethical collaboration, solidarity, movement building across borders, and epistemic hierarchies; it has shaped multiple cohorts of feminist scholars. But transnational feminism has also met with criticism from some quarters and has been portrayed in the United States as exclusively focused on "elsewhere" and unconcerned with domestic questions, in spite of its early theoretical commitments. Some critics have cast it as an artifact of the past. We believe otherwise. Amid the increasingly unregulated voracity of capital for global consumer markets, labor, land, and other resources, and the ascension to power of right-wing nationalist leaders and movements intent on racist exclusion, it is important to foster feminisms that hold capacious collective visions for sustainable futures. The premise of this volume is that in our current era, a transnational feminist lens is needed more urgently than ever.

With that in mind, we pursue a simple question: What can two decades of transnational feminism offer to contemporary analysis and activism around the globe? We gathered scholarship set in five continents—North and South America, Africa, Australia, and Asia—to explore how transnational approaches are being taken up within and outside the academy. In particular, we were curious about the salience of the nation as a unit of theoretical analysis and activism: How are scholars currently examining the power of nations in ordering economies, cultures, and forms of social justice activism? How are transnational political relationships configured in relation to the changing power of nations? In what way do feminist and other social movements traverse the spaces within and between nations? And how do powerful economic actors work with/in nations to shape the terrain of transnational political action? The chapters in this volume are written by a dynamic group of scholars from universities in Brazil, Mexico, Mozambique, South Africa, and the United States who convened at the triennial Women's Worlds Conference in Brazil in August 2017 for a symposium titled "Whither Transnational Feminisms?" The material presented at this symposium has been revised over a two-year conversation since the conference and, along with some commissioned work, offers new directions for thinking about transnational feminism's pasts and futures.

Connections across borders figure centrally in each chapter. Rather than only describing feminisms in discrete nations—an international approach—our authors stress the power-laden networks, material linkages, and discursive flows that characterize our contemporary world, which a transnational approach typically connotes. The term *transnational* both acknowledges and questions the nation as a source of constraint and a locus of identity and possibility. As we note in the first chapter, transnational feminism not only marks connections that cross national borders but also places those articulations under critical scrutiny to diagnose how power operates within them in asymmetric and multidirectional ways.

We view transnational feminism as a flexible and evolving framework rather than a rigid set of prescriptions frozen in time. It is an analytic lens that, we insist, has been constructed through mutual engagement between scholars and activists in many parts of the world, and our book draws on the insights of those within the academy as well as their counterparts in non-university-based activist settings. The primary interventions of *Transnational Feminist Itineraries* are both conceptual and empirical, based on engagement with theory as well as observation of feminist activism on the ground. First, we claim that the grim contemporary global political and economic scenario that confronts those who struggle for racial, ethnic, geopolitical, economic, environmental, and gender justice calls for the very tools that transnational feminism offers. Most important, these tools include (1) a specific mode of thinking across national and digital boundaries attuned to the politics of scale, (2) critiques of nationalism and novel forms of transnational capital with an eye to their gendered and racialized causes and effects, (3) a processual and historical approach to thinking about identity categories,

Ashwini Tambe & Millie Thayer

and (4) an expansive imagining of solidarity that presumes differences rather than similarities.

Our coauthored first chapter elaborates these four features of transnational feminism. Chapters by Srila Roy, Carmen L. Díaz Alba, and Rafael de la Dehesa each reflect on scale, while Inderpal Grewal, Cara K. Snyder, and Isabel Maria Cortesão Casimiro and Catarina Casimiro Trindade address nationalism and forms of fundamentalism. Laura L. Lovett, Kathryn Moeller, Nancy A. Naples and Mary Bernstein, and Amrita Pande each discuss the role of transnational capital, while Jennifer C. Nash and Cricket Keating and Amy Lind consider how solidarity can be expressed in ways that creatively engage differences.

Second, our collective theoretical framing of transnational feminism refuses to place it in opposition to other approaches. We carefully explore the relationship between transnational feminism and parallel perspectives—especially intersectional feminisms and postcolonial and decolonial feminisms—and seek to illuminate overlaps and disjunctures. We argue that these perspectives are complementary rather than antagonistic and that their disjunctures, rather than signaling deep divides, provide fertile ground for mutual learning and new elaborations. In this spirit we also call for greater clarity about transnational feminist work on racialization, colonialism, and identity. The chapters in the first section, by Tambe and Thayer, Nash, and Grewal, each reflecting on the relationship between intersectional and transnational feminist theory, carry out such clarificatory work.

Third, we situate transnational feminism in the changing history of cross-border feminist activism that precedes and accompanies it. In relation to the activism of recent decades, we find that the rise of the political right has largely forced feminists to retreat from the global stage they occupied in the late 1990s and has partially displaced the institutionalized actors that dominated it. While we claim that transnational activism has largely shifted from an "embodied" to a "spectral" form—a trend that the pandemic has for now intensified—our book illustrates continued commitment among activists to cross-border solidarities and transnational analytic perspectives. In our view, what may have begun as a pragmatic and defensive move away from venues such as the United Nations has generated opportunities for creative new forms of transnational politics. In this regard, de la Dehesa discusses "embodied" forms of activism, while Díaz Alba and Lovett focus on cross-border digital campaigns—the "spectral." Tambe and Thayer also address the challenges of forming solidarity in digital contexts.

Fourth, noting that social media platforms drive political polarization and empower the right, even as they also enable progressive mobilizations, we argue that the current scenario calls for "scaling out" across social and ideological boundaries, as well as "scaling up" across geographic ones. As feminists increasingly renew their attention to domestic politics, we find this kind of lateral movement beginning to occur, although not always in predictable ways, as Roy's chapter illustrates.

Finally, we address the critiques of transnational feminism in the academy, finding that some of the valid concerns about US-centrism, elitism, and the inaccessible style of some written work are common to many fields, though more visible in the feminist field, given its diversity of actors. In any case, these obstacles have not deterred marginalized activists from forging and actively participating in transnational feminist alliances, as Casimiro and Trindade, Díaz Alba, and Lovett show in their chapters.

This volume is structured along thematic lines. Part I offers provocations about the current state of transnational feminism. Tambe and Thayer provide an overview of the arguments reflected in the book, place transnational feminist activism in historical perspective, and argue for new approaches to theorizing scale. Nash delves into the troubled relationship between intersectional and transnational feminism, also exploring how women's studies job advertisements participate in cleaving these two approaches apart. Grewal, coeditor of *Scattered Hegemonies* and an early participant in conversations on transnational feminism, provides a historical perspective on the field and offers a transnational analysis of corruption and patriarchy under the Trump presidency.

The next two parts of the book represent new takes on debates within transnational analysis. Part II features work that recasts the concept of scale in analyses of social movements. The chapters featured in this section are each about forms of women's social mobilization in distinct locations: Roy on new forms of mobilization "in the name of women" in India, Díaz Alba on the shifting fortunes of the World March of Women in Mexico, and de la Dehesa on the history of reproductive politics around mass sterilization in Brazil. Each chapter shows how national movement building articulates in complex ways with transnational discourses: Roy shows how a "protest assemblage" in India was shaped by a mediatized environment shaming the country, while de la Dehesa explores how circulating condemnations of mass sterilization in Brazil shaped national laws regulating sterilization in what he describes as "network ecologies." National-level organizing within a transnational network can reproduce hierarchies and elitism, as Díaz Alba's

Ashwini Tambe & Millie Thayer

chapter reveals in describing the consequences of shifting the local coordination of the World March of Women from the capital, Mexico City, to San Cristóbal de las Casas in Chiapas.

Part III showcases nuanced transnational critiques of what J. K. Gibson-Graham (2006) called the "rape script" of inexorable global capitalist penetration. Moeller, who writes about Nike's "Girl Effect" campaign on the ground in Brazil, and Lovett, who discusses patterns of international consumption and feminist resistance to gendered scripts in children's toys, each recount and critique examples of corporate attempts to construct gendered subjectivities. They note that forms of standardization—whether of children's toys or of targets of development intervention—meet a far-from-certain fate: transnational activists undercut the messages toys convey, and the ideal adolescent girl can prove an elusive target for Brazilian NGOs contracted by Nike to implement its program.

We then turn in part IV to a paired set of case studies of a thorny issue debated among feminists: commercial surrogacy. The chapters by Pande (on caste, religion, and race in the practice of transnational surrogacy in India) and Naples and Bernstein (studying the unequal relations shaping cross-border commercial surrogacy exchanges from the perspective of Australia) show how and why there are no easy answers or ways to resolve the moral and political dilemmas that this practice throws up. Naples and Bernstein apply a reproductive justice lens to studying the practice of gay couples in Australia seeking commercial surrogate mothers from the Global South, noting how the impulse of fighting heteronormativity grates against the principle of contesting racialized/economic reproductive coercion. Pande takes up, from a transnational feminist angle, the principle of "epistemic honesty" in conveying the voices and perspectives of surrogate mothers.

Our part V includes chapters by Keating and Lind (on plurinationalism in Ecuador), Snyder (on the transnational migrations and imaginations of women soccer players from Brazil), and Casimiro and Trindade (on the struggles of Mozambican feminists against the control of women's bodies by a patriarchal state). This part of the book offers an array of critical engagements with how states and nationalisms shape feminist politics, how the discursive power of nations is actually being entrenched through the process of transnational migration, and how transnational networks serve as resources in domestic struggles. Snyder explores how both Brazilian media and women soccer players participate in constructing the United States as a sanctuary and how such constructions obscure the workings of global capital and homonationalism. Casimiro and Trindade offer a detailed account of a

2016 crackdown on feminist protest in Mozambique, pointing to the specific mix of Christian and authoritarian Marxist influences that vilify feminism as a foreign intrusion. We close the volume with Keating and Lind's account of the innovations underway in theorizing the Ecuadorian nation and the family in new diverse and pluralistic ways that dismantle colonial legacies.

OVER THE TWO-YEAR PERIOD when we wrote this book it became increasingly clear that our globe was experiencing a rightward political tilt. A number of events underscored the electoral resurgence of nationalism: Britain formalized its economic-nationalist exit from the European Union in a messy referendum in 2019; in that same year, the reelected Hindu nationalist Bharatiya Janata Party (BJP) government in India formally revoked the autonomy of Muslim-majority Kashmir and redrafted criteria for citizenship to deepen the exclusion of Muslims; in Brazil elected president Jair Bolsonaro, a former military officer, openly endorsed antidemocracy protests and favored a return to dictatorship; the Turkish president, Recep Tayyip Erdoğan, who imposed vicious censorship on the press, social media, and intellectuals, was reelected in 2018; hard-liner Benjamin Netanyahu's victory in elections in 2020 made him the longest-serving Israeli prime minister; and Vladimir Putin proposed a constitutional amendment that would allow him to stay in power in Russia until 2036. Authoritarian strongmen like Trump seemed to act with impunity, emboldened by massive electoral boosts—and they were shameless in seeking to bend unfavorable election results to their will. The global pandemic bolstered xenophobic turns inward, with foreigners viewed as vectors of disease in multiple parts of the globe, and the fortressing of nations, cities, and homes occurred with renewed fervor. At the same time, the inadequate responses of autocratic leaders to the spread of the virus, deploying exclusionary rhetoric rather than public health guidelines, actually threatened to undermine their own power. It was precisely a moment that called for robust feminist understandings of nationalism—and an analysis of how solidarity can and must work.

The genuinely transnational collaboration we fostered—even before the onset of the pandemic—thus emerged out of a sense of political urgency. It has been important for us to feature the expertise of specialists from varied locations, including some whose work is not easily available in English. The outcome, we believe, is a set of geographically diverse voices engaged in theoretically rigorous conversations. Our process, which has been a mix of interpersonal meetings and presentations, email exchanges, phone calls, and detailed commenting on files, has exemplified the joys of feminist intellectual

Ashwini Tambe & Millie Thayer

collaboration. For the coeditors—situated in two different institutions and on two different continents over 2018 and 2019—the tasks of coordinating a conference in a third country and coauthoring a chapter together has been a reminder of how a deliberate effort to maintain fragile connections yields not only intellectual rewards but also personal and political resilience in tough times.

NOTES

1 For details on events outside the United States, see Gregory (2020).
2 Widespread protests over the killing of Breonna Taylor present a striking example of such public attentiveness to violence against women; see Wood (2020) and Patil (2020).

PROVOCATIONS

Part I

The Many Destinations of Transnational Feminism

ASHWINI TAMBE & MILLIE THAYER

IT HAS BEEN NEARLY TWENTY-FIVE YEARS since the term *transnational* entered the feminist lexicon in a positive register. Supplanting earlier uses of the term *transnational* that typically referenced giant cross-border corporations, *transnational feminism* signaled an approach focused on building critical and careful solidarities between feminists in various locations. Transnational feminism did not just mark connections that cross borders; rather, it placed networks under critical scrutiny to diagnose how power operates in asymmetric and multidirectional ways (Grewal and Kaplan 1994; Modern Girl around the World Research Group 2008). It argued that national frameworks can limit research and movement agendas, but even as it drew connections across national locations, it was critical of universalizing border-crossing narratives that obscured imperial or parochial interests (Sangtin Writers and Nagar 2006). The impact of transnational feminism has since been widely felt, with the term now being used to define activist and scholarly projects, courses, and jobs in the academy.

One specific reason for the term's rapid acceptance was its implicit correction of tendencies within US feminism to center white women's perspectives and adopt a salvationist approach to women in other parts of the world. Transnational feminism offered a new modality of solidarity, one that sought to both acknowledge and undercut US feminism's power. Yet, over time, this specific critical edge of transnational feminism has dulled; the most common sense in which the term *transnational feminism* is used today is simply to signal its non-US referents. In contemporary US feminist circles, *transnational feminism* is presumed to refer only to feminism from and about an elsewhere—to a context beyond a US locale. This assumption, while partially true, is incorrect in its emphasis. While transnational feminism certainly has explicitly featured movements, ideas, goods, and people that cross borders, its goal has not simply been to connote non-US feminism. The term *trans* in *transnational* implies, as it does in other academic uses of the term, an effort to question the stable boundaries of the term it precedes—and we argue that this means a questioning of both nations and nationalism. The goal of transnational feminism is not to chide theorists for not looking beyond their own immediate geographic horizons. It is to question the extent to which the nation and nationalism structure, and limit, our thinking. Transnational feminism, then, is not, as is sometimes claimed, a simple celebration of a geographic "scaling up"; rather, it is a lens focused on critically examining the very practice of scaling up.

This chapter is an effort to clarify key features and histories of this approach and to also generate new possibilities for its future. We open with a focus on defining the distinct features of transnational feminism, noting its varying uses across disciplines. We explore other terms to which *transnational feminism* is adjacent, such as *intersectional, decolonial,* and *postcolonial feminism,* and explain its relationship to these approaches. Given the frequent mischaracterization of transnational feminism as inattentive to race, we pay particularly close attention to transnational feminist understandings of racialization and identity formation. We then situate transnational feminist theory as a distinct moment within a longer history of cross-border women's activism. We offer a typology of different forms of cross-border activism around the globe since the late nineteenth century. Following this history, we turn to the contemporary resonance of transnational approaches at a time of increasingly virulent nationalisms. We reflect on the digital environment within which activists function and call for transnational practices of "scaling out." We close by engaging with a range of criticisms of transnational feminist approaches.

Ashwini Tambe & Millie Thayer

Transnational feminism is at once a perspective, a set of theories, *and* a set of activist practices, networks, and discourses. Transnational feminist movements and transnational feminist theory are certainly different arenas of action, but they have developed in explicit and implicit dialogue with each other. In many parts of the world, such as Latin America and South Asia, activism and academia are not as separate from one another as they are in the United States. Scholars and activists engage with one another, often as a community—whether at gatherings such as regional, national, and UN conferences or in cyber networks and virtual campaigns, where theories and strategies about consequential matters are engaged.

In some cases, productive tensions between scholars and activists have pushed each to articulate their thinking more clearly. For example, a rift between academic feminists and digital activists emerged in India in 2017 about the politics of #MeToo in higher education: Dalit-rights activists and young women advocated the value of posting anonymous accusations of sexual harassment online as a means to protect vulnerable accusers, while more established Indian feminist academics expressed caution about the abuse of anonymity by the religious right to target left-leaning male faculty members. In the eyes of digital activists, the calls by academic feminists to respect the legal principle of due process and allow the accused to respond to accusations appeared conservative and overly protective of the upper-caste men named on the list (Kappal 2017). The rift exposed and prompted deeper conversations about generational and caste divides within Indian feminism (Deo 2018; Roy 2017). In other cases, the academic/activist divide produces constructive differences that nourish both sides in their distinct locations. A good example is critiques of NGOization in Latin America and South Asia: concerns about the political effects of NGOization on feminism have come from working-class and anti-institutional *autonomista* and grassroots activists as well as from feminist academic observers.[1] Those defending professionalized activism also represent diverse locations: both NGO activists and development scholars note its value in mobilizing expertise and ensuring continuity across time.

Within academic settings, the meaning of the term *transnational* varies across disciplinary locations. Sociologists focus heavily on cross-border social movements and on a specific form of activism that is critical of formal, elite, national-level organizing. In historians' circles, the term *transnational* implies an attentiveness to the impact of the nation as a unit of analysis and a focus on circulation—of people, goods, and ideas. There is also emphasis on critically studying nationalism and colonialism. In women's studies, it includes the senses used in sociology and history, but it especially implies a specific orientation toward identity formation: transnational feminist approaches treat identities as specific to place and time and also as emergent; they see components of identity such as race, sexuality, and gender as constitutive of each other rather than as discrete vectors (Grewal and Kaplan 2001; Swarr and Nagar 2003).[2]

Within activist settings, the term *transnational* has also sometimes been a slippery category, with its boundaries defined in varying ways. For some, especially those who participated in UN conferences and other institutionalized processes, *transnational* has meant international policy advocacy aimed at shifting global norms to gain leverage in local struggles for gender equality. Others have contested what they see as an elite, top-down approach to advocacy and call instead for forming connections between locally rooted, issue-based groups. For them, *transnational feminism* signals a preference for movements focused not on national groupings but on less formal, cross-border issue-based networks, such as the Latin American and Caribbean Women's Health Network; #Dalit Women Fight, an online solidarity network focused on Dalit women across South Asian countries and the South Asian diaspora confronting caste-based oppression; or Women in Black, which emerged in protest against Israeli occupation of Palestine and became a coalition of groups holding vigils against militarism. In this understanding, transnational activism seeks solidarities that are distinct from international advocacy. Like transnational feminist theory, then, transnational feminist activism articulates a specific modality of cross-border connection that is attuned to differences of power.

TRANSNATIONAL FEMINIST THEORY'S ADJACENT FORMATIONS

Within the US academy and specifically within women's studies, there is a peculiar sedimented division of labor between transnational feminism and other feminist theoretical approaches. Transnational feminism is presumed to cover research on geographic sites beyond the United States, while other approaches, particularly intersectional feminism, are presumed to be focused on the United States, and especially on US women of color. As a result, transnational feminism is frequently depicted as uninterested in US racial politics (Soto 2005; Desai, Bouchard, and Detournay 2010). Jennifer C. Nash, in this volume, engages with a cluster of scholarship in the mid-2000s that worried

Ashwini Tambe & Millie Thayer

that transnational feminist scholarship erased US women of color. While transnational feminist writings did specifically seek to decenter US-centric knowledge and categories, the presumption that transnational feminism was inattentive to race actually obscured the important contributions of transnational feminism to understanding racial formations in their geographic, historical, and national context.

Transnational feminism emerged as a critique of imperial modes of practicing feminism, and its intellectual foundation included a focus on the relationship among colonialism, racial formations, and gender/sexual regimes. Work on the racial/sexual politics of colonialism by scholars such as Antoinette Burton (1994), Ella Shohat and Robert Stam (1994), Anne McClintock (1995), Mrinalini Sinha (1995), M. Jacqui Alexander and Chandra Talpade Mohanty (1997), and Ann Stoler (1995) formed its bedrock. Such scholarship is implicitly committed to both tracing the violence of racisms and denaturalizing racialization, to show how racial formations were historically and geographically contingent. Demonstrating that the meanings of whiteness and Blackness varied across borders underscored how racialization is connected to social imperatives and historical forces such as capitalism. Doing so rendered racialization inherently contestable, even as it recognized its violence as real and immediate.

The earliest generation of transnational feminist theory was committed to examining multiple categories of oppression in conjunction with one other, very much in keeping with the tenets of intersectional feminist theory. For example, Anne McClintock's (1995) *Imperial Leather* articulated nation, race, sex, and class as mutually constitutive categories, and the central concern in *Scattered Hegemonies* (Grewal and Kaplan 1994) was an exploration of gender in relation to nation, class, and race. Transnational feminism, like intersectional feminism, presumed that categories of identity emerged in complex, intertwined ways. However, it did not predetermine which categories were most important, out of an attentiveness to locally specific social hierarchies. As a result, transnational feminism did not articulate the relationship between categories in the same concise way that the term *intersectionality* conveyed. *Intersectionality* as a term mandates taking account of a wide range of structures of power (around race, class, sexuality, generation, ability, etc.), but because its genealogy is specifically tied to critical race feminists' call to address the invisibilization of US Black women in the law, it is most commonly taken to refer to race in conjunction with gender (Nash 2019).

The category of "women" may have been the starting point for intersectional analysis, but it can lend itself to an expansive approach; intersectional orientations seek to understand interconnections and relationships, as well as the struggles that have emerged alongside them. In Nash's view (see chapter 2 of this volume), intersectionality had a "field-defining capacity" that transnational feminism did not (see page 40). And in our view, the role of activists, including those explicitly critical of US empire, has been an important part of this expansive growth—women of color pushing white feminists to address race, innovating intersectional analyses on the ground—taking academic work back to the community of scholar-activists.

Like us, several authors in this volume, particularly Nash, Inderpal Grewal, Nancy A. Naples and Mary Bernstein, and Cricket Keating and Amy Lind, seek to also think the transnational and intersectional in conjunction, rather than in opposition. We argue that the two approaches are connected in being attentive to the ways that differences of power shape feminist practice: if intersectionality presumes a particular critical orientation toward the normative subject of feminist efforts, a transnational feminist approach signals a particular critical modality of *connection*—one focused on difficult solidarities and "dissident friendships," as Elora Halim Chowdhury and Liz Philipose (2016) have explored. It is an understanding of solidarity that presumes differences rather than sameness as its starting point.

What, then, might distinguish transnational from intersectional approaches? Transnational feminist theorists' emphasis on the historical and geographic mutability of race and nation leads to treating such categories as always in formation and geographically variable, rather than as vectors of oppression whose meanings are preordained. Sylvanna M. Falcón's (2016) research on the UN World Conference on Racism in Durban in 2001, for instance, explores how delegates negotiated national differences in how Blackness was experienced; in this setting, US women of color frequently encountered a different sense of their place in the world. Ashwini Tambe's (2019b) work on brothels in colonial Bombay examines hierarchies of whiteness in this extractive (rather than settler) colonial context, where eastern European women were not seen as adequately white—even though in settler colonial societies such as Argentina, eastern European brothel workers were targets of rescue and rehabilitation for marriage because there was a premium on whiteness and reproduction, as Donna Guy (1995) has explained.

Apart from intersectional feminism, another theoretical approach to which transnational feminism is sometimes counterposed is *decolonial feminism*. Decolonial feminism centers Indigenous epistemologies in explicitly contesting Eurocentric structures of knowledge production, including those related to understanding gender (Lugones 2010). We think of transnational

Ashwini Tambe & Millie Thayer

feminism as a precursor to decolonial feminism because of how the former stresses the importance of colonialism in shaping structures of knowledge. Transnational feminism practices what could now be termed a decolonial sensibility in the way that it questions the Anglocentrism of feminism and, relatedly, the ways in which settler colonialism, the Atlantic slave trade, and missionary practices have contributed to feminisms around the globe.[3] It contributes trenchant critiques of how contemporary systems of law and governance are inherited from European empire.[4]

In its attention to the impact of colonial histories, transnational feminism draws closely on earlier currents of postcolonial scholarship formulated in the late 1980s and 1990s that critiqued the enduring legacies of European imperialism. (To clarify, the *post* in *postcolonial theory* does not imply a chronological relationship to colonialism but rather a focus on the impacts of colonialism; it does not claim to be "after" colonialism so much as a "tethering to" colonialism.) However, transnational feminism more directly critiques the national frameworks within which postcolonial critique was advanced, as well as a critique of the colony/metropole binary that structured postcolonial thought. One of Inderpal Grewal and Caren Kaplan's (1994) innovations in *Scattered Hegemonies* was to refuse the rigid bifurcatory logics of postcolonial thought in favor of conceptualizing multidirectional flows of power.

To be sure, our effort to stress the resonances between these varied approaches is not to deny their distinct force and appeal; decolonial feminism clearly derives its power from asserting its distinctness from postcolonial approaches. The appeal of decolonial critique lies in its call to change the very foundational categories and language of scholarship. In centering the recovery of Indigenous and subaltern perspectives marginalized in settler societies, it positions itself as explicitly antiassimilationist. Nonetheless, it is worth acknowledging, as Grewal does in her chapter in this volume, that a common central problematic shapes each of these critical approaches: that of transcending colonial legacies. In a similar vein, the 2017 special issue of *Feminist Studies* demonstrates that postcolonial, decolonial, and transnational feminism are far more connected in their concerns than is recognized, given their shared attention to the epistemological violence and sedimented practices of colonialism. The imputed regional division of labor between the two approaches, with postcolonial approaches presumed to refer to South Asia and the Middle East and decolonial approaches to the Americas and settler colonial societies, is also worth interrogating (Ramamurthy and Tambe 2017). Even though the histories of settler and extractive colonialism follow different trajectories and entail different forms of violence, such regionally inflected intellectual silos obstruct scholarly conversation more than they should. In the spirit of upholding transnational feminist ethics of complex solidarity, then, we reassert the points of connection transnational feminism has with each of these distinct but adjacent approaches.

THE HISTORICAL ARC OF CROSS-BORDER FEMINIST ACTIVISM

As a theoretical lens, transnational feminism emerged in the early 1990s. However, cross-border feminist relationships, mutual influences, and coordinated action long predated transnational feminism's self-conscious theorization. Cross-border feminist activism, which began in an organized way in the nineteenth century, is a much broader and more variegated phenomenon than transnational feminism, which embodies a specific critical mode of cross-border connection. Cross-border feminist activism has itself moved through four spatialized moments occurring at different times in different parts of the world: *porous national activism, asymmetric internationalism, embodied transnationalism,* and *spectral transnationalism.* These different moments overlap one another, and earlier eras continue to shape those that follow. We offer them as a schematic, rather than descriptive, typology of the shifts happening in women's movements around the globe. There may well be examples of women's movements that do not follow this trajectory; we draw primarily on our collective understanding of movements in Latin America, South Asia, and the Anglo-American world.

Porous National Activism

The first efforts by women's movements at cross-border activism were conducted on behalf of nations because of how deeply imbricated such movements were in nationalism. In nineteenth-century Latin America, for example, what were then called "feminine" movements were, for the most part, contained within national boundaries and/or targeted their demands toward local polities. Feminist periodicals sprang up beginning in the 1830s and instigated the agitation for women's education and other issues in their respective countries (Greenberg 1990). In spite of their national focus, however, the educated elite activists who led these efforts were not entirely isolated from one another. They made connections across borders through letters and visits to one another, seeking advice, sharing experiences, and acting as "godmothers" to one another's movements, as Katherine Marino (2019)

Ashwini Tambe & Millie Thayer

and Christine Ehrick (1998) demonstrate. Across Asia, Kumari Jayawardena (1986) has noted, feminism grew up alongside anticolonial nationalist campaigns, but its ideas also reached across national boundaries: Jayawardena describes how Egyptian women were influenced by secular reforms in Turkey and how Chinese women were inspired by stories about "new women" in Japan. These processes occurred through active communication via travel, letters, and talks and also through the circulation of reports in women's magazines.

Divisions of race, class, and colonial status remained very stark in these early phases, however. In Britain and the United States, women's groups organized crusades for temperance and against slavery, trafficking in women, and other issues, which reflected a mode of elitist aid to the less fortunate. They traveled the world promoting their causes, secure in their confidence in the moral and intellectual superiority of their own national cultures and societies. British suffragists sought inclusion in their imperial polity by demonstrating their fitness for citizenship through a defense of race and nation that excluded their colonized "sisters" (Burton 1998). Imperialist worldviews affected the organizations of working-class socialist women and women of color as well—those organizations based in Europe and the United States tended to also take a paternalistic stance toward the women in Africa, Asia, and Latin America whom they aimed to uplift. In effect, nation trumped race and class, highlighting the power of nationalism to undermine transnational alliances (Evans 1977; Neverdon-Morton 1989; Barnett 1978). Postcolonial and transnational feminist histories have highlighted the problems with this form of cross-border activism (Burton 1998; Spivak 1988).

Asymmetric Internationalism

The second type of cross-border women's activism tended to be more formally internationalist and drew on the culture inculcated by intergovernmental organizations such as the League of Nations and the United Nations. Both of these organizations, based on ostensibly egalitarian relations among the representatives of diverse nations, offered a model of international engagement and opportunities for feminists to make claims on a world stage. The organizations themselves were responses to wars among imperial powers and coincided with waves of decolonization in the Middle East, Asia, and Africa. Although class gained purchase as an axis of organization, with the extension of socialist and communist movements, national identity remained a primary form of identification.

A series of international women's organizations were founded in the early and mid-twentieth century to lobby states and institutions such as the League of Nations and the United Nations around issues including suffrage, peace, protectionist legislation, and women's rights to citizenship in marriage.[5] But the domination of international women's organizations by white, middle- and upper-class, Euro-American, Christian women persisted; Orientalism and universalist assumptions pervaded missionary-style efforts. Some feminist activists in the Global South resisted such overstepping and used intergovernmental venues to make the case for their national visibility, independence, or sovereignty. Nova Robinson (2016) has tracked how Arab feminists used the League of Nations and the United Nations to pursue such goals. In the early years of the United Nations, efforts to agree on a common minimum age for marriage produced heated exchanges between delegates on questions of national sovereignty, as Tambe (2019a) has noted. This was, then, a phase of uneven and sometimes contentious internationalism, one that excluded many from the colonized periphery, except a select few. From a critical transnational feminist angle, such activism pursued the fiction of a world of equal and intact nations collaborating harmoniously around common ends—a fiction that frequently overlooked those suffering from internal colonization within nations.

Embodied Transnationalism

When the United Nations, responding to pressure from development activists in the North and South, launched its Decade for Women in 1975, it unleashed a wave of collaborations, networks, and campaigns. These novel forms of cross-border action coincided with the end of Fordism and the increased reach of global capital fueling the exploitation of young women workers in free-trade zones across the world (Harvey 1990). In many parts of the Global South, middle-class women experienced increased access to education without concomitant access to public employment. This gap, in addition to the frequent exclusion of women within left organizations, widened the constituency for feminism. Middle- and upper-class women's access to affordable means of travel and electronic communication made possible the creation of a potentially mobile activist class. In turn, such feminist mobilization in both the North and the South contributed to nongovernmental, bilateral, and multilateral aid agencies opening their coffers to gender-based organizations. The explosion of a feminist NGO sector not only attended to advocacy and empowerment but also filled the gaps left by retreating states.

Ashwini Tambe & Millie Thayer

Beginning in the 1980s and especially in the 1990s, feminist movements became more professionalized, using aid-industry resources to fund not only local projects but also a coordinated lobby targeting the United Nations and other international institutions. In these venues they carried out a series of discursive struggles designed to lay the groundwork for feminist campaigns to guarantee implementation of policy changes at the level of individual states, a move seen as particularly important in countries with regimes hostile to women's rights. Other feminists rejected institutionalized politics, spending their energies on more site-specific efforts to organize against violence, foster gendered awareness among youth, and draw on forms of art and culture. Then, too, advocacy on behalf of women, which used a range of distinctive appellations, was diversifying, as racial and ethnic minorities, professionals, religious women, working-class women, lesbians, and trans and queer people organized in and across multiple countries, coming together in horizontal gatherings, networks, and campaigns around a host of issues and concerns.[6]

In this period, feminist activism became more transnational in the sense that it involved stitching together alliances that transcended national borders while also recognizing their continuing relevance. The national differences—and inequalities—that divided feminists in varied contexts were recognized and examined. Connections were also forged between feminist activists focused on issues rather than on representing nations. While some feminists worked within hierarchical state or multilateral entities, as international activists had done before them, most, and especially the new feminist constituencies, exerted power from outside such organizations. During this period, the initiative and creative energy passed to the Global South, and the emphasis shifted away from individual political rights to collective social and economic entitlements.

We refer to this political moment as *embodied transnationalism* for several reasons. First, beginning with the 1975 UN women's meeting in Mexico City, cross-border feminist interactions were often literally face-to-face, in *encuentros* (gatherings), meetings, performances, marches, or lobbying activities. When they were not, they often involved email or phone conversations that linked people in different countries in direct communication about goals, strategies, and tactics. As we argue in the following section, this latter characteristic has shifted dramatically in the era of social media that defines our contemporary times. Second, we use the term *embodied* because so many of the issues under debate were rooted in the bodily experiences of sexual and racial minorities; HIV-positive, disabled, working, and poor women; sex workers; and rural and young women, rather than in the abstract conceptualizations of political rights fought for by suffragists and those who lobbied the League of Nations earlier in the century.

The academic field of transnational feminism—with its specific theoretical approach—was founded during the epoch of embodied transnationalism. Its emergence was a direct critique of the Eurocentric modes of earlier cross-border activism. Its confident articulation of perspectives from the Global South was also related to the wider geographic growth of women's studies as an academic field. Christine Min Wotipka and Francisco O. Ramirez (2008, 89) argue that international women's conferences shaped when new academic programs were established and that the UN World Conferences on Women in Mexico City, Copenhagen, Nairobi, and Beijing (1975–95) spurred the growth of women's studies programs in many sites in Latin America, Europe, Africa, and East Asia. Women's studies gained legitimacy as not only forming the academic arm of women's movements, documenting movements and providing knowledge necessary for policy, but also demystifying the patriarchal structures of academic knowledge production (Montague and Tambe 2020). In its early years, scholars in these new institutions, like the movements they identified with, focused on body politics and critiqued the interventions of the state in and against women's bodies. For instance, in Latin America feminists resisted both state-sponsored torture and efforts to restrict reproductive rights (Alvarez 1990; Ewig 2006; Mooney 2012). In South Asia there was a movement against dowry-related killings and state inaction (Kumar 1993). By the 1990s, with the advent of transnational feminist theory, feminism in the academy had changed its focus from the body itself to the relations that linked bodies across borders and critiques of universalized and Eurocentric understandings of the category of "women." This emphasis on relations and hierarchical modes of creating connections became the centerpiece of transnational feminist theorizing.

Spectral Transnationalism

The turn of the twenty-first century has presented new challenges to transnational feminist approaches. In the United States, the 9/11 attacks, and the military response to them, contributed to exacerbating right-wing fundamentalisms of various kinds: religious, racist, military, and economic. In the past decade, waves of dislocation and displacement in the wake of wars, persecution, and economic crises have sent refugees across borders in a desperate

Ashwini Tambe & Millie Thayer

search for safety, where they are met by security states intent on shoring up their borders by violent means. Since the late 2000s, democratic institutions have also come under threat by authoritarian regimes, which are rekindling the flames of nationalism among their electorates. Kleptocratic states have returned brazenly to the fore as handmaidens to and beneficiaries of global capital (Merino 2011). New forms of colonialism are evolving as extractive industries take possession of vast expanses of formerly sovereign territories and the resources contained in them.

Feminist movements are at this time confronting serious challenges to their ability to engage across differences. The shift from direct communication via email and phone to the ideological silos created by social media exacerbates the fragmentation of political spaces and the hollowing out of an internally diverse communal life. In the era of "fake news" and growing social distrust, we find ourselves grappling with the question of truth as the common grounds of knowledge are increasingly contested. It is an awkward space for feminist poststructuralists and social constructionists, who have long struggled against positivism and the tyranny of factualism and who now find themselves compelled to defend the wisdom of science against extremists who, for instance, doubt claims of a warming climate, the effects of a virus, or the plasticity of gender.

What are the implications of this bleak context for transnational feminist activism? In the early 2000s, feminists began to encounter the resurgence of the right in international venues like the United Nations, which had previously proved hospitable to their advocacy. Global alliances of right-wing states and religious forces dominated debates over the language of resolutions, threatening to roll back earlier victories and even erase terms such as *gender*, which had served as a means to challenge essentialist and oppressive conceptions. At the same time, the funds on which feminist NGOs depended for embodied transnational activism were drying up as international aid agencies themselves confronted demands to turn their attention to crises at home and away from social issues in the Global South. A handful of feminists were left to confront an onslaught of well-funded and well-prepared right-wing activists at UN preparatory meetings. Not surprisingly, many concluded that it would be best to expend their energies elsewhere.

In the 2000s both shrinking funds and attacks from the right drew traveling feminists back home to defend earlier gains and saw some NGOs shut their doors or devolve into online activism. Autonomous feminist collectives and local grassroots initiatives struggled to survive, as they always had. Meanwhile, a new generation of young feminists and LGBTQ activists staked their claim to the streets, engaging in creative but ephemeral modalities that reached new constituencies but left open the question of how to sustain strategies and address enduring forms of power (Sorj 2017). Digital activism was less costly in terms of resources and even lives, yet it sometimes led to the kinds of dangerous liaisons that Srila Roy in this volume calls "protest assemblages," where ideologically incompatible groups coalesce briefly around particular issues and use one another in a furious effort to gain advantage for their point of view.

In this context, transnationalism persists but becomes spectral, still present but in out-of-body form. Activists far less often meet face-to-face, coordinate campaigns across borders, or engage in networks as actively as they once did.[7] The specificity of place is reasserted, as domestic politics become the focus for many feminists.

Yet the practices of embodied transnationalism have left their mark, and local struggles, such as African women's critiques of the role of global capital in the extractive industries that are destroying their communities, often take a diasporic perspective or deploy a transnational analysis. As Carmen L. Díaz Alba suggests in this volume, local movements have been strengthened by the forums that transnational events, such as the World March of Women in Mexico, generated. Some of the most promising current forms of transnationalism are the alliances being forged between Black Lives Matter, a movement founded by US Black queer women, and efforts to contest violence against subordinated people in other parts of the world, such as Brazil and India.[8] Whether we are seeing embodied transnationalism "in abeyance," to borrow Verta Taylor's (1989) term, assuming temporary new forms in the face of the current virulent nationalisms and fundamentalisms that rove the planet, or a longer-term trend toward digital politics and away from corporeal forms of transnational alliance, it is too soon to tell.

TRANSNATIONAL FEMINISM'S
CONTEMPORARY POLITICAL CHARGE

Transnational feminist theory is particularly valuable for its trenchant critiques of the disturbing political developments of our time. Among the most worrying of these developments is nationalism, expressed in right-leaning trends in contemporary electoral politics around the globe. In the 2010s a number of countries—India, Turkey, Britain, the Philippines, the United States, Venezuela, Brazil, Russia—have witnessed the rise of authoritarians such as Recep Tayyip Erdoğan, Vladimir Putin, Rodrigo Duterte, Donald

Ashwini Tambe & Millie Thayer

Trump, Jair Bolsonaro, and Narendra Modi. They have commonly been termed *populist* because their rise is premised on campaign promises to the poor (despite often being beholden to corporate agendas). These leaders have nonetheless employed antidemocratic means to consolidate their power, such as muzzling the press and mobilizing violent vigilante groups. What makes their rise especially disturbing is that they have been placed in power through electoral means. Their popularity makes them appealing to party establishments that stand to gain from increased votes, even when their positions are out of step with the established norms of the party and of democratic practice. Once in power, such candidates have undermined constitutional protections in their respective countries. They have criminalized protest and systematically attacked academics and universities harboring critical voices.

Such politicians owe their striking success in no small part to their effective trafficking in virulent nationalisms—white nationalism in the United States, the United Kingdom, and Europe; economic nationalism in the United Kingdom and the United States; religious nationalism in India and Turkey; and militarist nationalism in Russia and the Philippines. The appeal of such narratives—whether about nations with wounded majorities, external enemies, or vulnerable economies—is premised on the coherence and viability of economically sovereign and internally homogeneous nation-states. Their proclaimed national sovereignty and internal homogeneity are, however, fictions—both in the current context of global trade and financial interdependencies and also in the history of colonialism and immigration. The states on which these nationalisms are based are themselves the products of the occupation of minoritized groups in boundary areas, such as Kashmir, Baluchistan, or Kurdistan (Ali et al. 2019).

While a critical assessment of nation formation and nationalism has been staple fare in a range of fields from history to anthropology to literature, transnational feminism adds sharp insights into the gendered and sexualized nature of nationalist discourses. Cynthia Enloe's (1990) and Nira Yuval-Davis's (1997) analyses of the relationship between gender and nationalism, and specifically the patriarchal investment in territorial domination through militaristic methods, defined this topic for decades. Transnational feminist approaches recognize the importance of analyzing nationalism through the lens of gender but move beyond essentialist truisms about militaristic masculinity and peaceable femininity. They have been especially attuned to how the appeals to security and protection are mobilized by men but also championed by right-wing women in many parts of the world. For instance,

Paola Bacchetta and Margaret Power (2013) have tracked the participation of women in fascist, racist, and antifeminist movements in various parts of Europe, the Middle East, Australia, South Asia, and the United States. Grewal's (2017) analysis of how white women are important actors in post-9/11 security discourses offers an important departure from femininity as a mere object of masculine manipulation. Instead, there is a critical focus on how the investment in stable national boundaries is a patriarchally sanctioned heteronormative imperative advocated in the name of women's protection and reproductive futures. Transnational feminism's attention to the shifting configurations of nationalism, gender, and homoeroticism—including nationalism's mobilization of convenient feminine identities (such as the security mom or the mama grizzly in the United States), ascetic masculinities (such as those of Modi in India), and virile authoritarians (such as Putin), as well as homonational discourses in the United States that draw LGBT constituencies into the arms of the nation even as they feminize and sexualize foreign "terrorists"—is vital to accounting for the present moment (Puar 2007; Berlant 2000; Puri 2004).[9]

The success of many authoritarian demagogues is not just owed to their virulent nationalism; it is specifically also an outcome of the social media environment of the 2010s. It is widely accepted, particularly after the publication of the 2019 Mueller Report, that the manipulation of Facebook ads influenced the 2016 US election results. Donald Trump would never have captured and sustained the US presidency without the existence of Twitter, the platform that allowed him to create a fan base of millions (at last count, his followers number over 80 million, although these numbers include critics and bots); he shuns the conventions of public communication via press statements and two-way interviews and instead mostly issues one-way proclamations on a daily, if not hourly, basis. Modi, who at last count had over 64 million followers, uses Twitter to mobilize what can be termed an army of trolls, who, like Trump's supporters, savagely harass critics of the administration.

The key features of social media platforms that can make them pernicious are the speed of direct communication and their capacity for preserving homophily via self-selected and self-amplifying social groups. They whip up political storms and circulate rumors at an unprecedented pace—a prime example being how WhatsApp messages led to a wave of lynchings in India in July 2018 (Elliott 2018; BBC News 2018). Worryingly for the future, such platforms sustain politically homogeneous bubbles that prevent genuine dialogue across constituencies. Even in less homogeneous public forums

Ashwini Tambe & Millie Thayer

such as newspaper comments pages or YouTube video comments sections, anonymity makes grandstanding more common than empathetic engagement. Politicians who entertain with hyperbole amplify the nationalistic, misogynist, and racist character of this social media environment. Trump's appearance on the US political scene is of a piece with the polarizing digital environment around the globe.

As the political forces confronting us raise novel challenges for political practice, the impetus to push our theorizing in new directions is increasingly urgent. Many contemporary accounts of our political moment present only two choices: corporate globalization, which depends among other things on the exploitation of female labor, or insular protectionist nationalism laden with patriarchal assumptions about women's place. We are asked to choose between options that serve only their elite advocates, increasing either our vulnerability to transnational economic oligopolies or our subjection to nationalist leaders who share a dangerous delusion of bounded economies locked in hostile competition.

In this scenario, transnational feminist perspectives are more important than ever because they offer critiques of these models' costs to democracy, the environment, and human life and suggest an alternate set of values on which economies and communities could be constructed and coalitions stitched together across differences (Gibson-Graham 2006; Harcourt 2013; Thayer 2017). Transnational feminists expose the fiction of sovereign bounded economies, nations, and cultures, and point to the work done by specific gendered and sexual orders in sustaining them (Alexander 1991). Rather than treating the nation as a historical artifact that can be wished away or transcended in a postnational mode, transnational feminists offer critical accounts of how and why nationalisms have power and can be refused. They also expose the hierarchies and violence undergirding corporate networks (Ramamurthy 2004). The status of this body of theory as a flexible framework, rather than a rigid set of prescriptions, has allowed it to evolve in new directions and take account of novel developments, such as those discussed here, as they occur.

TRANSNATIONAL PERSPECTIVES ON SCALE

How, specifically, does transnational feminism critique nationalism? For decades, it has been a feminist maneuver to denaturalize the nation by cutting across scales: refusing the divides between the private and the public and, in the same vein, between the domestic and the international. A classic example is Enloe's (1990) move, in *Bananas, Beaches and Bases*, to treat intimate practices as vital to practices of statecraft. This model has been followed since in feminist international relations and in feminist geography, which frequently describe the mutual imbrication of the global and the personal. Geraldine Pratt and Victoria Rosner's (2012) edited volume, *The Global and the Intimate*, offers a thorough account of feminist renderings of the relationship between these apparently incommensurate spheres across several disciplines. They note that conventional accounts of globalization contain flawed universalizing assumptions: "a global outlook can seem to speak from everywhere, from a god's eye view," and "economics trumps all other factors to define the global as little more than a network of markets and producers" (3). They note that the discourse of globalization is also heavily gendered by "the metaphorics of rape and victimization," as J. K. Gibson-Graham also observes (3).

The counterargument, Rosner and Pratt suggest, is to reengage the global with attention to processes of "subjective mediation" (Elizabeth Povinelli and George Chauncey's words), and to the body—by "holding on to emotion, attachment, the personal, and the body when we move into a more expansive engagement with the world" (11). Conversely, it also means a more expansive account of the personal: situated knowledges should be described in ways that are "material and site-specific, and that communicate the speaker's affiliations" (9).

Geographer Doreen Massey (1994) takes another approach to challenging the dominant view of the global, insisting on the connections between an apparently seamless global sphere and the specificities of daily life in particular places. She argues that the global, far from making place irrelevant, is instead constituted by the shifting web of links between localities. Sociologist Saskia Sassen (2000) traces the "counter-geographies of globalization," illustrating the ways that the global economy often rests on the invisible labor and/or exploitation of migrant women—domestic workers, sex workers, trafficked women. Philosopher Margaret A. McLaren (2017, 15) gathers a number of perspectives on solidarity that require "transversal" forms of connection.[10] Finally, in the field of history, books such as *The Straight State* by Margot Canaday (2009) demonstrate the scalar leap that makes such feminism appealing: from the intimate to the transnational, and vice versa.

Yet it is also important to acknowledge that many such scalar leaps are impressive because they center space as that which is transcended. They implicitly presume that traversing physical distance is a signal of power and importance. Transnational feminism's presumptive appeal lies in its facility with this kind of leap across geographic boundaries. As Leela Fernandes (2013, 21) critically describes it, there is a driving tendency toward "transcendence" in transnational feminist discourse, to move beyond the "borders of nation-states." Why, though, do we respect this form of scaling up? Transnational movement is, after all, not even always a reliable indicator of greater influence. Far too often, border crossing is the desperate response of those who face intolerable conditions in their home countries, rather than an expression of power. In the spirit of being more self-reflexive about transnational feminist practices, we ask, What would it mean to not center physical space and its transcendence? What would it mean to articulate a different sense of scale and transnational feminist politics? What would it mean to treat scalar differences as processual and actively produced through human action, as Díaz Alba proposes in this volume?

These questions are also motivated by new social and political formations in the digital age that render transcending physical space even less central as a metric of political value. Instead, there is a need to express and examine other forms of influence that pertain to the reach of digital sources. Given that social media use patterns suggest the consolidating and condensing of political constituencies, such that homophilic groups of people speak to each other, we should perhaps speak of *scaling out*, rather than *scaling up*, indicating not just when physical space is traversed but also (or rather) when established political constituencies (or bubbles) are transcended. Scaling up is commonly understood to occur in a vertical register, with greater command of space giving access to something closer to a panoptic view and the power that inheres in it. What we call *scaling out* involves making porous the borders between political identities. In particular, the rigidity of these borders, we argue, has often been reinforced rather than undermined by the workings of new technologies in the contemporary global context. When political-demographic-affective affinities are breached, those who inhabit distinctive subject positions and have often assumed opposing stances might find themselves in overlapping engagements with one another.

Power in such convergences is much more volatile and less predictable than it appears in scaled-up forms of activism. On the one hand, such scaled-out conversations have the potential to generate the kind of solidarities across difference to which feminists have long aspired, as in the case of actions around the globe inspired by Black Lives Matter, described in our introduction to this volume. On the other hand, they may also produce problematic and internally contradictory assemblages, such as those described by Roy in this volume, which included a variety of actors, from feminists to death penalty advocates, in response to a horrific rape case in India. They can also take on the perplexing contours of #MeToo-related ferment, which drew together in loose affiliation outraged Christians in Alabama, Hollywood movie stars, and community-based activists in scores of countries.

SHORTCOMINGS AND FUTURE DIRECTIONS
OF TRANSNATIONAL FEMINISM

In this chapter we have sought to weave together theoretical developments in transnational feminism with the cross-border activism that has repeatedly pushed it forward, acting in counterpoint, if not always in harmony. As we have shown, cross-border feminist activism began long before institutionalized forms of feminism existed; academic women's studies programs emerged in tandem with the embodied feminism of the 1970s and the connections activists articulated in UN women's conferences and parallel gatherings. Initially, scholarly and grassroots feminisms had a kind of synergy that made them difficult to separate, but, particularly in the Global North, the institutionalization of transnational feminism as an academic subfield within burgeoning women's studies programs often led to distinctive trajectories and disjunctive preoccupations between the two. In time, some scholars began to raise questions about the distance between scholarly approaches (and some forms of elite activism) and activist work.

One of the most interesting charges made about transnational feminist theory is that it is, paradoxically, US-centric. Fernandes (2013) observes that transnational feminism is a US-centric formation because it is a response to a specifically US problem: the limited field of vision of second-wave US feminism. The imperative of "paying attention to the global" has had cachet specifically because it was hitherto lacking in US feminist history. It actually flags how the US academy, by virtue of being a central node of English academic circulation, could afford to be inward looking and not engage with a beyond or an outside. Yet we also note that the transcending of the national, which is implied in transnational approaches, is also a luxury in which only those with secure nations can partake. In those cases where struggles for sovereignty are central, such as among First Nations, the transcending of the nation is an empty mandate.

A second charge is elitism. Those who focus on geographically distant problems often do so with blithe disregard for problems in their own backyard, to put it colloquially. Transnational feminism can perpetuate an elitism both of activist practices and of academic language. For some, to be a transnational feminist implies a connection to other feminists by virtue of personal mobility. It takes money to travel to meetings and attend conventions. Many movements sign on to a transnational mandate in order to look au courant, but as Millie Thayer (2010b) has shown, not all movements have the means to participate in transnational campaigns or to make their meanings heard in the same way.

Another kind of elitism is that of the theoretical language used: poststructuralism has been an influential force in transnational feminist thinking in many quarters. Janet Conway (2017) has noted the inaccessibility of the language used by some poststructural feminist analysts as well as the related gap between this kind of transnational feminist theory and transnational feminist activism.

There is certainly much of value in the criticisms described here. While largely agreeing with the need to address the problems just summarized, we would like to offer some alternative perspectives, based on lessons from the cross-border activism we have observed, and to propose future directions for feminist scholars. We do need to recognize the US-centrism (or Eurocentrism) that characterizes much of the scholarship and some of the activism produced in the Global North. There are indeed groups for whom the nation is still an unattainable rallying cry. But transnational connections, which may be a luxury for some marginalized peoples, have been experienced as a necessity by other vulnerable groups. The eagerness with which participants from countries in the Global South created or signed on to transnational networks of LGBTQ, Afro-descended, indigenous, Muslim, anti-neoliberal, and other groups of women; joined or organized advocacy campaigns; and made their presence felt at international events, such as the unofficial parallel gatherings at UN meetings, or regional congresses and collaborations, testifies to this fact (Thayer 2010a; Robinson 2016). Some, such as Falcón (2016), argue that those feminists who are vulnerable in their home societies—for example, in countries in sub-Saharan Africa or the Middle East—are the most likely to seek the legitimacy of the United Nations; they find the safety in numbers in horizontal networks to be crucial for advancing their cause.

The elitism of some forms of transnational activism has also been correctly noted by many observers, with particular reference to the "femocrats" (from North and South) working or lobbying in the formal spaces of international institutions. For most women around the world who lack the cultural or financial capital to participate, these arenas are out of reach; there are also legitimate critiques of the lack of accountability of the people who circulate in them. And yet the presence of Black, Indigenous, working-class, and gender-nonconforming people and sexual minorities in the mobilizations outside the official venues, such as the UN World Conferences on Women, speaks to the value they see in exerting pressure on those institutions. Sonia Alvarez and colleagues (2002) cite complaints by the *históricas*—feminism's often-elite founding mothers—about the large numbers of working-class women who crashed the party at Latin American regional feminist gatherings. And, in more recent years, the appearance of working-class and trans women at these meetings has ruffled the feathers of the more privileged attendees. But these are, in our view, welcome changes. The World March of Women, discussed by Díaz Alba in this volume, is an important example of a transnational movement whose participants are primarily working-class, "popular" feminists, including many women of color (Lebon 2013).

Finally, in relation to language, critics accurately observe that some of the poststructuralist and/or postcolonial academic writing on transnational feminism is inaccessible to the large majority of women whom transnational feminists hope to include. And much of the academic work that circulates is in the English language. Even in the case of this volume, we recognize the limitations of writing in English about contexts across four continents— Africa, South Asia, and South and North America—many of which, such as Brazil and Mexico, are not primarily English-speaking locales. But we would submit that this is a challenge for many fields and is not unique to feminist scholarship. The difference may be that feminist scholarship and activism exist in closer relationship with one another than they do in other fields, bringing the problems of communication and accountability into view and demanding effective "translation" in a way that does not occur in other fields (Alvarez et al. 2014). And, we would argue, transnational feminism, with the energies it draws from feminists in the Global South, is especially well positioned to counter Anglocentrism in the academy through more consistent translation practices.

It is especially well positioned to do so via the format of the edited volume, which has become a signature genre for transnational feminist scholarship. Some of the most influential examples of transnational feminist theory are edited volumes—*Third World Women and the Politics of Feminism* (Mohanty, Russo, and Torres 1991), *Scattered Hegemonies* (Grewal and Kaplan 1994), *The Modern Girl around the World* (Modern Girl around the World Group Research Group 2009), *The Global and the Intimate* (Pratt and Rosner 2012), *Decolonizing Feminism* (McLaren 2017), *Translocalities/Translocalidades* (Alvarez et al. 2014), *Critical Transnational Feminist Praxis* (Swarr

Ashwini Tambe & Millie Thayer

and Nagar 2010), and *Dissident Friendships* (Chowdhury and Philipose 2016). And many that are not strictly edited volumes, such as *Playing with Fire* (Sangtin Writers and Nagar 2006), also innovate new modes to convey collaborative work.

The gaps between non-university-based movements and their academic counterparts, whether with regard to Anglocentrism or inaccessible theory, become—as they should—the object of critique and debate. They are an opportunity to articulate with greater precision more egalitarian visions of collaboration. Transnational feminist work is clearly a heterogeneous set of movements, constituencies, strategies, sites, and political stances drawn together in often-uncomfortable proximity. It is simultaneously an opportunity to confront and work across differences, contest inequalities of power, and take advantage of distinctive strengths. Transnational feminist theory has theorized difference, power, and the challenges of honoring heterogeneity while recognizing the urgent need for solidarity. The distinct locations its participants engage, and the very clashes that can emerge, are a crucible for producing new tactics, language, and visions that can us move toward greater justice.

NOTES

1 See Sangtin Writers and Richa Nagar's *Playing with Fire* for an example of a collaboration between activists and academics critically examining NGOization.
2 On this point, see the critique of intersectional approaches articulated by Grewal and Kaplan (2001).
3 Margaret A. McLaren's 2017 edited volume *Decolonizing Feminism* presents transnational and decolonial feminism as kindred approaches, both committed to vigilance about how universalizing discourses are deployed.
4 Lisa Lowe's *The Intimacies of Four Continents* (2015) is an example of genuinely transnational scholarship on the relationship between classical liberal political thought and European imperialism.
5 Examples include the Inter-American Commission of Women and the Women's International League for Peace and Freedom.
6 For a view of this process from the perspective of Brazil, see Thayer (2010a).
7 There are certainly exceptions, such as the work of Women Living under Muslim Laws with the UN human rights system in their campaign "The Violence Is Not Our Culture."
8 See, for example, the Vidas Negras Importam, a series of protests in Brazil following the police killing of an unarmed Black man, Pedro Henrique Gonzaga, in February 2019, modeled after Black Lives Matter. See also references to the conversations between members of Dalit Women Fight, mentioned earlier in the chapter, and women from #BlackLivesMatter and #SayHerName.

9 For examples of early feminist critiques of nationalism and masculinity's place within nationalism, see Yuval-Davis's *Gender and Nation* (1997) and Enloe's *Bananas, Beaches and Bases* (1990). For an account of how feminine identities are mobilized in nationalist cultures, see studies of right-wing women by Bacchetta and Power (2013).

10 Transversal politics typically implies a form of antiassimilationist dialogue that presumes both the difference and the equality of its participants. Yuval-Davis (1997, 1999) is usually credited for first explaining this concept from Italian politics to wider feminist audiences.

2

Beyond Antagonism

Rethinking Intersectionality, Transnationalism, and the Women's Studies Academic Job Market

JENNIFER C. NASH

IN 2005 Sandra K. Soto posed a now-famous question: "Where in the Transnational World Are US Women of Color?" This critical query suggested that feminist investments in the transnational levied a heavy cost on US women of color, particularly Black women, as transnational feminist theory was imagined to perform its analytic and political work apart from US racial formations and apart from US Black women. Karla F. C. Holloway also amplified this concern, arguing that the transnational "manifests a profound and troubling discomfort with the local" and that transnational frameworks often act as permission for "local body-politics" to remain "underinterrogated" (2006, 2). Shireen Roshanravan echoed these anxieties about "global feminist" frameworks, noting, "Dismissing the politics and subjects of Women of Color as US-centric in the move to a 'global feminism' can easily be seen as strategic evasion of local critiques that would decenter white/Anglo perspectives and knowledges still anchoring the field" (2012, 6). Taken together, these texts cast transnational feminism—at least as practiced in US women's studies—as a feminist regime that renders Black women anachronistic, out of time and place.

In the decade since Soto's provocative query, US feminist scholars, including Anna Carastathis, Sylvanna Falcón, and Leela Fernandes, have begun a very different line of inquiry, considering what it means to think transnationalism and intersectionality, an analytic emerging from Black feminist theory, side by side. Put differently, this recuperative move has fundamentally challenged the notion that transnational feminism, at least as institutionalized in US women's studies, necessarily inflicts a kind of epistemological and representational violence on Black women. Falcón and Nash (2015, 9) call for a vision of transnationalism and intersectionality as both engaged in similar kinds of antisubordination work, a view that recognizes their overlap "without rendering invisible [their] distinct genealogies, histories, and epistemologies," a way of bridging them that problematizes the logics of the neoliberal university, which, they argue, have wedged them apart in the service of making each a valuable area of curricular development and faculty hiring. Similarly, Carastathis advocates a decolonial intersectionality and argues that "the identity-based specialization of labor that these divisions [between transnationalism and intersectionality] imply has implications for their deployment in institutional projects of diversity management and the training of 'difference' into colonial demographic categories, which women-of-color and Indigenous scholars are then called upon to naturalize with their embodiments" (2016, 199). Sara Salem (2014) also champions a "decolonial intersectionality," one that centers "women outside of privileged locations in the West where neoliberal imperialism continues to play a large role in producing and reproducing patriarchy [because] concepts that have their history in imperial centres are seen as unlikely to act as tools for meaningful change. This is why an intersectional approach needs to be combined with a decolonial framework." We can, then, think of these critical sutures as attempts to name a disjuncture and to repair it, to imagine a radical feminist politics rooted in both intersectionality and transnationalism, oriented toward complexity and solidarity, invested in a robust and nuanced conception of power's myriad forms. Often the suturing of these analytics unfolds through rhetorics of returning to a *before-time*, through genealogies of these terms that highlight how they have long been bound up. For example, some scholars center texts like M. Jacqui Alexander and Chandra Talpade Mohanty's (1997) *Feminist Genealogies, Colonial Legacies, Democratic Futures*, a transnational feminist anthology invested in theorizing US racial formations, as "early" texts thinking intersectionality and transnationalism together. Put differently, these critical sutures often unfold through "unforgetting" certain key feminist texts and through centering those texts as ones that performed a kind of intersectional transnationalism long before the terms became divided (Wald 2009).

This chapter aspires to historicize a moment when feminists labor to reconnect transnationalism and intersectionality. This chapter is a critical meditation on how we—feminists laboring in the US university—arrived at a moment when intersectionality and transnationalism were constructed as antagonistic, separate, and irreconcilable and when we had to engage in the intellectual and political labor of putting them back together. In this chapter I consider that question through a close engagement with the US academic job market, particularly the job market in women's studies, which has, I argue, produced—and continues to produce—the conception of these analytics, tools, methods, frameworks, and politics as separate. To be clear, the job market is not the only space that narrates intersectionality and transnationalism as analytics that are in tension. In other work (Nash 2019), I tell this story through a close engagement with the National Women's Studies Association, the field's professional organization, arguing that this has been another institutional space that has, in a variety of ways, pitted intersectionality and transnationalism against each other. But in this chapter my focus is on the women's studies academic job market, precisely because its capacity to produce and shape the discipline's intellectual and professional life, to value (and perhaps even devalue) certain analytics, remains underexplored. Though critical university studies scholarship has offered an important vocabulary for naming precarity and competition as ethics shaping the tenure-track job market, and tools for thinking historically about the emergence and entrenchment of ethics of corporatization in the contemporary university, there is far less attention to how the academic job market has come to shape disciplinary knowledge production precisely because of its capacity to articulate what analytics, keywords, methods, and frameworks confer value on scholarly work. There has been far too little analysis of how intersectionality and transnationalism's respective "citational ubiquity" in women's studies unfolds alongside the job market's valuation of these keywords (Wiegman 2012). If naming one's scholarly work *intersectional* or *transnational* gives it legibility and value on the job market, then it is unsurprising that *intersectionality* has become a keyword in women's studies, a term around which program building—hiring, curricular development, mission-statement drafting, and priority setting—unfolds.

This chapter advances two claims: first, rather than engaging in the definitional move where I succinctly capture intersectionality and transnationalism, I aspire to consider the institutional work of each term in the context of women's studies. I ask: What do these terms *do* for women's studies programs and departments, and what do we—feminist scholars—think we are doing when we mobilize these terms? Here I follow Robyn Wiegman's (2012) call to think about the "critical aspirations" that undergird our attachment to our objects of study and Clare Hemmings's (2011) plea to think about the "stories we tell," and I probe the meaning-making work both analytics perform for a field still—and perhaps forever—haunted by US Black woman, by the specter of so-called racial difference, and by the threat of "white feminism," which seems to forever hold the potential to undermine feminist theory, politics, and practice. The second portion of the article analyzes the academic job market in women's studies, with a particular interest in thinking about recent advertisements for tenure-track and tenured positions in women's studies. I closely read these texts for their engagements with transnationalism and, to a much greater degree, intersectionality, probing how these terms appear together—or separately—and how they are constructed by the market. I am particularly interested in tracing how these terms are produced in job ads as fundamentally separate, as terms that attach to different scholars, to different objects of study, and perhaps even to differently raced or ethnicized scholarly bodies who are called on to perform and embody these analytics. To be clear, my meditation on the job market in women's studies is not meant to fall into the now-familiar tradition of bemoaning feminist institutional politics or feminist desires for university recognition. As someone who labors in the university and who has spent most of my academic career laboring in women's studies programs working intensely for both visibility and resources, I am not at all opposed to the process—the fight, even—of seeking institutional recognition. I am, though, invested in a feminist reflexive practice about the costs, perils, and complexities of our institutional longings, a critical practice that does not end with a call for abandoning the project of academic feminism but instead with a plea for a continued interrogation and reimagination of the structures in which we have decided, often quite radically, to forge homes in the institution.

READING THE ANALYTICS

Though I have, in other projects, described intersectionality and transnationalism as "twin analytics," intersectionality has had a field-defining capacity that transnationalism has not. Indeed, intersectionality has had a popular and academic reach that is unprecedented among feminist analytics. As James Bliss notes, "No black feminist concept, save perhaps identity politics itself, has been as widely institutionalized in this milieu as Kimberlé

Crenshaw's formulation of intersectionality" (2016, 728). In other work, I think of intersectionality's move to the center of women's studies as linked to intersectionality's intimate connection with Black woman, the sign that, as I have argued elsewhere, fundamentally (if anxiously) shapes critical aspirations in women's studies (Nash 2019). Following Bliss's insight that "Black women are the object(s) of desire marking the limit that constitutes the field of women's studies," I view the ongoing feminist preoccupation with intersectionality's critical promise as necessarily linked to the discipline's sense that reckoning with Black woman, with her imagined demands for a feminist praxis that accounts for her "difference," can liberate feminism from its racial exclusions and violence (731). I describe intersectionality's promise to exculpate women's studies in my earlier work, noting, "Intersectionality is regularly envisioned as *the* paradigmatic analytic that stands for both black feminism and black women (indeed, the two are regularly collapsed and conflated), the theory that requires women's studies to reckon with black woman and her imagined complexity. It is intersectionality's ostensible capacity to remedy all that has ailed feminist theory, to provide 'political completion,' that gives the analytic its analytical, political, theoretical, and even administrative-programmatic muscle" (Nash 2017, 118).

Intersectionality—a term, analytic, method, and ethical and political commitment—gestures to both an antisubordination commitment to capturing, describing, and dismantling how structures of domination are made in and through each other and a recognition of the particular location of multiply marginalized subjects, particularly Black women, in these overlapping and mutually constitutive structures. In recent moments, intersectionality's critical genealogies are traced to a wide array of Black feminist scholar-activists, including Kimberlé Crenshaw, Patricia Hill Collins, Frances Beale, Deborah King, and the Combahee River Collective, and to women-of-color feminists like Gloria Anzaldúa and Cherri Moraga. Increasingly, intersectionality is hailed as an intellectual and political gift, something that Black feminism (and sometimes, problematically, feminism itself) has given critical theory, social movements, and feminist politics. For Leslie McCall, intersectionality constitutes "the most important contribution that women's studies . . . has made so far" (2005, 1771). Jean Ait Belkhir describes intersectionality as "one of the greatest gifts of *black women's studies* to social theory as a whole" (2009, 303). Intersectionality's "gift" or "contribution" is construed in myriad ways by different scholars, with some treating it as the analytic that rescues feminism from its history of racial exclusions, as the framework that reimagines conventional disciplinary knowledge and infuses it with a commitment to so-called difference, or as the primary tool that describes the complexity of hegemonic power.

In response to both the feminist fantasy of global sisterhood (and its attendant rescue narratives) and visions of feminism that entirely elided non-US settings, transnational feminism sought to transform feminism's theories of power's workings.[1] As Inderpal Grewal and Caren Kaplan explicate, the term *transnational* "problematize[s] a purely locational politics of global-local or center-periphery in favor of . . . the lines cutting across them" (1994, 13). In many ways a corrective to the feminist casting of race, class, and gender as the "holy trinity," transnational feminist approaches call for an engagement with "other complex categories of identity and affiliation that apply to non-US cultures and situations. US feminists often have to be reminded that all peoples of the world are not solely constructed by the trinity of race-sex-class; for that matter, other categories also enter into the issue of subject formation both within and outside the borders of the US, requiring more nuanced and complex theories of social relations" (17). This demand for attention to "complex categories of identity and affiliation" often—incidentally—shored up certain sites (and not others) as loci of transnational feminist investigation. Jennifer Suchland's (2011) work, for example, reveals that the so-called Second World often falls out of transnational feminist analyses, precisely because it is not imagined as a transnational space and because the Global South has been imagined not simply as *a* transnational space but as *the* transnational space.

Both intersectionality and transnationalism have been hailed as transformative analytics, though the ethical and political value of each is often described differently. As I have argued elsewhere, intersectionality is often hailed for its capacity to yield a particular kind of feminist "complexity," even as the nature of that complexity is described differently. Some scholars imagine it as a methodological complexity (Nash 2019).[2] Others imagine it as promising an alluringly complex "political completion," and still others imagine it as distinctly able to capture "complex personhood" (Wiegman 2012, 240; Gordon 1994, 4). Or, as Patricia J. Williams describes, "that life is complicated is a fact of great analytic importance" (1991, 3). As Leslie McCall notes (in a now-canonical article aptly titled "The Complexity of Intersectionality"), "The terms complex, complexity, and complexities appear frequently and are central in key texts on intersectionality" (2005, 1772), and yet complexity's particular meanings and virtues are never fully defined. It is never entirely clear if intersectionality's complexity yields complexity for complexity's sake or if complexity is part of a larger effort to do justice to something, perhaps the messiness of the social world.

If intersectionality's value comes from its capacity to gesture toward complexity, transnational feminism produces a different kind of ethic: solidarity. As Catherine Sameh notes, "Solidarity attempts to build ethical relationships based on equity while acknowledging and challenging the economic and political structures that create inequality between people. As a set of feelings and aspirations, solidarity might be imagined as a bridge that enables people to connect to or meet each other across significant divides" (2016, 181). Solidarity, then, upends both ideas of global sisterhood and notions of an "enforced commonality of oppression" and replaces them with what Mohanty terms "communities of people who have chosen to work and fight together" (2003, 7). If solidarity creates an aspirational goal for different forms of relationality, it also calls for new kinds of feminisms, with renewed attention to power's workings, including feminism's power. Grewal and Kaplan, for example, argue, "Feminist movements must be open to rethinking and self-reflexivity as an ongoing process if we are to avoid creating new orthodoxies that are exclusionary and reifying. The issue of who counts as a feminist is much less important than creating coalitions based on the practices that different women use in various locations to counter the scattered hegemonies that affect their lives" (1994, 18). It is, then, worth noting that the imagined value of these analytics has been constructed differently, one around a newly complex feminism and one about the practice—and promise—of what Chowdhury and Philipose term "dissident friendship" (2016). Perhaps we can sit for a minute with how analytics imagined to be associated with Black women are presumed to be challenging, difficult, and complex, even if reckoning with that complexity is imagined to be a feminist virtue, a challenge worth tackling.

Finally, both intersectionality and transnationalism have been subjected to various forms of *post*-ing, with scholars and activists noting their imagined incompletion or shortcomings, calling for either replacing them or complementing them with other key terms.[3] *Postintersectionality,* a term that emerged in the legal academy and has been championed by Peter Kwan (1997) as well as Robert S. Chang and Jerome Culp (2002), is an attempt to think through intersectionality's limitations and the variety of intersections it leaves untheorized, particularly sexuality. Thus, postintersectional scholars have often developed new terms like *multidimensionality* and *cosynthesis* to bring new forms of imagined complexity to intersectionality. As Kwan notes, these new forms of complex analysis are "dynamic model[s] of the conditions of categorical formations whose ultimate message is that, since the multiple categories through which we understand ourselves are implicated in complex ways with the formation of categories through which others are constituted, political emancipation and the achievement of justice are realizable only when we recognize that we all have a stake in finding ways of seizing control over the legal and cultural forces that shape all of the categories that are formed to maintain systems of oppression" (1997, 1292). Thus, the term *postintersectionality* seems to anticipate a desire to jettison intersectionality that this work has not manifested. The notion of *post*intersectionality has most famously unfolded around the theoretical concept of assemblage. Jasbir Puar's (2007, 215) now-famous call for assemblage as an analytic that interrupts intersectionality's imagined status and identity politics, a framework that "underscores feeling, tactility, ontology, affect, and information," has been taken up as the primary and most significant critique of intersectionality. Indeed, as I argue in my most recent book, despite Puar's critical engagement with intersectionality's utility and institutional politics, her investment in assemblage is primarily interpreted as a critical call for displacing intersectionality, for moving beyond it (Nash 2019).

In the context of transnational feminism, decolonial feminism is often hailed as a crucial *post-* (or perhaps even anti-) transnational politic. The call for decolonial feminist theory and politics is rooted in the notion that decolonial analytics are more attentive to indigenous subjects, to settler colonialism, and to processes of racialization in and beyond the Americas. In many ways, the call for a decolonial feminism links scholarly conversations in women's studies and Black studies, demanding a critical interrogation of categories like "human" and their racialized, gendered, and sexualized construction. As María Lugones notes, there is a "need to understand that the colonized became subjects in colonial situations in the first modernity, in the tensions created by the brutal imposition of the modern, colonial, gender system. . . . The behaviors of the colonized and their personalities/souls were judged as bestial and thus non-gendered, promiscuous, grotesquely sexual, and sinful" (2007, 187). Of course, this conception of decolonial feminism as the transnational's present and future tense necessarily relegates transnational feminism to feminism's embarrassing past. Priti Ramamurthy and Ashwini Tambe place critical pressure on the tendency to narrate the decolonial as the productive present tense of the past tense of transnational feminism. They write:

Jennifer C. Nash

The distinctions that are frequently drawn between the two approaches (postcolonial and decolonial) however have been a source of disquiet. . . . A common temporal marking that concerned us was the eclipsing of postcolonialism, which was increasingly becoming viewed as passé, and a setting up of decolonial feminism as always already better in time. . . . The depiction of postcolonial feminism as deconstructive, abstract, elite theory confined to the ambit of modern colonial knowledge systems overlooked the important quandaries that postcolonial feminism raised about how to represent marginalized people ethically and, indeed, how to understand the very desire to represent the marginalized—whether or not we claim belonging to them. (2017, 510)

Much like "critiques" of intersectionality, then, decolonial feminism positions itself as appropriately and productively attentive to multiple and complex vectors, including gender, race, coloniality, sexuality, and nation.

For my purposes, what is crucial about both analytics is the work they have performed institutionally for academic feminism in the US university. Indeed, myriad women's studies programs and departments define themselves—at least rhetorically—through their commitments to these twin analytics, to coursework, pedagogical tactics, and approaches that center these analytics. The Ohio State University Women's Studies Department, for example, notes, "The mission of the Department of Women's, Gender and Sexuality Studies (WGSS) is to generate interdisciplinary forms of knowledge about the complex interplay of power and difference, especially as inflected by categories such as gender, sexuality, race, class, age, ability, and nationality, across a vast array of contemporary and historical cultures" (The Ohio State University, online). The University of Minnesota Department of Gender, Women, and Sexuality Studies notes, "While gender and sexuality are fundamental to our field, we recognize that our lives and identities as gendered beings are also deeply and inextricably informed by other differences (such as race, nation, caste, and disability) that intersect at the core of who we are and how we function. And so we are committed in everything we do—our research, teaching, and engagement with communities—to fostering an inclusive understanding of human experiences that explores and embraces these differences" (University of Minnesota, online) And The George Washington University "offers courses that examine the world from diverse vantage points—gender, race, age, class, sexuality, ethnicity, nationality, etc.—and encourages students to explore and voice varying points of view, from a multidisciplinary vantage point" (The George Washington University, online).

These various quotes indicate how deeply women's studies programs and departments have rooted themselves in intersectionality and transnationalism as ethics and mandates that orient the institutional lives—hiring, curriculum, degree programs—of the field and their particular departments. (It exceeds the scope of this chapter, but this also aligns with larger institutional mandates around diversity, which also compel women's studies programs and departments to speak these languages to signal their viability and importance.)

THE POLITICS OF DISTINCTION IN THE JOB MARKET

"Who hires a PhD in women's studies?" asks Susan Stanford Friedman in a 1998 *Feminist Studies* article. She writes, "For the most part, not sociology, literature, history, political science, or economics departments. None of the traditional departments is likely to hire a feminist teacher-scholar who is not trained in a 'regular' discipline" (304). The anxieties undergirding the women's studies PhD, particularly around job placement, continue even as the question "Who hires a PhD in women's studies?" is now posed in relationship to the fact that graduates *do* secure tenure-track employment. Indeed, the women's studies job market is its own job market, with the National Women's Studies Association acting as a space of conference interviewing, with various institutions sponsoring postdoctoral fellowships in the field, and with a number of tenure-track positions open each year (not even counting jobs in traditional disciplines that seek scholars working on gender/sexuality or feminist/queer theory).

The women's studies job market—like all academic job markets—is a site that makes evident, and perhaps even produces, what terms, methods, frameworks, and analytics are valuable in a particular historical and institutional context. This value unfolds in multiple ways—at times certain approaches are valuable because of their intellectual or political contributions to the field and allied disciplines, and at times value is conferred because analytics align with larger institutional priorities and demands (we can think, here, about interdisciplinarity, global learning, service-based learning, and diversity as institutional demands that circulate with particular intensity in the US academy in this moment and that are often thought to align with intersectionality and transnationalism). Moreover, as Falcón notes, the job market becomes a space in which disciplines jockey for resources in the institution, making demands for tenure lines by naming (and valuing) important subfields, analytics, terms, and methods that the department currently does not cover. Falcón writes, "The job ads are interpreted and simultaneously scrutinized by department faculty and administrators, respectively, but for different ends. Administrators are the ones who have final approval of a faculty hire. Yet, faculty have to translate and justify to the administrators, who are often outside of our fields, why a particular position is needed. So for me, the dislodging of intersectionality and transnational feminism began, in part, during that moment in which they had to be made distinct rather than mutually inclusive" (Falcón in Falcón and Nash 2015, 10).

My impulse here is to suggest that the job market—which in some ways evidences the success of institutional feminism—has both reflected and produced precisely the separation that I charted at the beginning of the piece, an insistence that intersectionality and transnationalism are wholly distinct analytics. To engage in this analysis, I offer a close reading of US academic job market ads from the past five years. I follow Hemmings's citational practices—I do not attribute advertisements to particular universities—and instead seek to treat the collective performances of intersectionality and transnationalism's value as reflective of a disciplinary common sense even as job ads are produced in and through particular institutional priorities. Why is it, I want to understand, that so many job advertisements in our field look the same, sharing the same preoccupation with either intersectionality *or* transnationalism? What does it even mean that these are forms of knowledge production that are institutionally legible—and legible in their separateness—so that hiring can now happen along these axes?

Intersectionality is a keyword animating women's studies tenure-track job advertisements, even as the term is used in varied ways. For some departments, intersectionality is an area of focus:

> We invite applications from candidates with a research and teaching focus in gender, sexuality and/or LGBTQ studies and a strong emphasis on intersectionality.
>
> Preference will be given to candidates who can fill department needs in any of the following areas: 1.) Intersectionality; 2.) Research/activism of communities and women of color; or 3.) Sexuality studies; or 4.) Gender and STEM.
>
> The appointee will have interdisciplinary research and teaching interests and/or experience in the intersectionality of race, gender, and sexuality (LGBTQ) as it relates to new/social media.

Here intersectionality reflects a substantive area, a subfield that falls under the rubric of feminism/women's studies. For others, intersectionality is a method or approach: "Assistant Professor of Women's, Gender, and Sexuality Studies. PhD in humanities or social science with an emphasis in an intersectional approach to women's, gender, and sexuality studies." In this case, intersectionality seems to be a (preferred) mode of engaging in feminist inquiry, analysis, and scholarly pursuit. And yet, for others, intersectionality seems to constitute both a commitment to analyzing interlocking structures of domination *and* a political and ethical investment in capturing and dismantling structures of oppression. Three advertisements that perform this labor note:

> This position requires teaching or research in the intersectionality of gender, race, ethnicity, nationality, class, sexuality, and/or other social justice issues.

> We are particularly interested in candidates whose work is intersectional, understanding intersectionality not as descriptors of identity, but as a critique of structural inequalities.

> The hiring committee welcomes applications from qualified candidates working in critical approaches to intersectionality and social justice.

And yet, for some, intersectionality is a cross-cutting theory, method, and practice that supersedes feminist practice, that must inform all teaching and research. One job advertisement simply notes, "Candidates must demonstrate the ability to include intersectionality in all of their syllabi." Perhaps nowhere is intersectionality's inherent value more visible than in this command that intersectionality must be included in all teaching, that intersectionality is the single principle, method, theory, and political commitment that unites and drives all feminist teaching. These advertisements are marked by a sense of intersectionality's singular importance to the field, apart from transnationalism, with the exception of one advertisement that notes: "Candidates must have experience teaching core women's and gender studies courses through an intersectional lens and be qualified to develop courses in either transnational feminisms and/or queer theories." Even here, although intersectionality and transnationalism appear together, they are kept separate, with intersectionality constituting a "lens" and transnational feminism, like queer theory, constituting an area of intellectual inquiry. Intersectionality and transnationalism are not treated as equivalent forms of inquiry in the advertisement, even as the university seeks a scholar who can engage in research with an "intersectional lens" and teach transnational feminism.

Jennifer C. Nash

Similarly, advertisements seeking transnational feminist scholars move apart from intersectionality but largely emphasize an investment in non-US feminist and queer inquiries. Put differently, *transnational* is treated as a place-based marker and indicates a desire for scholarship that centers non-US locations. Some universities note:

> We seek a teacher-scholar (preferably with Ph.D. in hand) with advanced training in women's, gender, and/or sexuality studies and social science methods whose work focuses on transnational feminism and areas and/or populations outside the U.S.

> We seek a social scientist working at the intersections of gender, race, and social justice whose research is located outside of Europe and the Americas or who incorporates transnational or diasporic approaches to these regions.

> We invite applications for a tenure-track joint position at the rank of Assistant Professor in Transnational Sexuality Studies. Candidates must have native or near-native fluency in one of the foreign languages . . . : American Sign Language, Arabic, Chinese, Czech, French, German, Hindi, Italian, Japanese, Korean, Portuguese, Russian, Sanskrit, Spanish, and Swahili, and be willing and able to deliver instruction at all levels of the graduate and undergraduate curriculum.

In the case of all three advertisements, "transnational feminism" is aligned with "populations outside the U.S." and seems to stand in for a desire for a scholar who both uses transnational feminist theory/methods *and* applies them to non-US locations. Certainly, some advertisements push against the conflation of transnational with a particular geographic elsewhere. One notes,

> The specific area of specialization within the field of transnational feminism is open, but preference will be given to candidates whose transnational work and perspective concentrate on the Asias in the comparative sense. We furthermore understand "transnational" not only in a geographic way, but also in terms of flows and intersections across established boundaries and bodies of knowledge.

Yet this advertisement notes its investment in the transnational as exceeding the "geographic" alongside its desire for a scholar who works "on the Asias in the comparative sense." These advertisements share a sense that transnational feminist work does not center questions of race (at least in the United

States) and that transnational feminist approaches bring their value to the institutional spaces of women's studies by enabling a robust and detailed engagement with non-US spaces.

While the vast majority of advertisements separate transnational and intersectionality, a few suture them:

> We are seeking candidates who specialize in intersectional and/or transnational queer, feminist studies, with an emphasis on queer theory. We particularly welcome candidates with research areas that include—but are not limited to—critical race theory and sexuality studies, settler colonialism and indigenous studies, imperialisms, and postcolonial studies. The department also seeks a colleague who will build innovative pedagogical and research connections to antiracist, feminist social justice work within (either) local, regional, or transnational networks and communities.

> We seek a scholar with teaching and research interests in African-American, black diasporic, or non-western feminisms, particularly as they intersect with analyses of gender and sexuality. The program is especially interested in scholars whose work engages feminist thought broadly defined, with emphasis on transnational feminisms; colonial, decolonial, and postcolonial thought; critical race studies; or other relevant bodies of theory.

In both cases, intersectionality and transnationalism are treated as overlapping approaches, theories, and methods that inform feminist and queer inquiry. These kinds of articulations of the field's critical aspirations suggest strategies for disrupting the tendency to pit intersectionality and transnationalism against each other and for unsettling the tradition of assuming that intersectionality refers to Black/women's bodies while transnationalism refers to Global South/women's bodies.

CODA: THINKING DIFFERENTLY

While this chapter has lingered on a consideration of how the women's studies job market reflects and perhaps reproduces transnationalism and intersectionality as separate analytics, imbuing each with value and creating capacity building in women's studies through their separateness, it ends by asking what it might mean to shift from a conception of a women's studies job market to a feminist job market. The idea of a feminist academic job market might seem strange. How can a market marked by precarity, competition, and scarcity,

Jennifer C. Nash

construct itself in feminist ways? Yet, to me, it seems odd that women's studies—as a feminist discipline—surrenders its feminist principles and commitments in the face of hiring, tenure, and promotion, in the face of building our ranks. It is equally troubling that we refuse to imagine the possibility of building the ranks of women's studies faculty in universities as a task that could unfold in feminist ways, even as it unfolds in institutional space uninvested in feminist politics. What might our job market look like if we aligned it with feminist principles, including a radical critique of the logics and discourses of diversity that make hiring a site where liberal multiculturalism makes its practices most visible, where transnationalism and intersectionality code as much for bodies of scholars as for fields of study?

NOTES

1 In her canonical *Feminism without Borders*, Chandra Talpade Mohanty notes, "It is the praxis-oriented active political struggled embodied in this notion of solidarity that is important to my thinking—and the reason I prefer to focus attention on solidarity rather than on the concept of sisterhood" (2003, 7).

2 Ange-Marie Hancock, for example, describes intersectionality as yielding "causal complexity" (2007, 15).

3 My use of *post-ing* is indebted to Tiffany Lethabo King's (2015) formulation of it in her provocative article "Post-identitarian and Post-intersectional Anxiety in the Neoliberal Corporate University." Writing about intersectionality, she notes, "This 'post-ing' of intersectionality transforms it into a backward, Black moment in a postmodern and perhaps post-Black time. The rhetoric of 'post' announces an exhaustion with Black feminist thought that is a concern. Critiques of intersectional work are important because they are what keep analytics dynamic and useful, but a call to move beyond, and not with intersectionality risks circumventing generative conceptual work. Black feminist intersectional politics is useful in that it enables a conceptualization of power as both always in motion and as the hardened effects that make ontological differences appear on the landscape (or grid). Intersectionality can be used as a way of reading for unpredictable expressions of power, as well as for subjects who narrate power in legible ways" (133).

3

Rethinking Patriarchy and Corruption

Itineraries of US Academic Feminism and Transnational Analysis

INDERPAL GREWAL

US FEMINISM SEEMS TO HAVE BECOME newly powerful through opposition to Donald Trump and to right-wing American conservative ideologies, particularly around reproductive rights, the advancement of women of color in politics, and the #MeToo movement. This activist turn emerges amid a wealth of scholarly vigilance about the forms that feminism can take. Scholars have offered sharp critiques of feminisms as forms of power, state or otherwise: "imperial feminism" (Amos and Parmar 1984), "white feminism," and varieties of national and religious feminisms, as well as "governance" (Halley 2006), "carceral" (Bernstein 2007), or "security" (Grewal 2017) feminisms, have become resonant in research showing how empires, colonialisms, and racisms pushed particular feminisms to flourish, often through comparison and control of women from colonized spaces. We see emerging and contending constructs of "white feminism," "women-of-color feminism," or, in the case of India, "savarna" (upper-caste) (Da Costa 2018) or Dalit feminisms (Mehta 2017). Marxist and liberal philosophies run variously and multiply through these emergent formations, and the question whether these are identities or political subjectivities is always up in the air.

Gendered inequalities remain—women are still targets of violence and discrimination in numerous places, including the Global North, though we know that many groups of men and other genders are also targeted. And gendered forms of masculine power continue as well, from the predations of patriarchies becoming oligarchic to right-wing nationalisms that empower some groups of men by giving them power over women and other genders and by disenfranchising and racializing Others. At this historical juncture, these oligarchies and patriarchies signal the inequalities that mark the result of more than four decades of neoliberal policies and authoritarian nationalisms. The continued relevance—albeit with some differences—of many kinds of feminist research helps us to understand what shifts, continuities, and differences emerge at every historical juncture (S. Roy 2012).

In recent times, feminist research has become mobilized to critique the politics of gender and sexuality in the news, as sexual, racial, and religious politics and questions of economic inequality continue to roil many institutions that have supported male power. As much as there are groups of women who align themselves with revanchist masculinities, in the context of the United States feminisms have emerged that are working to oppose the authoritarian tendencies of the Trump regime and its global counterparts.[1] Across the globe, we see feminisms critiquing circulations of male heteronormative power that is fundamentally patriarchal and that operates by neoliberal logics of privatizing capital and property to increase dominant male ownership of capital on a massive scale. Young people are aligning themselves with LGBT and trans movements more widely, though with fears that these too will be taken over by liberal rather than radical potentialities (Eng 2010). The #MeToo movement protests sexual harassment not just as a form of power over sexuality but also as power over education, employment, and all sorts of mobilities and opportunities that foreclose the futures of women and differently gendered persons. Online lists naming sexual harassers, street protests, and confrontations with authorities have come to question liberal feminist remedies, seeking more public disclosures that hope to name and shame and thus challenge the foundational gendered structures of institutions.

What sorts of feminist directions are becoming visible in academic research at the present time after these shifts that I have mentioned? How is scholarship contending with the diversity of feminist politics that are variously liberal, radical, religious, imperial, or capitalist? Are there feminisms that can address the question of rights and advocate for the nonstate and noncitizen formations that are emerging globally, as empires wax and wane and climate extinction looms? What is the theorization of capitalism and gendered inequality that we can offer at this historical juncture of what I have elsewhere called "advanced neoliberalism," which includes emergent processes of connection and exclusion, in which inequalities and exclusions increase and generate protest and repression (Grewal 2017)? How might feminist research contribute to addressing the continued appropriation of indigenous lands and communities by transnational corporations and national capitalisms at the same time as the language of women's empowerment, as feminists such as Aradhana Sharma (2008) and Sarah Banet-Weiser (2018) point out, has become widespread? In this chapter I discuss some problems for contemporary academic feminist politics and analysis through examining how political subjects are imagined through research and approaches that we term *transnational*, *postcolonial*, and *intersectional*. I offer a case study of patriarchy in the United States to reveal how such an analysis helps to understand the relation among corporations, capitalism, gender, and race in America.

FIELD FORMATIONS: POSTCOLONIAL, TRANSNATIONAL, AND INTERSECTIONAL FEMINISMS

Postcolonial feminism engages global histories, examining gendered identities and modernities as connected with colonial categories. Early postcolonial studies scholars worked to dismantle the "tradition-modernity" divide that had existed in area studies before postcolonial studies and had seeped into social science, global health, international relations, and development studies—all with profound impacts. They critiqued the production of universalized categories, the overwhelming power of US and European knowledge production in the making of empire and even in anticolonial nationalisms (Narayan 1997; Jayawardena 1986; McClintock 1995; Spivak 1999; Mohanty 2003; Alexander 2006; Carby 2000). While postcolonial theory brought to light the problem of development and modernization, of geopolitical and national inequalities and commensurabilities, many of its (mostly nonfeminist) practitioners also had their blind spots, such as a reliance on national and territorial boundaries; even the construction of differential modernities, for instance, focused on bounded cultural and historical difference between nations and cultures (Chakrabarty 2007). Another problem in postcolonial studies in its turn toward the nation was an underemphasis on race, despite so much work on the writings of Frantz Fanon, for example, by some scholars. The complexity of race or caste as globalizing categories, with multiple histories of relationships that are not just about labor, is an ongoing problematic that demands collaborative and transnational research across a variety of regions, groups, and historical periods.

Some feminist postcolonial theorists, however, did address the relations across boundaries, across cultures and international domains, that produced different, gendered subjects in relation to global and other projects (national and subnational as well as regional) in historically specific ways. Gayatri Chakravorty Spivak, for instance, was distinct from subaltern studies theorists precisely because her approach also engaged with thinking of the "worlding" of women and their global circulation (Spivak 1985). The questions of how modernity made different subjects globally and how the subject "woman" varied historically and regionally were both examined critically, over and against the continued disavowal of difference by a powerful global/liberal feminist project (Weinbaum et al. 2009). The contribution of postcolonial feminism was critical to transnational cultural politics—such as the critique of comparisons of North and South, for example, or of "saving brown women from brown men," as Spivak (1988) famously called it, which has now emerged in feminist transnational studies as an important analytic and political project. The work of prominent theorists of postcolonial studies was frequently marked as "area studies" without being seen as generalizable; for instance, the common claim in US academia was that postcolonial studies was bounded by its South Asianness. Such arguments ignored broader claims from postcolonial theory about the colonial underpinnings of contemporary knowledge formations: the problem of representations of "Orientals" or Africans or Arabs and of non-Western women (Mudimbe 1988; Said 1978; Kandiyoti 1995; Oyěwùmí 2003; Abu-Lughod 2015; Yegenoglu 1998), the "provincialism" critique (Chakrabarty 2007), the "underdevelopment" thesis (Rodney 1981), or the critique of knowledge production (Spivak 1999; Mbembe 2001). The emergence of the "decolonial" paradigm, though valuable in its insistence on indigeneity as a central question of justice and settler colonialism, seems to promise a method of transcending the colonial processes and sedimentations that postcolonial theory took on as a central problematic (Mignolo and Walsh 2018). Postcolonial theory's concern with the problems and theorizations of nationalisms, and the desires and difficulties of decolonization, cannot be ignored, given the emergence of new authoritarian populisms that emerge as religious and racial nationalisms but use colonial legal and policing mechanisms.

Drawing on varied contributions from postcolonial studies but addressing difference in terms of the varieties of gendered and racial formations and the linkages across them through many empires, a transnational approach foregrounded both difference and the making of difference. Critiquing the Euro-American feminist power to adjudicate whether women in other regions are sufficiently modern or "empowered" has led to calls for such feminism to recognize its own patriarchal and racial formations and limits. Understanding how the production of the "unfreedom" of women in the Global South was necessary for establishing the "freedom" of white women in the North (Grewal 1995b; Burton 1994) has remained valuable in the imperial wars of the twenty-first century, which are increasingly deterritorialized and territorialized around racial and religious identities.

What we now call a *transnational* approach in feminist research emerged to make connections across feminisms and national boundaries by theorizing how feminist scholarship and feminist formations needed to contend with a history of colonialism, culture, and empire that spanned continents and nations. Drawing on the work of the journal *Public Culture*, created by Arjun Appadurai and Carol Breckenridge, as well as the emerging interest in travel and mobility studies (Clifford 1997; Adey et al. 2017; Creswell and Merriman 2013), it was a way to understand the relations among diverse feminisms created by myriad institutions and contexts globally, many of which resulted from European imperial cultures. It hoped to bring attention to the connections and links—rather than commonalities and differences, as in the prevailing comparative approach—between the anticolonialisms and antinationalisms that emerged as "resistance" to those empires. In the US context, it posed the problem of reducing the study of feminisms to a context of nationally bounded area studies. This transnational approach emerged out of a recognition that national comparison and comparative political and literary studies were a colonial project, seldom able to break out of the North-South binary, which was variously metaphorized as modern-traditional, advanced-backward, or mobile-static. The project was to have feminist theorizing more focused on the *making* of difference, and the disavowal of that process, across spaces that could not be seen simply as global/local but that were linked across different spatialities and temporalities. Studies of sexuality have also become engaged with thinking through transnationalisms. Many scholars have now taken these approaches to critique nationalisms, border practices, contemporary resonances of colonialisms, and the making of difference that is racial or cultural.[2]

In our anthology *Scattered Hegemonies*, published in 1994, my coauthor and coeditor Caren Kaplan and I attempted to bridge understandings of subject populations in the United States with those outside it and to think about how histories of colonialism, feminism, racism, and modernity linked gender constructs across nations and nationalisms. We employed the insights of what is called *mobility studies* to think outside national boundaries. We were inspired by how "Western feminism" was being challenged by black feminisms and postcolonial feminisms. Reading texts by British feminists such as Hazel Carby (1999) and Valerie Amos and Pratibha Parmar (1984), and the work of Angela Davis (1983), bell hooks (2014), Audre Lorde (2007), and Gloria Anzaldúa (2012), had given us an understanding of the problematic of empire itself as raced and classed in its creation of imperial subjects. But we also found it necessary to address national and local hierarchies created by caste, religion, or any of the many vectors of difference existing across diverse cultures. By calling it "transnational feminist cultural studies," we argued that hegemonies were different but connected through imperial projects. We learned to critique "ethnic absolutisms" through the complex circulations of culture described by Paul Gilroy (1990) and the Birmingham school. Scholars such as M. Jacqui Alexander and Chandra Talpade Mohanty (1997) worked in a related but somewhat different framework, offering highly influential critiques of categories of "non-Western" women and Western development regimes and a powerful version of anticapitalist and antiracist scholarship.

Most so-called comparative work operated through comparisons between the Global North and Global South as separate, bounded entities and civilizations that could be mapped onto existing nation-states; transnational studies hoped to overturn this diagnosis of colonial epistemologies. In particular, we critiqued the erasure of the connections and linkages among empires and nationalisms, among the forms of power that circulated globally to create both colonialisms and anticolonialisms. Epistemologies of flows (Appadurai 1996), oceanic connections (Gilroy 1995), intimacies (Stoler 1995), and historical diasporas (Chow 1993) had also emerged on the academic scene to disrupt the traditional disciplinary and interdisciplinary formations of area. We also encountered a similar problem in working on histories of colonialism and slavery in the United States: the domestication of the "third world liberation" projects of the 1960s had turned race into a cultural project of an American ethnicity and produced notions of culture that were nationally bounded (Gilroy 1990). The question that remains even now is how to think race as a project of many Euro-American empires contending with disjunctive and different imperial histories and anticolonial movements.

The term *intersectional* was important as an answer to the diversity of and differences among gendered and feminist subjects based on race and gender. It addressed the problem of understanding race and gender as producing separate identities, showing that institutions relied on both gender and race (as well as citizenship status) to produce forms of subordination. It drew from the interventions made by legal scholarship in critical race studies to include considerations of gender in the making of legal subjects. Kimberlé Crenshaw's (1991) innovative use of this term was a means to address the problem of the gender-versus-race argument forged by white imperial feminism, on the one hand, and cultural nationalisms, on the other. Crenshaw proposed a method rather than an identity, one that saw institutions of power as formed by multiple intertwined forms of power and suggested that those institutions could be opposed and understood only by intersectional analytics. While other approaches using analytics of articulation (Hall 1996) or multiplicity remained powerful, the language of intersectionality soon emerged as dominant in activist and academic spaces in the West.

While in the United States intersectionality has become the means to address the imbrication of gendered and racial power and identities, there is a danger, when ignoring transnational formations, of leaving out the rapid dissemination and power of ideas of race that cross and reify national boundaries and empires. That white supremacy and white nationalisms are transnational movements with American and European (extending to Australia and New Zealand) connections and differences means that greater attention needs to be paid to transnational and imperial logics. Intersectional analysis can suggest the power of the term *race*, but it is surely not necessary to limit its analytic power to the US context or to the history of race as it emerged through Atlantic slavery. As scholars of Asia, Africa, Latin America, and the Caribbean have amply demonstrated, race is dynamic and unstable and also historically quite heterogeneous, even as it crosses regions and continents through globalizing networks and processes. Different colonialisms—Portuguese, Spanish, Japanese, British, French, US—all created overlapping and divergent racial and gendered categories.

Jennifer C. Nash (2019) has suggested that the "intersectionality wars" indicate that the term has been institutionalized in ways that reduce its original claim of complex identities; it has become a way to signal race and black feminism (in the United States), without paying attention to all the problems of seeking to ground this theory in one particular subject and only on the intersection of race and gender. One might recall that Crenshaw's original essays on the term also referenced the condition of immigrant women and described how issues of violence toward those women could not be understood

Inderpal Grewal

without addressing their immigration status as enabling the violence (e.g., Crenshaw 1991). Moreover, given that the histories of indigeneity and settler colonialism are connected to broader processes of extraction of land and labor, intersectionality can be useful and has been taken up in divergent ways. I have now seen the term *intersectional* used in the context of India as well in order to insist on caste as a category that, akin to race, is essential to understanding gender in India, for instance.[3] It has become useful for critiquing a kind of feminism that is being called "savarna," or upper-caste, feminism (Soundararajan and Varatharajah 2015; FirstPost staff 2018) and also for proposing that white feminism can also be critiqued intersectionally (Grewal and Roy 2017, 254–62).

TRANSNATIONAL FEMINIST STUDIES: PROSPECTS

At this point, many disciplines in the US academy have institutionalized transnational feminism and intersectional feminism, generating academic positions and many journals and books on these topics. The term *transnational* is, however, not without its problems. It may be difficult to continue to use it if its possibilities become overly reduced, for instance, to a study of American or other imperialism, rather than including the ways that different genealogies and histories of subjectivities coming from all sorts of locations produce subjects and institutions. It is difficult, requiring new connections and networks to carry out, or expensive collaborative projects, including historical ones. Yet it remains valuable, given that terms such as *postcolonial* and *intersectional* are unable to address the diverse global-international-geopolitical networks and alliances, as well as the histories of past regional and global connections and genealogies. I see its possibilities as an analytic and descriptive category whose political project is recognizing the power of the global and national that is made through relational and boundary-making and boundary-transgressing projects that have historically reorganized space, place, and territory. Given that there are mobile economies, cultures, worlds, and people, transnationalism allows us to begin from the foundational concept that people, boundaries, and histories are not fixed. An ever-growing group of scholars and researchers is doing transnational projects; for these scholars, it is important to critique area studies and Western comparative analysis as an imperial project, to understand nationalisms' myriad problems, to investigate transnational and nonprovincial histories that uncover pasts that go beyond comparative analysis, to create new projects of oceanic and interregional studies, and to claim the centrality of migration and displacement.[4] How far such work will go toward countering imperial epistemologies and ongoing inequalities is uncertain. But we do have to keep at it.

While some have come to think of transnational feminism as an identity, we (Caren Kaplan and I) saw it as both a scholarly paradigm drawing on new theories of mobility and also a political project intended to fracture notions of national tradition or culture, or global capitalism and its institutions, as well as hegemonic forms of power that would be differently articulated in the making of place and nation. The critique of the national as the global-national, that is, a kind of national that both relies on global capital and also denies its relationship to geopolitics and colonial/modern histories, allowed us to think about forms of power that produced transnational elites, geopolitics and international relations, corporate and capitalist collaborations, and networks of power and privilege that have produced inequalities the world over. It was useful to understand affiliations, solidarities, and power, both in feminism and in other political projects. As a term that shared its key term with transnational corporations, *transnational feminism* was a politics that hoped to not claim vanguardism or purity. It was a theoretical project and a scholarly paradigm that could also be politically useful in critical and creative ways to puncture universalisms and Eurocentric normative ideas. We could see that the "common" struggle of women that is understood as a universal in some Western feminism was a matter of power and influence rather than a natural outcome of gender difference. We could also understand solidarities and differences as both constituting feminist networks and struggles.

Transnational feminist cultural *politics*—rather than cultural *studies*—had to be thought through with reference to context, region, and temporal and spatial politics. It enabled a focus on the national in the transnational, in order to argue that the transnational did not transcend nationalism even if it produced international and transnational alliances. We could understand how nationalisms were produced by forces external to it. Such a politics remains important to think about nationalism, not just in relation to the nation-state but in relation to other nationalisms—religious, cultural, racial—many with repressive sexual and gender politics. Transnational cultural politics is a means to connect processes of imperialism, colonialism, and capitalism that make national-racial and gendered subjects. It emphasizes both the operations of transnational capital in the present and also the histories of modernization, globalization, and colonization as foundational institutions of the modern world and as genealogies for subjects everywhere.

CASE STUDY: TRUMPISM, CORRUPTION, AND PATRIARCHY IN THE EMPIRE

While so much of transnational feminist cultural politics focuses on understanding empire, it also has become a method of seeing whether imperial constructs can be dislodged by using categories that emerge in the study of what are seen as the peripheries of empire—but are, in fact, spaces that enable empire or even places that are laboratories of its power (Amar 2013). Drawing on this notion of laboratories of empire, Jean and John Comaroff (2012, 113–21) argue for "theory from the South" to examine how the millennial capitalism imposed on the Global South has now come to bear on countries in the North. This is a method of doing transnational work that reverses the itinerary of empire by moving terms from the South to the North, rather than in the other direction (as a center-periphery analysis suggests), and by drawing on postcolonial analyses to recognize the continued colonial processes of extraction that subtend the direction of these itineraries. Such a reversal of the itineraries of terms undercuts the exceptionalist claims of American empire, for instance, and sees much of its operations as banal to millennial capitalism (Comaroff and Comaroff 2001). Yet it is not just in the Global South that these concepts are instrumentalized for imperial power; places and spaces that are described as "Third World" and colonial methods of control and exploitation exist within the empire itself.[5] Thus, the process of producing "theory from the South" has a more complex itinerary, one that moves processes of exploitation from within the empire to its peripheries and then back again. The abjected populations within the imperial nation then become the site of simultaneous disavowal; the foreign and the domestic are separated, and migrants then are seen as the foreign Others infiltrating the empire rather than as those displaced by it.

There is thus a need to examine the spatialities, direction, and itineraries of concepts to also ask why and how some terms were disavowed in the North in the first place, or defined in ways that have often been racialized and that have supported continued exploitation, and how such a politics of disavowal is used hegemonically by powerful groups. Another important project is to understand how these concepts that are used to define the Global South were most pertinent to the colonizing North. This is a process of disavowal I have called *outsourcing*—a kind of imperial cultural arbitrage (Grewal 2013) in which terms become valuable and useful because they are deployed outside the United States. I suggest that Western exceptionalism is upheld through such process of displacement and differentiation, especially with the use of terms such as *patriarchy* and *corruption*.

These two terms have come into use in the United States to describe the Trump presidency, but they do not apply uniquely to Trump since these terms can certainly be used to describe the collaborations between private and transnational corporations and the US state. However, they have erupted into use to describe Trump as an anomalous US president, while the Trump era is in fact a culmination of longer processes that have enabled a more authoritarian mode of government. The Trump presidency must also be understood as a particular kind of capitalist authoritarianism that has been seen in many other parts of the world and that is also not that foreign to the United States. One might argue that Trump is best understood as a transnational networked capitalist firm, as Trump Corporation, found around the world but specific to Euro-America in harnessing the power of racial empire. Such a patriarchal capitalism was believed to be outmoded in the West with the advent of the corporation as a collection of shareholding persons who did not necessarily have kinship ties, but it has long been a powerful formation forged by ties to the US state. It has been enabled, as Thomas Piketty (2014) has pointed out, by the tremendous power of inherited private and corporate wealth transmitted within families toward the end of the twentieth century and into the new century and found within both monarchies and democracies in Europe and America. Sylvia Yanagisako's (2002) research on such firms in Italy has shed some light on their operations and their gendered and patriarchal dimensions, and feminist anthropologists have called for greater attention to the use of kinship and gender in studying capitalist societies (Bear et al. 2015). Such corporate kinship became normalized to capitalism and wealth accumulation. While US liberalism justified such accumulation as individual and American exceptionalism, on the one hand, and American empire, on the other, Trump's vulgar exercise of power and wealth explodes these narratives to reveal how race, gender, and kinship explain inequalities.

The Trump family firm, then, with all its advertising, use of media, and desire to use the law for itself, makes open and visible what has been central to US power: the maintenance of racial patriarchies through privatized accumulation. The accumulation by the family is the main project of the Trump presidency, for which it uses racial populism to stay in power. All

Inderpal Grewal

of Trump's cabinet came from the corporate sector, and worked to further their own corporate profits. Employing his children and family as key advisers, and not trusting anyone except family, Trump revealed through his actions how the American presidency was captured by a family firm. Many of Trump's travels included visiting his own properties, and the American taxpayer then reimbursed the Trump companies for his visits. Those visits served as publicity for these properties, such as his house in Florida, which functioned both as a presidential vacation spot owned by the Trump corporation and as a hotel where businesspeople and politicians around the world paid for access to the president. Donald Trump Jr. used his position as the son of the president to create business opportunities during his visit to India and other places, and Jared Kushner, Trump's son-in-law, was a key adviser emboldened to make deals for his family and the Trump family under the guise of doing foreign policy. Newspapers reported Kushner's dealings with the families of other authoritarian leaders around the world (Kirkpatrick and Lipton 2019). Trump's own financial interests remain murky and are a topic of conjecture as his former staff and supporters are discovered to have engaged in criminal conduct.

While Trump's travels and deals were noted as corrupt by watchdog organizations in the United States, a large number of politicians in Congress or other branches of government were unwilling to condemn this behavior. Critics of Trump have spoken of similarities to the operations of mafia, thus again portraying an invisible norm as an exception. The term *lobbying*, which obscures the difference between democratic access to representatives and bribery by the wealthy and corporations, is an ongoing practice in the political culture of the United States, though Trump ratcheted nefarious accumulation to spectacular heights. For example, the appointment of corporate lobbyists to his cabinet was not just about a "business-friendly" administration but reveals how the state has been captured by this capitalist class, which is white and male, for the most part. Such racial and masculine power is also appealing to many Americans, as white supremacy has been both a campaign tactic and a mode of accumulation.

The Republican Party's refusal to disclose the Trump Corporation's and Trump's tax filings and the extent of the holdings and finances of this privately held firm means that they have protected the Trump Corporation and ceded the presidency to this family firm for their particular agendas. This regime, then, most obviously requires a set of terms that are most often used for the Global South: the vocabulary of corruption and patriarchy seems suited to the power being exercised in the United States today. That which liberal empire strove to hide in the making of American exceptionalism is now laid open. Further, in exceptionalizing Trump, the power of patriarchies during more liberal presidencies is made invisible, as Lorna Finlayson (2019) argues in her critique of new books discussing "patriarchy's resurgence" under Trump.

The adjudication of the scale and understanding of corruption has been a mainstay of the production of difference between the Global South and North. Organizations such as Transparency International offer an example of such work. Their famous index of corruption is now entitled "corruption perceptions"; although it still includes the poorest states as the most corrupt, it now also includes Russia and China, with European democracies as the least corrupt.[6] This is the key way in which the Global South is held accountable for its own nondevelopment, for its powerful authoritarian leaders, even as large-scale corruption and bribery of foreign state officials has been a regular practice for companies from the Global North seeking large contracts.

Using terms such as *corruption* and *patriarchy* to describe the American president can undercut US exceptionalism and help us to think transnationally. Much is problematic about the discourse of corruption—its focus on legality rather than inequities of power, its preference for the needs of the bourgeoisie rather than those of the poor, and its inability to address questions of other forms of power, including race and gender. *Corruption*, like *transparency*, harkens to a desire for a democracy that never was—one that can be mobilized against governments too. Witness how it was used in Brazil against former president Luiz Inácio Lula da Silva (popularly known as Lula), for instance, to bring back neoliberal and predatory capitalism under Jair Bolsonaro's authoritarian regime. Yet it is useful in helping understand the nature of authoritarian and imperial power in the United States as banal rather than exceptional.

Another reason *corruption* is useful to think through but not to deploy uncritically, and not just with reference to the West, is that it pays little attention to the gendered and sexualized nature of authority; sexual and economic violence remain unconnected in most articulations of corruption, scholarly or popular. Patriarchy is often a hidden partner—as both cause and effect—of corruption, as some men become powerful through patrimonial capitalism and ongoing privileges, including access to careers and wealth. Abuse of power, via sexual harassment and sexual assault that subordinate groups of people, remains outside the ambit of the term. Unless a sexual scandal involving a high-level official becomes a topic of media coverage, such as

Trump's payments to cover up his affairs and allegations of sexual assaults, the everyday advantages of sexual transactions that are claimed by powerful males or groups escape media focus as forms of corruption. Furthermore, the targets of anticorruption campaigns globally remain mostly the state and its representatives—either politicians or bureaucrats. People still hold public officials rather than private businesses responsible for corruption—a situation that is deployed and exacerbated by neoliberal projects of privatizing public institutions. The erasure of contemporary accumulation as enabled by public-private partnerships between states and corporations is enabled by a neoliberal targeting of the state as corrupt and the corporation as efficient.

What is excluded in the uses of the term *corruption* is therefore instructive. Indeed, the advantages of upper-class and upper-caste white male privilege—of a hegemonic masculinity that gives some men the power of patriarchy and the ability to exert violence over others—are highly desirable to many and often well known. But these patriarchies and powerful groups are not solely national/local powers but include transnationally connected elites. The social advantages of corruption are thus not simply in the realm of work or capital but rather spread across public and private divides, as domestic and professional realms become continuous in so many ways—family networks; marriage alliances that continue race, caste, and upper-class power; educational opportunities and global networks across corporations and political infrastructures; and the support and enabling of sexual predation by powerful corporate elites. The production of new patriarchies, their class compositions, and their collaborations with traditional authorities such as the police and the military increase social and economic insecurity and disenfranchisement, especially among poor and historically stigmatized communities.

It is time, then, to examine both corruption and US patriarchy in new transnational ways. Masculinities, toxic or otherwise, are not just about family but also about the family as a network, and specifically as a transnational network intertwined with geopolitics, capitalism, and nationalisms. The family, the patriarch, and the oligarch are key to thinking about Trump's attempt to capture the US government for the advantage of the Trump family firm. This is one way in which as feminist scholars we can address the question of the state, corruption, and power. Oligarchs embody the male privatization of extreme concentrations of power and capital and reveal how capital is gendered and, in the West, racialized. Such patriarchs are not all white globally, as much as we can comfortably say this about the United States, and their power is not just limited to one country. The recent exposés in the United

States about sexual harassment and sexual assault are instructive in this regard, revealing how gender and sexuality are central to these regimes of power. These patriarchies are also not just about power over the household, or women and the family, but about power, including sexual power, over all sorts of other bodies and genders.

If I have suggested that though *corruption* and *patriarchy* have historically been used to describe the Global South but should be used to describe political and economic power in the United States, it is not just because of Trump as an example but also because of the predations in the corporate workplace. The stories of sexual harassment and sexual assault in the corporate workplace expose the ways that capitalist firms are linked to states and use kinship, gender, and elite white male networks to accumulate wealth and power. Powerful heads of media corporations, such as Harvey Weinstein, film producer, and Les Moonves, the CEO of the media corporation CBS from 2003 to 2018, had the power to destroy the lives of women who rejected their sexual advances at work or who refused to be silenced. Moonves reportedly promoted white male writers and masculine stories that put white men as protagonists on millions of TV screens (Thomason 2018), and the power of such masculinist media representations cannot be discounted. Corporate boards and legions of lawyers from powerful law firms constituted a transnational network of business interests protecting these men. Journalist Ronan Farrow (2017, 2019), reporting on the Harvey Weinstein case, noted that Black Cube, an Israeli security company, was hired by Weinstein's lawyers (in particular the extremely wealthy law firm of Boies Schiller Flexner) to spy on women such as actress Rose McGowan, who was accusing Weinstein of sexual assault. In this case, the "intelligence gathering" was done by a female employee from Black Cube pretending to be sympathetic to McGowan but actually gathering information on McGowan to help suppress lawsuits. Black Cube was started by ex–Israel Defense Forces personnel, and its website claims that it "protects" business internationally through surveillance and information gathering.[7] In this case, the Israeli security state's expertise was used to protect sexual predators. The Harvey Weinstein–Black Cube story brings to light all the ways that whiteness, patriarchy, capitalism, and empire are transnationally networked. None of these stories of capitalist and patriarchal networks are nationally bounded, since the infrastructure of corruption is transnational, including tax shelters in remote regions and money laundering through real estate transactions that in urban spaces have led to skyrocketing prices that locals cannot afford.

This kind of securitizing of the powerful that enables sexual predation subtends the legal process—the process protects patriarchy, and its standards of evidence often discourage women (and men) from going to the authorities. It works to produce doubt about a witness and destroys their credibility in myriad ways. Controlling subordinate groups and their stories is the work not of a single man but of a capitalist patriarchy that is protected by security states, the extralegal machinations of complicit companies, offshore shelters, media corporations, and kinship relations. The predations are networked into the infrastructure of patriarchy and empire. At the same time, the Western control over and criticism of African or Latin American dictators and patriarchies continues, as Western countries encourage authoritarian power in the Global South to enable ongoing expropriation.

The advent of Trump has brought greater attention to theorizing patriarchy, but there is still a danger of nostalgia for a liberal version of the theory, particularly a version that universalizes patriarchy. Some of the recent feminist research in the United States again presumes that patriarchy works as a universal, using a psychological approach based on immutable characteristics of masculinity and femininity (Gilligan and Snider 2018). Though patriarchal power seems to be present in many places, how it functions and maintains itself, who it includes and excludes, depends on the structure of particular societies. Patriarchies change over time as masculinities and femininities and genders change spatially and temporally. The US examples I have described from a transnational feminist angle reveal a particular racial empire producing itself as exceptional. Trump exemplifies a particular American version of patriarchy that shores up white masculinity in its illiberal attempts to maintain an empire losing its power.

Such a patriarchy, determined to use race and capital to maintain its power, is not the same patriarchy everywhere though it is linked across regions by transnational corporations, colonial sedimentations of law and property, and geopolitics. History and its geopolitics produce differences in the ways that neoliberal capitalism and religious nationalisms engage with shifting structures of family and social reproduction in specific spaces. Although I suggest that corruption is everywhere intertwined with the hierarchies generated by patriarchies, how these relations are maintained and contested depends on heterogeneous hierarchies of time and place. The disavowal of patriarchy and corruption is a particular and peculiar mode of power deployed in the US, and it seems time to end this version of American exceptionalism.

ACKNOWLEDGMENTS

My thanks to the editors of this volume, Ashwini Tambe and Millie Thayer, for their sharp and extremely helpful comments on this chapter, as well as to the Duke University Press reviewers. My thanks also to the terrific feminist group gathered by the editors at the international conference in Florianópolis, Brazil, for their comments and feedback.

NOTES

1 Many different feminist antifascist and antiracist movements have now emerged around the world, becoming visible in protests all over the world—including in Brazil, the United States, the United Kingdom, India, and many other countries, though these may form somewhat different local political alliances. See, for one example, Wade (2018).

2 A short list would include the work of Lila Abu-Lughod, Sylvanna Falcón, Eda Pepi, Miriam Ticktin, Nadera Shalhoub, Richa Nagar and Amanda Lock Swarr, Neha Vora, Attiya Ahmad, Denise Brennan, Deborah Thomas, Aisha Beliso-De Jesús, and the editors of the present volume, Ashwini Tambe and Millie Thayer.

3 See, for instance, the digital magazine from India *FII*: *Feminism in India*, which has the banner "Intersectional feminism: Desi style" and states that its mandate is "to learn, educate and develop a feminist sensibility among the youth. It is required to unravel the F-word and demystify the negativity surrounding it. *FII* amplifies the voices of women and marginalised communities using tools of art, media, culture, technology and community." *FII*: *Feminism in India*, accessed June 6, 2020, https://feminisminindia.com.

4 There is now a large literature that has taken these projects in different and related directions, some within gender and sexuality studies but others in anthropology and critical race and sexuality studies. See, for instance, the work of Millie Thayer, Sylvanna Falcón, Richa Nagar and Amanda Lock Swarr, Attiya Ahmad, Neha Vora, Sahana Ghosh, Samar Al-Bulushi, Catherine Sameh, Sima Shakhsari, Deborah Thomas, Denise Brennan, and so many other scholars who are working to think about the processes and politics of culture and power.

5 My thanks to Ryan Jobson for making this important point.

6 Transparency International. Accessed December 15, 2020, https://www.transparency.org/en/research.

7 Black Cube. Accessed December 15, 2020, https://www.blackcube.com/. Black Cube has now responded to the revelations of its action by stating the following on its website: "We do not undertake any projects involving violent crime of any kind, including sexual harassment. We never use intimidation, blackmail or hacking to obtain information, and we only ever record conversations that we are a party to. We do not put words into people's mouths and our recordings are never edited to change the meaning of a conversation. Full, unedited transcripts of our recordings are always provided to the court."

SCALE

Part II

4

Transnational Feminism and the Politics of Scale

The 2012 Antirape Protests in Delhi

SRILA ROY

THE BRUTAL GANG RAPE AND MURDER of twenty-three-year-old Jyoti Singh Pandey in Delhi toward the end of 2012 constituted a "critical event" in India.[1] The mass protests that broke out in the wake of this rape brought an unprecedented number of protesters onto the streets in the capital and across the nation. The protests transformed the judicial, affective, and discursive landscape by forcing the Indian state to respond and by bringing discussions on sexual violence into news channels, living rooms, and Parliament. They were accompanied by unusually high levels of international media interest, making Pandey's rape, over similar acts of gender-based violence, an "international cause" (Roychowdhury 2013). These protests had significant global currency insofar as they traveled farther than events of a similar nature. This "scaling up," where a crime committed in a South Delhi neighborhood provoked conversations and activism well beyond national boundaries, also interpellated a range of individuals across ideological and social divides, in a form of "scaling out," as Ashwini Tambe and Millie Thayer write in chapter 1 of this volume. In other words, multiple kinds of audiences—feminist, antifeminist, and those unfamiliar with South Asia—were mobilized by this episode to speak about sexual violence. The antirape protests of 2012–13 constituted, then, not just a critical event nor an international cause but a "protest assemblage." In framing it as such in this chapter, I foreground the scalar dimensions of feminist politics in the Global South.

The 2012 Delhi protests were not novel in their scale and potential to travel. Other events (and scandals) relating to women, sexuality, and race have often exercised the imagination of global publics. Transnational feminist scholarship has firmly established how, across the North and the South, categories of gender, sexuality, and race, on the one hand, and feminist theories and political imaginations, on the other, are constituted in and through connected historical processes, colonialism, or global capitalism. As I explain in the first part of this chapter, transnational feminist scholarship has situated and theorized women's movements as being historically constituted through national and supranational processes. Contemporary instances of mobilization in the name of women—such as the 2012 Delhi protests—also demand a transnational feminist lens given their scaling-up and scaling-out capacities. Viewed through what Leela Fernandes (2013) calls the broadest geographic unit—the transnational—historical and current moments of feminist protest trouble "the scalar divisions of conventional scholarship" (Tambe 2010, 3).

In this chapter I unpack the scalar implications of transnational feminist perspectives by prioritizing the politics and ethics of scale in reading women's movements in the Global South, particularly the Indian women's movement (IWM). The first part of the chapter draws on feminist scholarship that (re)historicizes feminism and women's movements in *relational* terms. It reminds us that women's movements have always been simultaneously national and global and are materially, if not always imaginatively, constituted by interconnected histories of colonialism, imperialism, and the uneven effects of development, globalization, and neoliberalism in both the periphery and the metropole. Such an analysis hinges on multiplicities and connections that decenter hegemonic versions of feminism at varying scales, be they national, subnational, regional, or global.

I then turn to the changing scales and sites of the IWM as epitomized by the mass protests around the rape and murder of Pandey. The protests embodied the widespread dispersal and diffusion of feminism in India away from the traditional stronghold of the IWM.[2] I use the concept of the "protest assemblage" to emphasize this sense of dispersal and diffusion given the multiscalar dimensions of the protests, especially through the determining influence of the media, both old and new. Such a protest assemblage produced endless possibilities for mobilization in the name of women but not always in ways clearly recognizably as feminist (Knudsen and Stage 2014). Hegemonic feminist voices jostled with counterhegemonic or even nonfeminist ones, producing a sense of crisis among metropolitan activists as to what constitutes feminism in the Indian context. Against this sense of anxiety, I argue that the disaggregation of Indian feminism decenters dominant metropolitan and majoritarian narratives while bringing into focus nonmetropolitan minoritized feminist voices that have always existed within the nation-state. My reading of the 2012 antirape protests rests on media reportage and some published commentaries analyzing the protests, analytically enabled by the transnational feminist toolbox that I detail in the section that follows.

TRANSNATIONAL FEMINISM: A SCALAR ANALYSIS

Feminist scholars adopting a transnational and postcolonial perspective have long uncovered complex, albeit uneven, linkages in the production and circulation of feminist thought, knowledge, and political imaginaries, thus "emphasizing subnational and crossnational cultural formations" (Tambe 2010, 2). They have rewritten the history of feminism itself as "a set of circulating ideas" in ways that confound easy divides between the global and the local, the center and the periphery, and the self and the other (Tambe 2010, 2). Indeed, a range of feminist scholars, from Inderpal Grewal and Caren Kaplan (1994) to Amanda Lock Swarr and Richa Nagar (2010), have presented transnational feminism as a conceptual and political advance over international or global feminism, which reproduces power along Eurocentric lines by centering the European nation-state and universalizing European women's experience to the rest of the world (Alexander and Mohanty 1997). Transnational feminism instead attends to differences rather than commonalities among women while situating those differences and inequalities in historical formations and globalizing flows that are cross-cultural and cross- or even postnational. Women are, in other words, different but inhabit an interconnected and interdependent world riddled with clear asymmetries of power and privilege.

Transnational feminism is ultimately set apart by practices that can foster South-South feminist dialogues and collaborations as opposed to privileging northern feminist agendas and perspectives. Mary E. John (1999) emphasizes such a possibility in the name of a new feminist internationalism under globalization, even as she notes some tensions *within* feminisms of the Global South. These tensions stem not just from the politics of location (Latin America versus Asia, for example) but also from internal asymmetries of power, such as caste in India, to which I return later on. Implicit in these efforts is the attempt to move beyond nation-centric visions of the world or the tendency to think of the local as being contained within the national and defined in nationalist terms, an analytic perspective that has been theorized and criticized as "methodological nationalism" (Fernandes 2013; Chernilo 2006).

Scale is an implicit theme of transnational feminist analyses. Scalar and spatial investigations of women's movements do not merely reflect the truism that women's movements are very much the product of both local and global forces. Instead, they think of the local and the global as relational concepts—as continuously produced in and through an active and constitutive relationship to and with each other (Mohanty 2003; Go 2013). While globalization has made the transnationalized nature of feminism and women's movements more obvious, there is an older history to the constitutive internationalism of feminism as a political movement. The history of colonialism proves critical here: both in terms of overturning a wave model that has rendered commonsensical the idea of feminism as originating in the West and emanating from there to the rest of the globe and also in terms of foregrounding relations across space. It has become common in critical women's historiography to insist "that, like gender, the category of feminism itself emerged from the historical context of modern European colonialism and anti-colonial struggles, and that therefore histories of feminism must engage with its imperial origins as well as its national(ist) legacies" (Burton 1998, 558).

But well into the 1970s, attempts to speak on behalf of *all* women in calls for an international or global sisterhood were plagued with problems of Eurocentrism, imperialism, and racism (Amos and Parmar 1984). Works like Robin Morgan's (1996) *Sisterhood Is Global* were unable to appreciate the local contexts in which women's movements emerged and flourished, a task that Amrita Basu (2010) set out to fulfill in documenting local feminisms' challenge to macro understandings of women's movements that ignored postcolonial particularities (such as the influence of nationalism and the state on their nature and functioning). Basu called for this attention to local feminisms at a time "in which the global was ascendant over the local in defining the character of feminism" (quoted in Abeysekera 2013, 210)—during the 1995 UN Fourth World Conference on Women in Beijing, the culmination of a series of UN-sponsored conferences that began in 1975. For many

Srila Roy

commentators, these conferences provided the material conditions for the evolution of a framework of transnational feminism, for the building of genuine solidarity, collaboration, and exchange, especially among activists from the Global South (see Thayer 2010a).

This is not to say that past tensions or northern dominance of the global platform of politicizing women's issues disappeared post-Beijing. But southern-based feminist organizations came to play a far bigger role than they previously had in defining the agenda of global feminism and transnationalizing particular issues, like women's rights as human rights. Nongovernmental organizations (NGOS) also emerged as the paramount form of representing women's interests, assumed to be better than the nation-state, which historically had underrepresented gender interests in the postcolonial period (Alvarez 1999, 2009). The transnationalization and NGOization of women's movements in the South bespeak an ontology of relatedness that makes it difficult to posit the local, the nation, the home, and the self as stable categories outside of the global and transnational.

With these spatial and scalar considerations in mind, I now turn to a women's movement that has historically been framed in national and nationalist terms, the IWM. The national framing of this movement is less sustainable in the wake of globalization but also with respect to the challenges it faces from minoritized feminist voices from within the nation-state, especially Dalit and queer feminisms.[3]

THE TRANSNATIONAL INDIAN WOMEN'S MOVEMENT

Feminist struggles in the period of economic liberalization can be broadly characterized in terms of deterritorialization, dispersal, and diversity—that together account for the scalar expansion of the IWM from the national to the global owing to the twin processes of transnationalization and NGOization. In India these processes are traceable to the opening up of the Indian economy to global market forces, or to forms of economic liberalization, beginning in 1991. The availability of foreign funds for development and social justice work meant a transformation in the scales and orientations of the IWM. The transnationalization of the IWM is especially significant given the imbrication of this particular social movement in histories of colonialism and nationalism and the manner in which, well into the postindependence period, the nation-state served as its primary point of address (Sunder Rajan 2003). The so-called autonomous IWM worked solidly within the parameters set by the newly independent nation-state, addressing recognizable constituencies of poor grassroots women and relying on the nation-state as the main source of redress. Deterritorialization entailed the literal and imaginative severing of feminism from the episteme of the nation-state (John 2014).

The process of NGOization is a key signifier of the deterritorialization of the IWM and the expansion of its boundaries.[4] In truth, NGOs played an enormous role in the organizational transformation of Indian feminism from the autonomous feminist formations of the 1970s, which spearheaded major legal changes, especially around violence against women, to transnationalized and professionalized NGOs that provide a range of services on behalf of and for women and are not necessarily populated by feminists. As detailed elsewhere (S. Roy 2015), NGOization is the locus of several anxieties in India. First, and paradoxically, the IWM became a funded enterprise precisely when (neo)liberalization was driving Indian women further into poverty. Second, the donor dependency of NGOs meant a shift in the scale of intervention: to the global from—and eventually, many argued, at the cost of—the grassroots. Finally, NGOization was seen to cost the IWM its radical edge, given that a precise demarcation of the boundaries between Indian feminism as a social movement and that of funded NGOs was no longer possible.

The deterritorialization and dispersal of feminist struggles in the liberalization period have been accompanied by their reterritorialization in the new spaces made possible by India's globalization, such as NGOs but also the media and cyberspace. These new spatialities of feminism resulted in the broadening of concerns and strategies—away from a primarily state-centric legal feminism—and have been able to hail a variety of gendered subjects, such as the young middle-class women and men who took to the streets in Delhi in 2012. There is, however, a prehistory to the kind of urban mobilization around women's issues that we saw in Delhi; it can be traced to protest actions in the early 2000s. These include self-consciously feminist protests such as the Pink Chaddi or Pink Panty campaign, the Slutwalk marches, and innovative online campaigns around women's public safety (such as Blank Noise), all of which galvanized largely metropolitan middle-class and upper-caste women and men, primarily through online platforms and the use of social media.[5] In a sharp break from an earlier discourse on women's vulnerability to violence in the public sphere, these mobilizations have generated widespread debate on women's sexuality not in terms of violence and victimization alone but also with respect to sexual freedom, pleasure, and agency.[6] Organizationally, they are mostly contingent, provisional, and still-evolving feminist formations that have yet to be consolidated into a coherent framework, so that their outcomes cannot be anticipated in advance.

These mobilizations and especially the 2012 antirape protests are emblematic of just how porous the boundaries of Indian feminism have become and of their interpellative ability to hail multiple subjects and constitute a range of publics under its sign. Such a heterogeneous and shifting activist landscape makes it difficult to conceptually clarify what or who a feminist is, what can be counted as feminist knowledge and practice, and whether the IWM can be thought of as a self-contained social movement or a "field of protest" (Ray 1998).

A PROTEST ASSEMBLAGE

The 2012 antirape protests defy being labeled as either a field or a movement given their highly contingent, unstable, shifting, internally diverse, and non-homogeneous nature. As I detail in this section, the protests were constituted by a multiplicity of heterogeneous agents, a large section of whom had no history of political mobilization and were described as "otherwise indifferent middle-class youth" (Dutta and Sircar 2013, 294). Their actions were disaggregated across different spaces and sites (the street/the web) and operated on multiple scales (metropolitan/national/global), and even in terms of different temporal registers, such as the immediate demand to hang the rapists versus the long-term demand for structural change (Baxi 2013, 2015).

Thus, they might be more productively understood as an assemblage, which Gilles Deleuze describes as a multiplicity made up of heterogeneous terms with its only unity existing in a contingent sense of alliance and co-functioning (Bignall and Patton 2010). In contrast to perspectives that produce social movements as the constant while accounting for variations in different fields, there is no constant in an assemblage but variation to variation (Deleuze and Guattari 1987). Simon Tormey, for instance, writes of the difficulty in calling the anticapitalist movement a movement, given that it functions as an "'assemblage' of different currents of thought, different groups and organizations, some allied to the interests of the nation-state or regional agendas, others genuinely 'global' in scope and orientation" (2013, 140). Britta Timm Knudsen and Carsten Stage (2014) use "global protest assemblage" to describe and explain how internet technologies mediate antistate protests in contemporary Iran in ways that can be both transgressive and normative. And Aradhana Sharma speaks of contemporary state-led interventions into women's empowerment in India as "an assemblage ... made up of heterogeneous elements that are not necessarily internally coherent but are brought together for specific strategic ends" (2008, 2).

While all social movements and mass protests can be characterized by a degree of heterogeneity, what makes the 2012 protests different from previous feminist struggles in India is the inability to reduce them to a singular or coherent ideological or discursive formation, even in the name of feminism. This particular protest assemblage comprised different, divergent, and even oppositional publics. Some saw the state as the singular oppressor of women, while others regarded the state as a protector and savior of women. Indeed, many prominent Indian feminist activists recoiled with horror at some of the calls for chemical castration and execution of rapists that were heard on the streets of the capital and were louder than the more progressive calls for *azaadi*, or unconditional freedom for women. While the protests might have been aimed at some loose sense of justice on behalf of a rape victim, the affective articulation of this demand—whether through empathy, loss, rage, or fear—was not consistent or unified. Consequently, and departing again from previous protests around sexual violence, there was no singular vision of how to combat India's rape culture, given the disparate understandings of rape as injury, harm, or crime. Ultimately, the protests cannot be reduced to the divergent publics and oppositional ideologies that constituted it; they were something more. The heterogeneous, shifting, conjunctural, evolving, and excessive nature of such a protest made it impossible to know its outcome—one that could not, moreover, be reduced to the agency of the actors involved or to their intentions.

The media, old and new, shaped how this protest assemblage came together and transformed in its unfolding and aftermath. The media and the internet did not create the 2012 protests, but the protests would have looked rather different without the intervention of the media and communication technologies, especially if we compare them to previous moments of protesting violence against women in postcolonial India, of which there is a long history.[7] Not only did the media environment shape and shift Pandey's story as it traveled—transforming a local rape victim into a global icon—but it also constituted and channeled the outpouring of affective responses in particular ways. Given the disproportionate attention that was given to the calls for execution and castration on the 24/7 news channels, for instance, it is not surprising that a retributive public came to represent much of the face of the 2012 protests (Baxi 2013). The state's carceral response to Pandey's murder—in the deployment of the death penalty—has been traced to the demands of such a public, suggesting that mediatized affective responses fed into concrete forms of redress (Baxi 2013). Affective responses to this critical event were structured by the media in ways that closely aligned the protests, at the domestic level, with the concerns of the "securocratic state" and, at the international level, with the global community's Orientalist readings of India's unique "rape problem" (Kapur 2013; Roychowdhury 2013).

In the afterlife of the protests, their global significance has become even more apparent but not in straightforwardly Orientalist or Eurocentric ways. Feminists from other parts of the world contrasted the quietism that surrounded sexual violence in their locales with the national outrage around it in India. In these discussions India became the benchmark against which mobilization around sexual violence in other parts of the world—for instance, South Africa but also the United States—came to be measured, rather than simply being the index of non-Western inferiority. In comparing the scales of protest around sexual violence in the United States and India, Krupa Shandilya writes, "In viewing the Delhi case through a global lens we see that, contrary to popular opinion in the West which painted the Delhi rape as yet another instance of the backward, regressive East, the Delhi case swiftly ignited a robust movement that galvanized a nation to protest against sexual assault" (2015, 483).

It appears, then, that the indeterminate nature of the protest assemblage around Pandey's gang rape produced a transnational circulation of multiple meanings, some of which reproduced Orientalist framings of saving Third World women while others inverted these power relations in unexpected ways. It produced what Fernandes (2013) calls transnational knowledge about violence against women—knowledge that is produced in a certain context that ends up having a differential impact in another context owing to its transnational circulation and take-up. The documentary *India's Daughter* (Udwin 2015), which I now turn to, was one of the most directed attempts at producing knowledge around the Delhi rape and ended up being a transnational object par excellence, consumed by global publics over local elites, who were prevented from doing so by their government and feminists alike. In reflecting on the controversy that surrounded the documentary and its ban in India, I underscore—in this final section—moments of critique and solidarity in even the most short-lived and transitory moment of political friction.

The BBC documentary *India's Daughter* told Pandey's story, featuring close looks at Pandey's parents and, most controversially, at one of the men convicted of the crime, Mukesh Singh (whose case was then pending appeal). The film was quickly banned by the government of India for being "offensive" toward women, a move that was more about international image building than about upholding women's rights. But the controversy surrounding the film and the ban also brought to the fore surprisingly sharp differences *within* the IWM over the issue of representing sexual violence and its subjects and perpetrators through the lens of an English female filmmaker, Leslee Udwin (herself a rape survivor). Amid angry dismissals of the film as Orientalist for patronizing India's "daughters" (already framed by the title in patriarchal paternalist terms) and predictably linking rape to Third World poverty, critique and censorship converged on the unparalleled screen time the film affords a convicted rapist. A group of influential Indian feminists called for restraining the film's release, initially on the grounds that Mukesh's misogynistic statements constituted hate speech, while later arguing for the right of the accused to a fair trial. The countercritiques to this feminist position—which coalesced around a number of concerns relating to freedom of speech, mediatized representations of sexual violence, and the (limited) influence of the media on legal process—identified the real danger in how the feminist demand for restraint ultimately fed into the government's reactionary move to ban the film.

Not only did the film create a new assemblage of discourses, meanings, practices, and affects around sexual violence, but the Indian government's attempt to censor it created new capacities for protest even within the media. The popular private news broadcast channel NDTV telecast a "tribute" to *India's Daughter* by blanking its screen for a full hour, thus making "the ban . . . the object of protest" (Baxi 2015). A final moment in this new assemblage of meanings around Pandey's rape and murder involved the mass lynching of a man accused of rape in Dimapur in Nagaland, an economically and politically marginalized Indian state in the northeast of the country. This event was linked, by metropolitan feminists and the media, to the incitement to avenge sexual violence that both the 2012 protests and the controversy around *India's Daughter* had constituted. "Dimapur" is another key moment in the journey through which Pandey's story has traveled and been transformed in the long afterlife of the Delhi gang rape—in protesting publics that exceeded national frontiers, in digital and broadcast media, in its filmic rendition for a global audience, and in the silencing of this testimony by national elites, including metropolitan feminists. In tracing this journey, we see how a singular event is transformed and has limitless capacities to assemble meaning, affect, and action; it scales out (and not just up) across highly oppositional publics.

Let me end with a final point that goes back to the feminist frictions I began with: while the clamor of disagreement around the film remained limited to a group of influential (largely Delhi-based) feminists, an important intervention was staged by Dalit activists on their online forum, *Roundtable India*. In it, Karthick (2015) called out elite upper-caste feminist hypocrisy in questioning the right of a Western woman to make a documentary on Indian women while effectively masking—and thereby naturalizing—their own privileged position in caste terms. Karthick underscored sharp differences among Indian feminists across caste lines; he accused upper-caste feminists for uncritically valorizing anti-imperialist politics while reducing anticaste positions to nothing more than "identity politics." He further asserted, "But in condemning western universality, who gave these members of an ultra-elite closed group the right to condemn in the name of all brown women and men? If it was not for the intervention of 'white imperialist capitalist patriarchy' women of a particular low caste in Tamil Nadu would not be allowed to cover their breasts. It was British colonialist legislation that put an end to the barbaric practice of temple prostitution in the state. All these moves were also fought for and welcomed by women of the concerned castes" (Karthick 2015). Dalit feminists were indeed some of the most vociferous critics of the publicity surrounding Pandey's gang rape. Their critique was posed on two levels: the first emanated from their struggle to accrue any visibility, whether from old or new media, for the routine acts of sexual violence to which they, as Dalit women, were disproportionately vulnerable. Second, they criticized how it served to render further invisible the intersectional contours of sexual violence in the Indian context, by highlighting the violence toward urban, aspirational, upper-caste women alone (the framing of sexual violence in terms of public safety also obliterated its caste-class dimensions, they argued). Their critique was directed not only at media representations but, as in Karthick's rebuke, toward metropolitan upper-caste feminists. Much like their Western/imperialist sisters, Indian feminists have tended to eclipse from view internal asymmetries of power pertaining to caste-class and sexuality in speaking on behalf of all Indian women. Consequently, the "Hindu middle-class woman, 'everywoman,' has become the de facto subject of Indian feminism," as Shandilya (2015, 465) writes of the

2012 protests. The upper-caste politics of metropolitan Indian feminists have been called out more and more in recent times, and Dalit feminist suspicion of the mainstream IWM has now become a given.

Karthick's critique also juxtaposes Western colonialism with caste-based (sub)colonialisms—and defends colonialism—in ways that radically shift the dominant registers of critique made by mainstream Indian feminists. By shifting the scales of protest from the colonial/global to the subcolonial/subnational, the Dalit feminist position fractures any claims by Indian feminists to speak on behalf of the Indian woman. In positing, moreover, imperialism as a historical antidote to caste and gender hierarchies, this critique also opens up the possibility of building solidarity on the transnational scale and countering the power of internal elites.

A final instance of a Dalit feminist intervention into the Delhi rape comes from the rural women's newspaper *Khabar Lahariya* (Waves of news; KL), which is run by Dalit women of the northern state of Uttar Pradesh. While occupying a position at the periphery, KL scales up and out, which is made clear in Shandilya's (2015) analysis of KL's representation of the Delhi gang rape as differing qualitatively from those of metropolitan feminists. Shandilya further points to the global relations that this instance of local feminism enables:

> Days after the Delhi gang-rape, KL ran an article about rallies in Canada, thus situating the readers of the collective [rural Dalit women] within a global women's movement. This reverse gaze—from the bottom up— suggests that one of the purposes of the newspaper is to educate Dalit women about their location in the world, in order to endorse their political mobilization but also to problematize the global feminist movement's relationship to them. This newspaper, unlike the urban feminist movements, posits a global analysis, in which sexual assault is seen as endemic to the world, in the spirit of second-wave feminists, but it also contains a recognition that its redress must arise from local epistemologies. (483)

Both the Dalit intervention into the Delhi gang rape and its representation in *India's Daughter* represent what Walter Nicholls, Byron Miller, and Justin Beaumont call "scale-shifting strategies" of political activism, or the manner in which "collectivities continually reshape scalar relations in an ongoing process of asserting and contesting power" (2013, 9–10). While mainstream metropolitan Indian feminists posit the national as the scale at which authentic politics is carried out, against the international as the domain of imperialist intervention, Dalit responses do otherwise. They problematize the idea that the national is the scale at which authenticity, representation, and political solidarity can be built, given the kind of power relations that criss-cross the national field and the marginalization that flows from it. Instead, they shift the scale at which Pandey's gang rape is posited and move beyond a simplistic northern-southern binary to subnational, subcolonial, and cross-cultural complexities. Just as Dalit feminists have critiqued national elites and decentered the national as the predominant scale of political intervention, they have long fostered solidarity networks across and beyond borders, as evidenced by the history of activist exchange between African American and Dalit feminists.

CONCLUDING THOUGHTS ON FEMINISMS' TRAVELS

The history of women's movements in the Global South is an archive of how feminism has traveled—not from the imperial heartland to the colonial periphery, as is invariably assumed, or, in an age of globalization, from global to local sites. Such ideas of linear progression are disrupted by the fact that feminism has always been implicated, as ideal and practice, in the transnational flow of ideas, concepts, and power relations, even as it has crystallized in relation to specific concerns within particular locales. As Tambe and Thayer note at the start of this volume, cross-border women's movements have a history going back over a hundred years, a history that is also marred by imperial hierarchies. The increased transnationalization of women's movements in recent years simply makes these processes and dynamics more obvious even as it has not entirely displaced from view the two default axes of our dominant frame of reference: the West and the nation-state. Still, owing to critiques made by minoritized feminists, within and across nation-states (and in solidarity with one another), it has become impossible to ignore the global dimensions of gender relations *or* to think of the local in terms of the national alone.

A scalar analysis of the 2012 Delhi gang rape shows complex interactions at national, regional, local, and global levels that together produced it as a transnational object forming the basis of prolific knowledge production around gender and violence. I have found it useful to make sense of this moment as a protest assemblage to emphasize its unpredictable nature, its ability to interpellate divergent publics, its internal heterogeneity and contestations, and its indeterminate effects. Instead of reading such a protest assemblage as representing the loss of feminism in postcolonial, liberalized India, I contend it to be its greatest strength: it undermines traditional power structures, whether of the nation-state or of hegemonic metropolitan and upper-caste feminisms, and produces, at the same time, much more diverse, contested, and multiple political responses and politicized identities (even if centered around a normative category of "woman"). A scalar analysis can, then, foreground significant aspects of feminist protest that are otherwise "left out of homogenizing representations of women's movements and transnational alliances" (Chowdhury 2011, 8). Inter- as well as intramovement tensions also become more evident through such an analytic, against the tendency to represent social movements as unified wholes, operating on a singular axis or scale alone. Emerging from these constellations and contestations of voices operating at multiple scales are also unexpected modes of solidarity and new feminist epistemologies and political potentials.

Rethinking feminism as a form of theory and praxis that circulates and travels does not simply disrupt a series of binaries such as the center and the periphery, the local and the global, the national and the transnational, and the self and the other in ways that leave historical power relations and inequalities untouched. Instead, it opens up the possibility to develop imaginative and actual relationships of solidarity that neither obfuscate nor remain paralyzed by those relations of difference, distance, apartness, and inequality within and through which feminism has traveled. Such solidarity has historically informed the production of feminist knowledge in the best instantiation of knowledge as a form of power and practice; it has also undermined conventional theory-activism binaries (Fernandes 2013). The relationship between power and knowledge that has been at the heart of transnational feminism should equally be at the heart of any attempt to retheorize gender and feminist politics in a highly complex, interconnected, interdependent, and unequal world.

ACKNOWLEDGMENTS

My thanks to the editors, Ashwini Tambe and Millie Thayer, for their inputs into this chapter.

NOTES

A longer version of this chapter appeared as "Women's Movements in the Global South: Towards a Scalar Analysis," *International Journal of Politics, Culture and Society* 29, no. 3 (2016): 289–306.

1 Pandey, a physiotherapy student, died battling injuries, including partial disembowelment, inflicted by six men aboard a private, off-duty bus, including

the bus driver. She was taking the bus home with a male friend after watching *Life of Pi* at a cinema in a popular neighborhood of Delhi. For more on this episode as a "critical event," see Anupama Roy (2014).

2 The term *feminism* is contested in India, as it is in most postcolonial countries, where it becomes an easy signifier of Westernization and elitism.

3 For an overview of these internal contestations and the ways they challenged and shifted the very subject of Indian feminist politics, see Menon (2007).

4 NGO*ization* is employed by feminists and leftists alike as an umbrella term to capture the many changes and transformations that have taken place in the IWM in terms of its form, its functioning, and the wider political context in which it exists. As economic liberalization occurred and state funding was withdrawn from key areas, NGOs stepped in to deliver—and not merely demand—development. See S. Roy (2015) for an overview of these debates.

5 For a sense of some of these campaigns, see S. Roy (2016).

6 This turn to politicizing sexuality in India is rooted in the very substantial challenges put forth by subaltern sexual identities and groups—sex workers, sexual minorities, and members of the queer movement—to the mainstream IWM, which traditionally shied away from the issue of sex or was even openly hostile to lesbian women and sex workers. See, for an overview, Narrain and Bhan (2005) and Menon (2007).

7 Since these protests, cyberfeminist interventions have grown exponentially, emerging as an important platform for a more self-consciously intersectional Indian feminist politics, especially at the time of India's #MeToo movement. See, for instance, some of the contributions to Jha and Kurian (2018).

5

Transnational Shifts

The World March of Women in Mexico

CARMEN L. DÍAZ ALBA

THE TRANSNATIONALIZATION OF FEMINIST MOVEMENTS has facilitated important alliances among women from very different regions of the world. In 2000 the World March of Women (WMW), a transnational network of grassroots women's organizations, opened a space for Mexican feminist organizations to articulate with social justice movements around the world. After some two decades, the WMW in Mexico offers valuable lessons. For what reasons did these organizations join this global movement? What challenges did the WMW face? In the current moment, is transnationalization still a meaningful strategy?

In this chapter I show that Mexican feminist organizations benefited from belonging to the WMW as a transnational platform that allowed them greater visibility, credibility, and prestige. Despite conflicts and difficulties, in the Mexican case the WMW strengthened local groups and allowed them to forge alliances with feminists across Mexico and beyond. I show why Mexican feminist organizations joined this transnational movement and the difficulties they faced in sustaining a national coordination that could articulate with the transnational scale. I address the complexity of building a movement with local-global dynamics, the interaction between scales, and the difficulties this involves, in order to understand why these groups remain (or do not remain) in the WMW.[1]

I argue that even in a context where movements cut across borders, the national level is still relevant. The transnationalization of struggles has played a major role for social movements, but these dynamics may change over time. The transnational scale is not given; it is constructed and therefore not permanent. In the first section, I briefly present my theoretical references regarding space and scale in transnational social movements. In the second part, I trace the trajectory of the WMW in Mexico, which was very active at the transnational scale from 2000 to 2008. I analyze the contributions of the WMW in Mexico and show why Mexican feminist organizations joined this transnational movement, despite the challenge of working at different scales. This case highlights the difficulties involved in sustaining transnational dynamics over time and the fact that these processes are episodic and discontinuous, rather than unilinear.

SPACE AND SCALE IN TRANSNATIONAL MOVEMENTS

Two concepts that have been problematized in the study of transnational movements are space and scale. Arturo Escobar identifies gaining space as a key element in the strategies of social movements. He defines space as "the experience of a particular location with some measure of groundedness (however, unstable), sense of boundaries (however, permeable), and connection to everyday life, even if its identity is constructed, traversed by power, and never fixed" (2001, 140). Following Doreen Massey, he argues that space is not fixed or permanent but constantly constructed; space is permeated by social structures and cultural practices that make the understanding of the relationship among identity, space, and power an essential task for anthropology. Space is not culturally neutral; it is produced through specific processes and narratives.

In the study of social movements, it is necessary to examine how space is constructed through participation in networks beyond the local. The local space appears subordinated to the global space, but as Escobar argues, both are connected to dynamics that are equally important. Boaventura de Sousa Santos (2009) also reinforces this point about the "monoculture of scales" to critique how the dominant scale, the universal and global, makes the particular or local scales less important. For Escobar, it is not necessary to choose between the local and the transnational space; he explains that there are social movements that originate in transnational networks but defend concrete spaces. Thus, in the field of social movements, defending the local space is as central as the networks that stretch across them (Escobar 2001).

Following this understanding, Escobar is critical of the "globalocentrism" in some disciplines that ignore the analysis of how space is produced in both theory and political action. He highlights the contributions of theoretical currents that avoid this globalocentrism, such as poststructuralist feminist geography and political economy, on the one hand, and some anthropological works that relate space, identity, and power, on the other.

In this vein, Janet Conway (2008), when discussing the World Social Forum, a series of annual meetings of civil society organizations and activists with a radical bent, argues that places should not be conceived as pregiven, since they are being produced through conflictual social relations and practices. The space where the social movement originates impacts its character, and many movements practice politics at multiple scales. For her, transnationalization is not just a strategy or a reaction against globalization. Transnationalization is a socially constructed scale that allows movements to go beyond the nation-state. It is not only global institutions that generate scalar jumps; movements create new spatialities when they are transnationalized, a prime example being convergence spaces such as the World Social Forum.

These arguments are relevant to understanding the emphasis placed by the transnational WMW on the local scale of women's struggles. The WMW, a multisited and multicentered network, engages in multiple scales of action. Although it has a common platform, the space where each group is located configures the WMW in a specific way, as Conway notes. In the case of the WMW in Mexico, I argue that a change in location from Mexico City to San Cristóbal de las Casas, Chiapas, significantly shaped the WMW both before and after the move. Like Conway, I find the WMW to be "a coordination of place-based feminisms, concretely engaged in specific geographies, on context-specific struggles pertaining to poverty and violence against women, in place-specific terms" (Conway 2008, 221). That is, the platform and the discursive framework of this movement are intimately linked to problems identified with the local scale. Building platforms of common action requires a continuous process of representation and deliberation through different spaces and scales.

For Pascale Dufour and Isabelle Giraud (2007), space is important to understanding the WMW at its different scales. Scale is not only related to the target of the protest. The configuration of power in a given space impacts the scale of the movement and the type of influence it can have on other scales of action. These authors also agree that local groups of women can transnationalize their discourses and claims, building multiscale alternatives to face social, economic, and political inequalities.

Dominique Masson (2010) shows that movements can organize their own spatial logics, independently of international institutions. Scales are dynamic, relational, and mutually constitutive, she argues; therefore, we need to take this into account in order to see the interactions between scales and the ways they influence each other. Space is an explanatory element, not just the scenario. Like any other collective action, the movement has to build the transnational scale if it wants to have an impact on it through its own organization, actions, mobilizations, and discursive frameworks. Masson's work reflects on what happens to the movement's relations and processes as they spread across the transnational space, what happens to discourses when scales change, what contradictions and tensions emerge, and what negotiations are necessary.

Framing my work within such arguments about the importance of space and scale, I argue that the WMW in Mexico is an example of how space and scale need to be taken into account to explain the changing dynamics of the movement. I build on the work of these authors to reflect on the ways the transnational is constructed and the difficulties of sustaining interscalar activism over time. This case shows that although transnationalization was seen as a desirable and needed strategy at one point, changes in space and over time brought a shift that put more emphasis on the local, rather than the global, scale.

GOING TRANSNATIONAL: MEXICAN FEMINISTS JOIN THE WMW

In 1998 a delegation from the Quebec Women's Federation, or Fédération des femmes du Québec, visited Mexico to invite women's organizations, mainly through trade unions they were already working in alliance with against the North American Free Trade Agreement, to be part of the WMW's global action in 2000. Around a hundred women's organizations joined this initiative. The organization that hosted the national coordination of the WMW was Mujeres para el Diálogo (Women for Dialogue), a feminist organization focused on popular education and based in Mexico City. The WMW in Mexico was organized in three geographic spaces: a central zone (coordinated from Mexico City), a northern zone (with headquarters in Chihuahua), and a southern zone (in San Cristóbal de las Casas, Chiapas).

The WMW is an interesting case for examining transnational networks because although this initiative had few financial resources, many groups decided to join. As Miriam Nobre and Sarah de Roure, from the international secretariat of the WMW, explain, "The participating groups assumed the March as a campaign without a financial counterpart. Thus, they had to mobilize the necessary resources to develop the activities they proposed to carry out, because they saw in it a possibility of strengthening as a movement. [The fact of] groups joining this international dynamic, driven by political commitment and without an economic counterpart, is in itself a point of differentiation" (2012, 59). Important elements helping the WMW to take root in Mexico were the preexisting networks and the trust already developed among organizations. Mujeres para el Diálogo, the organization responsible for the national coordination, had developed recognition, leadership, and legitimacy since the early 1990s. This organization also coordinated the Gender and Economy Network (Red Género y Economía) and was part of a wider network, the Latin American Women Transforming the Economy Network (Red Mujeres Transformando la Economía [REMTE]). According to the first national coordinator of the WMW in Mexico, Leonor Aída Concha (pers. comm., July 22, 2013), the WMW and REMTE often held joint seminars, and they published documents and mobilized together. After the first national meeting in January 1999, seven national workshops were held to plan, coordinate, and evaluate the actions of the WMW in Mexico, including the adaptation of the seventeen international demands of the WMW for the Mexican context.[2]

Many of the Mexican activists I interviewed saw the WMW as expressing an alternative to neoliberalism. It was also seen as an opportunity to connect at the national and international level to build a feminist movement. For Guadalupe Cárdenas, from the WMW in Chiapas, in the south of the country, the WMW was an opportunity to come together and create a broad movement: "We joined the World March because we had the need to be connected to the world" (pers. comm., November 14, 2014). Refugio Avila's organization, Centro de Apoyo para el Movimiento Popular de Occidente [Support Center for Western Grassroots Movement] (CAMPO), in the western province of Jalisco, also joined the WMW, because it represented an opportunity to join an international effort. Already working around issues of violence and poverty, this organization found resonance in the "Bread and Roses" slogan of the WMW and its international perspective (pers. comm., May 7, 2014). The analysis presented in the documents prepared by the WMW was relevant to the local experiences of women's lives. The transnational discourse of the WMW "matched very strategically with what we were already working on," according to Lourdes Angulo, from the WMW in Jalisco (pers. comm., May 9, 2014).

Carmen L. Díaz Alba

One of the strategies that brought together the efforts of the activists in constructing the WMW at the national scale was a national campaign on women's rights. The goal was to inform a broad public about women's rights and promote discussion, covering issues such as the rights to food, employment, and decent wages; equal pay for equal work; improvement of working conditions; women's education; the right to live without violence; physical, sexual, and psychological integrity; the fair distribution of domestic tasks; and the full exercise of citizenship (Ceregatti et al. 2008, 13). A Mexican delegation attended the demonstrations in New York in October 2000, as part of the first international action of the WMW. The national coordinator of the WMW at that time, Leonor Aída Concha, delivered a speech addressed to James Wolfensohn, president of the World Bank, in which she demanded radical change in the institution to effectively serve the poor, especially women (33–34).

After the first international action, many organizations that were part of the WMW in Mexico decided to continue working together within the country. Among their reasons, they mentioned that the WMW was a space that allowed them to share experiences and promote initiatives for the recognition of women's rights: "It was a tool that allowed us to strengthen our organizational processes in the women's movement" (17). This is an example of what Masson and Conway refer to when they suggest that scales are constructed by social movements. In this case, the WMW both allowed activists to bring transnational discourses into local experiences and also facilitated the interaction at the national and regional scale of organizations that previously were not working together.

International actions became moments of local activation and national-transnational visibility. In preparation for the second international action in 2005, two national meetings were held to reactivate WMW committees in at least eighteen provinces of Mexico. The goal was to receive the Relay March, which was traveling from country to country carrying the Women's Global Charter for Humanity.[3] On April 22, 2005, the Relay March arrived in San Cristóbal de las Casas. The Chiapas members of the WMW received the charter and a patchwork quilt, known as the "solidarity quilt," at the Guatemalan border. The caravan also held actions in Mexico City and Chihuahua.

For Graciela Ramos, who participated in the march and hailed from the northern Mexican state of Chihuahua, the Women's Charter became a very important tool in raising awareness as part of the local organizational process and movement building (pers. comm., March 18, 2014). A memorial was held at the cross for the victims of *feminicidio* (femicide), an installation that commemorates the women who have been murdered in this state. Their caravan finally moved to Ciudad Juárez, where an international forum on solidarity and a protest against feminicide were held. They then delivered the Women's Charter for Humanity and a solidarity quilt to US activists at the US international bridge (Ceregatti et al. 2008, 22–24).

According to the activists interviewed, the WMW was still an important convening power in 2005; however, many agreed that it was difficult to mobilize as many women as for the first international action in 2000. Some of the interviewees felt that this was because in 2005 it was a decentralized action, with many targets, whereas the previous one, in 2000, had focused on the United Nations, the International Monetary Fund, and the World Bank. Without a clear target, they argued, it was difficult for women's organizations to join the call.

SHIFTING BACK TO THE LOCAL:
A SECOND PERIOD OF THE WMW IN MEXICO

In 2006 Mexico participated in the sixth international meeting of the WMW in Lima, Peru. At this meeting, it was decided that María Quispe Nepo, a Mexican delegate, would become part of the International Committee to represent the Americas region. Back in Mexico, at the WMW's national assembly, the delegates decided to move the headquarters of the national coordination from Mexico City to San Cristóbal de las Casas, Chiapas, in order to promote decentralization and greater collective coordination.

In this same year, the elected president of Mexico, Felipe Calderón, declared the war on drugs. By 2008, in the midst of rising violence and militarization in the country, the WMW in Mexico decided to call for a national north-south caravan to address violence against women, from Ciudad Juárez to San Cristóbal de las Casas, two locales where violence was having a particular impact on women. The urgency of dealing with violence in Mexico pushed the WMW's activists to launch this action in 2008, while the other national chapters of the WMW at the international scale planned a global action for 2010. This caravan was the last action organized at the national scale by the WMW in Mexico. In 2010, for the third international action of the WMW, the WMW in Mexico was unable to coordinate a national action. The emphasis of this third action was the experience of women living in situations of armed conflict. While violence, militarization, the criminalization of protest, and armed conflict linked to the fight against drug trafficking were highly relevant to the Mexican context, the call of the march did not generate much of an echo. Faced with the decision about whether to join the third international action in 2010, activists expressed a feeling of burnout, little capacity or energy to continue, and a sense of disconnect with international demands. This is reflected in the testimony of Refugio Ávila, an activist from Jalisco: "Many felt exhausted. We proposed to pause the international articulation until the next action and review how we felt. We even proposed a mechanism to learn about our organizations' status, their main issues and how they related to new issues like militarization and criminalization of social protest. There were some who felt that this was not their cause, because military presence was more focused in Chiapas. We said that this affected us all . . . but the World March of Women turned to a lower profile and local scale" (pers. comm., May 7, 2014).

This quote indicates how national or local issues require the movement's energy, pulling it away from collaboration at the global level. Then too, as the quote illustrates, although the issues themselves were similar, the global framing did not resonate with local experiences. After the caravan of 2008, local groups were exhausted, and militarization seemed relevant only in Chiapas, in the southern part of Mexico; other regions in the country did not join the action. Even if, before, the transnational scale had been seen as an important element for movement building, changes in the local and national space forced activists to change their level of involvement outside of local issues. As Masson points out, scales are dynamic, relational, and mutually constitutive. A movement puts a lot of energy into building national and transnational scales of action, and it is difficult to sustain over time.

By 2009 the participants of the WMW in Mexico would attend few international calls, although the groups that had participated in the WMW continued their daily local work. There were some attempts to reactivate the WMW in Mexico City, but only in 2014 did a national assembly finally happen. Some of the interviewees referred to problems with the leadership of the national coordinator and to the lack of economic resources on the part of Chiapas's organizations, compared to the resources of the more metropolitan Mujeres para el Diálogo. According to Guadalupe Cárdenas, from the WMW in Chiapas, there were also organizational and communication issues with the national coordination based there: "In Chiapas, we had the idea that some of the *compañeras* were from the national coordination, others were from the state coordination and other *compañeras* were just local activists. . . . But we did not manage to separate the structure very well, and this was confusing, causing misunderstandings and omissions too. Because suddenly it was not very clear what had to be reported, where, how and who was involved" (pers. comm., November 14, 2014). In this excerpt we can see that a movement working at multiple scales requires a great level of organization. It is also interesting that she refers to compañeras who were "just" local activists, implying a hierarchization of scales. She does not see scales as interrelated but as separate spheres of action, causing tensions regarding who should address what at a specific level.

In addition, activists from other regions of Mexico referred to the lack of fluid communication at the national scale and few possibilities to get together. According to Guadalupe Cárdenas of Chiapas, "There were many omissions in information, they did not call us to meetings . . . lots of information gaps and disengagement" (pers. comm., November 14, 2014). In this regard, Graciela, from Chihuahua, argues that until 2008 the WMW had a lot of importance, but after this it became more and more difficult to coordinate with the WMW situated in Chiapas, specifically owing to a lack of resources (pers. comm., March 18, 2014). In the first stage of the WMW, the Gender and Economy Network provided the resources for these gatherings. With the move of the national coordination from Mexico City (under Mujeres para el Diálogo) to Chiapas, this network no longer carried out the WMW's agenda. Although the WMW was seen as a horizontal movement, differences in access to resources and the historical centralization of the country in the capital had an impact, reproducing hierarchies between groups and regions.

Trying to give the WMW a new chance, a new team took over the national coordination in Chiapas, as the former coordinator of the WMW moved out of San Cristóbal.[4] One of the activists who took on this responsibility noted that this was not an easy task: they faced conflicts and difficulties owing to the lack of guided transition efforts; it was confusing for the WMW's activists outside Chiapas: "It was a very ugly break with them [the previous coordinators]. . . . We had agreed that we were going to make a transition, that they would give us the World March contacts, and introduce us to state coordinators, the international coordination and the international secretariat, but they never did" (Guadalupe Cárdenas, pers. comm., November 14, 2014). On November 25, 2011, the WMW in Chiapas issued a public statement regarding the International Day for the Elimination of Violence against Women. In this same communication, they referred to the eighth international meeting of the WMW in the Philippines, but since the Mexican national coordination did not participate in this meeting, the representation of the Americas at the International Committee passed from Mexico to Guatemala. However, in 2012 the third Americas regional meeting of the

WMW was held in Guatemala City. Given the geographic proximity, three Mexican delegates attended (from Chiapas, Mexico City, and Chihuahua) and agreed to participate in the WMW's global action, "24 Hours of Feminist Solidarity," scheduled for December 10 of that year. The action was carried out in more than twenty-five countries, between noon and 1 p.m. (local time in each country).

In August 2013 the ninth international meeting of the WMW was held in São Paulo, Brazil. With resources from the International Secretariat, one delegate from Mexico was able to attend. Norma Cacho, from the national coordination in Chiapas, spoke at the opening ceremony on behalf of the Americas region. Finally, in 2014 two national assemblies took place, electing the vice president for gender equality of the National Workers' Union (Unión Nacional de Trabajadores), Marta Heredia, based in Mexico City, as the new coordinator of the WMW at the national level. In October 2015 the regional meeting of the Americas was held in the city of Cajamarca, Peru. Two trade union representatives from Mexico City participated, arguing that the WMW in Mexico was no longer active at the national level and that efforts were being made at the local scale (Mexico City) to reactivate the movement.

Despite many efforts by some of the WMW's activists in Mexico, it seems that feminist organizations previously engaged with the movement had decided to focus their attention on the local scale. As has been argued, the transnational scale is not given; it has to be constructed and can shift over time. Interscalar work can also generate tensions and unsolved conflicts, especially given the power inequalities between organizations and regions.

TRANSNATIONAL CONTRIBUTIONS VS. NATIONAL TENSIONS

Even though the WMW of Mexico is currently inactive, it is important to understand what elements allowed the transnationalization of the movement from 2000 to 2008. For many activists, the WMW in Mexico was an opportunity to connect across organizations, express local articulations of the movement, and thereby strengthen it. For Guadalupe Cárdenas, in southern Chiapas, the WMW made it possible to link with organizations at the national level: "We didn't have contact with the north. Through the World March we had contact with other states; it gave us the possibility to articulate" (pers. comm., November 14, 2014).

The WMW was also seen as an opportunity to build bridges between women, despite their many differences. Activists mention that the WMW allowed them to show that despite coming from very different countries and different contexts, they shared the same struggles in many parts of the world, as is stated in the following testimony from Graciela Ramos, from Chihuahua: "For many women, the March was a before and an after. It was like a watershed. It really did generate this awareness, the common causes worldwide. The feeling of sisterhood, with so different women. Although we could not understand our languages, we knew that we were sisters in dreams, in struggles, in suffering, in aspirations" (pers. comm., March 18, 2014). Graciela participated in several international forums representing the WMW. The possibility of weaving links at the international scale was, according to her, one of the main contributions of the WMW, which also influenced the national scale: "For me it was a very rich experience, being able to participate at international meetings on an equal level, with partners from all over the planet. That for me was really amazing. And how was this going to be translated at the national scale. I can tell you that I joined the World March with great hope, with great enthusiasm, and it was wonderful to be able to be in touch with comrades from all over the country" (pers. comm., March 18, 2014). Another element on which my interviewees agreed is that the impact of being part of a transnational movement cannot be measured only in terms of public actions. The WMW, they say, allowed them to develop elaborate reflections that connected the local scale with the international context, and vice versa. Thus, the transnational dimension developed their capacity for interscalar work and thinking.

From the beginning, the WMW at the cross-national scale had a strong component of popular education. This component was also present in the work of the WMW in Mexico with its popular-education methodologies and emphasis on working with grassroots women. A fundamental aspect of the work with the WMW was the popular-education materials it created aiming to make the WMW's international demands accessible to all women. One of these tools, which became an identity symbol, was the song of the WMW, built from pieces written in more than twenty languages. As Graciela Ramos recalls, for the case of Chihuahua, the song became a tool for popular education, singing about women's rights: "We recorded cassettes for all the *compañeras*. . . . We sang the same chorus in three languages, but there were verses from all over the world. It was a powerful thing" (pers. comm., March 18, 2014).

Another element mentioned by many of the activists interviewed was that the WMW recognized the movement's diversity and the possibility for multiple feminisms: "It was not one feminism, there were many feminisms"

(Guadalupe Cárdenas, pers. comm., November 14, 2014). The WMW was seen as a space where everybody was recognized as a feminist; all wanted respect for women and fought for their rights but with different approaches, depending on the context. This translated into initiatives that were launched together but took different forms in different spaces, according to the visions and possibilities of the organizations that constituted the WMW. This relates to what Conway (2008) refers to when she describes the WMW as a network of nodes of place-based activism and globally coordinated action, engaged in context-specific struggles rather than abstract terms.

In addition, the commitment to include all women in the movement, even if they did not necessarily describe themselves as feminists from the beginning, was also an important element. In the words of Graciela Ramos, "The WMW's great success at the beginning was that it was open to all women, feminists or not. All the women were there, the women of the grassroots, the peasants, of course the indigenous women" (pers. comm., March 18, 2014). This resonates with the transnational discourse of the WMW, aiming to build a broad movement for all women. Despite these elements in the transnational discourses and practices that facilitated a resonance among local organizations, many conflicts and tensions also arose at the national scale. Unequal financial resources were a key element in such conflicts. Lourdes Angulo, one of the activists from Jalisco, explained that while organizations did not wait for money to participate in the actions, that the WMW was mainly self-funded was a limitation (pers. comm., May 7, 2014). It was important to ensure the presence and participation of members of the WMW in the national forums and assemblies, especially if they were grassroots women: "At the end, the resource was the opportunity to participate, for national cohesion. And it was about who was able to get it and who wasn't" (Refugio Ávila, pers. comm., May 7, 2014).

Issues of inequality among regions and organizations once again proved to be important when building the national scale. Another source of conflict was the autonomy vis-à-vis governments, in a context of gender mainstreaming and institutionalization of gender policies. Alliances with antisystemic movements and the relation to the state's government were also a source of strong debate. The second national coordination, based in Chiapas, which was strongly linked to the Zapatista struggle, could not consider a dialogue with the federal or state government, while in Mexico City, the local leftist government was considered an ally of the women's movement. This became problematic in terms of accepting or refusing resources and dialogue spaces at the national scale.

Moving the national coordination from Mexico City to San Cristóbal de las Casas in Chiapas was seen, at the moment when the decision was made, as desirable to counter the heavy centralization of the women's movement. In practice, however, it implied very important challenges in terms of the leadership of the wmw and the resources available to continue the national coordination work. This reinforces the argument about how location is part of the explanation of the dynamics of social movements: many specific dimensions of space mattered. Unequal economic resources and differences in their relation to the state were crucial in shaping these movements. Faced with a national context of rising violence, and decreasing mobilization because of political repression, it became more and more difficult to match local agendas with the international agenda of the wmw.

CONCLUSION

All the activists interviewed agreed that the wmw in Mexico was a moment of important mobilization that connected local organizations with national and international efforts. For the women who participated in this movement, the reactivation of a national coordination that could articulate to the transnational scale was seen as important and necessary: "We must recover the mystique of the March. . . . For us, it was a reference. Not only in terms of analysis, of struggle, and proposals, but also a reference emotionally, and I think that was a great strength" (Graciela Ramos, pers. comm., March 18, 2014). Emotions seem to have played an important role as part of the glue that held the movement together at different scales of action. However, conflicts arising over time made it difficult for women dealing with different political contexts to sustain the movement at the national level.

My story shows how the wmw gave transnational visibility to the many alternative visions that women are fighting for around the world, and this was its fundamental contribution. As Refugio Ávila highlights, "We were addressing the consequences of an economic system, trying to counter the impacts. Now we are talking about alternatives to the system" (pers. comm., May 7, 2014). Local initiatives such as solidarity-based and food-sovereignty fairs promoted by the wmw were a source of inspiration for concrete alternatives to the hegemonic economic system all over the world. Between 2000 and 2008, the wmw in Mexico managed to articulate local efforts of women's organizations from the north to the south of the country, contributing at the same time to building a transnational movement. Accessing the transnational scale was successful when it connected with problems women experienced, and when there was resonance between the local and the international agendas (Guadalupe Cárdenas, pers. comm., November 14, 2014). Transnationalizing local struggles could empower and legitimize local actors to go beyond the national scale. Building these bridges between what the wmw raised internationally and what was done locally allowed continuity.

The specifics of the space that stretches across transnational and local scales are relevant in understanding a movement's dynamics; they are part of the explanation for the power of particular movements. Looking at the wmw in Mexico, we can argue that a shift in location explains, at least partially, the difficulties in sustaining the transnational scale of the movement. This case shows that dynamics at the national level are still of central importance, despite the globalization of movements and discourses. Coordination at the national scale seems to be crucial to participation at the transnational scale. Organizations from different regions may have very different relationships to the same state, as with the tensions between Mexico City and Chiapas.

The study of the wmw in Mexico also shows that organizing at multiple scales—local, national, and transnational—can be synergistic, as it was during the first national coordination of the wmw. But this can also reverse and shift to putting all the energy into the local scale, as happened with the second coordination in Chiapas. Alliances, synergies, and collaborations are episodic and discontinuous, not unilinear.

Although the wmw was seen as a possible means to critique neoliberal policies, it is difficult to sustain a movement with diverse actors and different scales of action. Some elements helped to build the transnational scale during the first period of the wmw in Mexico: the type of leadership, the preexisting networks, and the recognition of diversity within the feminist and women's movement. Through the wmw, activists scaled up the local struggles with transnational experiences, created training spaces for participants, used popular-education tools to show that women from many places of the world shared the same struggles, and proposed alternatives. Being part of this national and international platform legitimized and empowered many local organizations.

In a context of violence, increasing militarization, and criminalization of protest, it has been difficult to recharge the movement, as organizations seem to have prioritized the local scale, forced to do so by the political context. Scales are not permanent, and in the Mexican case, there was an important change in the dynamics of scale; during the first period of the wmw in Mexico, the national coordinators in Mexico City put a lot of energy into building the national and transnational scale through the march's framing and discourses. When the national coordination changed to the southern state of Chiapas, the emphasis was placed on local dynamics. Although the WMW managed to take root in this second space, this case shows that the construction of resonances across local, national, and transnational scales is a complex process, and its success is never guaranteed in advance.

ACKNOWLEDGMENTS

Gracias compañeras from the World March of Women, *muito obrigada* for all the conversations that led to this chapter. My gratitude as well to the Department of Socio Political Studies at Instituto Tecnológico y de Estudios Superiores de Occidente (Western Institute of Technology and Higher Education [ITESO]) for its financial support to attend the Women's World Congress in Brazil. Thank you so much Ashwini Tambe and Millie Thayer for your wonderful work organizing the seminar in Brazil, your thoughtful feedback, and the follow-up that made this book possible.

NOTES

1 These findings are the result of the fieldwork for my PhD thesis, which traces the history of the WMW in Mexico through internal documents and in-depth interviews with key activists from different regions of the country (Mexico City, Guadalajara, San Cristóbal de las Casas, Chihuahua, and Ciudad Juárez).
2 All interviews were conducted in Spanish, and all the translations are mine.
3 The Women's Global Charter for Humanity (2004) can be viewed at: https:// marchemondiale.org/index.php/who-we-are/key-documents/womens-global -charter-for-humanity.
4 It is difficult to determine whether there was an underlying conflict between local actors, since the former national coordinator was unreachable for an interview. Some activists said this was due to personal affairs.

　　　　　　　　　　　　　　　　　　　　Carmen L. Díaz Alba

6

Network Ecologies and the Feminist Politics of "Mass Sterilization" in Brazil

RAFAEL DE LA DEHESA

WHEN THE BRAZILIAN CONGRESS passed the country's Family Planning Law in 1996, about 27 percent of Brazilian women of reproductive age— almost half of those using any contraceptive method—had been surgically sterilized (Sociedade Civil Bem-Estar Familiar no Brasil [BEMFAM] 1997). This figure was notable, among other reasons, because the new law would for the first time legalize and regulate a practice that had become the most commonly used contraceptive method in the country even though it was largely performed in the shadows. Its costs generally not covered by the public health system or private insurance plans, the surgery was usually carried out in semiclandestine ways, often in conjunction with cesarean sections or other reimbursable procedures or through under-the-table clientelistic practices, for instance, by doctors-turned-politicians in exchange for votes (Caetano and Potter 2004, Caetano 2014). By bringing the practice of sterilization under the state's purview, the law's advocates hoped to finally offer a national response to a debate that had raged in the country for decades.

It was, to be sure, one of many issues on the feminist and women's health agenda in Brazil. But feminist condemnation of "mass sterilization" and "genocide" had been a particularly salient priority for the women's movement since it reemerged in the 1970s, still under the shadow of military rule

(1964–85). The ongoing political controversy surrounding the issue became evident in a dramatic final turn in the trajectory of the 1996 law. President Fernando Henrique Cardoso (1995–2002) used his line-item veto to retract the stipulations on voluntary sterilization, responding to a legal opinion issued by the Health Ministry that the procedure violated criminal laws against bodily injury. In response, feminists launched a campaign to overturn the veto, ultimately prompting Cardoso to renounce it as a mistake and call on lawmakers to overturn it. Congress did so in August 1997, legalizing and regulating voluntary sterilization (Libardoni 1996).

The decades-long contestation surrounding sterilization in Brazil was embedded in a transnational field in multiple and complex ways. Discourses condemning mass sterilization as genocide circulated broadly transnationally, within feminist circuits and beyond (Briggs 2003b). They repudiated the neo-Malthusian project of population control advanced by the so-called population establishment, an evolving network of international foundations like the Ford and Rockefeller Foundations, nongovernmental organizations (NGOs) like the Population Council and International Planned Parenthood Federation (IPPF), governments and bilateral aid organizations (most significantly the United States), and international agencies like the UN Population Fund. Many advocates of population control within this network regarded sterilization—and other long-acting contraceptive methods such as hormonal implants and injectables—as a particularly cost-effective means to address a perceived crisis of overpopulation. This was partly rooted in mistrust of the poor women and women of color generally prioritized by family planning policies, on the assumption that they would use other methods incorrectly or discontinue their use (Hartmann 1995; Connelly 2008).

For feminist movements in many countries and emerging transnational feminist networks, sterilization abuse became particularly salient as a way to shed light on systems of "stratified reproduction" across lines of race, ethnicity, nationality, and social class; to construct an expansive frame of reproductive rights; and to articulate feminist demands with other social justice movements and the anti-imperialist struggle (Alves and Corrêa 2003). At one level, then, Brazilian feminists' campaign against sterilization abuse reflected their participation in these emerging transnational networks. But feminists were just one of several globalized actors engaged in this debate. The political terrain they encountered was itself thoroughly globalized, constituting what might be conceived as a *network ecology* within which the regulation of sterilization and its place in "reproductive governance" in the country were negotiated and contested (L. Morgan and Roberts 2012).

This chapter traces the history of feminist mobilization against sterilization abuse and population control as it constellated around reproductive politics in Brazil, from the establishment of the first family planning organizations in the 1960s through the passage of the Family Planning Law three decades later. It draws on a larger research project on sexual and reproductive rights movements' engagement with health care that involved extensive research in archives belonging to social movement organizations, public health institutes, state agencies, and international foundations and included 100 interviews in Brazil with sexual and reproductive rights activists, health officials, and other relevant political actors. On the surface, the history of this mobilization presents two paradoxes: (1) it was directed against a military government that formally never adopted a national family planning program but rather instituted a program of comprehensive women's health care broadly inspired by feminist principles, and (2) the vast majority of women who were sterilized, across boundaries of class and race, actively sought the procedure.

In exploring this history, I use the concept of a *network ecology*. Feminist scholars have called attention to how transnational networks circulate resources, ideas, knowledge, policy innovations, and strategies, in ways that can create solidarities but that are also selective, uneven, and fraught with potential for misrecognition and mistranslation (Mohanty 1984; Thayer 2010a; Alvarez 2014). Much of this literature has focused specifically on the transnational articulations of feminist activists themselves. The concept of a network ecology expands the analytic lens to explore dynamics among multiple stakeholders engaged in these debates and their transnational articulations. It sheds light on the coevolution of networked actors, whether in coalitional or oppositional relation to each other, with attention to how these interrelationships shape the selection, (re)interpretation, and embedded salience of particular transnational discourses and practices (Oliver and Myers 2003; della Porta and Tarrow 2012). Networks are understood here as constellations of public and private actors at the local, national, and transnational levels, connected in ways that range from interpersonal relationships to formal contracts. Network ecologies are produced through the embodied practices of people from different movements and institutions occupying shared spaces and of "dual militants" participating in more than one movement, or through the more disembodied circulation of discourses and practices, producing a commonly understood, if contested, grammar. For a particular social movement, embeddedness in a network ecology can facilitate the "mainstreaming" of its demands, involving their vertical incorporation into political society, or the "sidestreaming" of its discourses and practices horizontally, across movements (Alvarez 2014).

THE POLITICS OF POPULATION BEFORE FEMINISM

When the first groups of a resurgent Brazilian feminist movement appeared in 1975 and began contesting population control, they entered a field already occupied by various transnationally articulated actors that had begun mobilizing around family planning a decade earlier. Key among these were private-sector family planning organizations. The most important was the Brazilian Civil Society for Family Welfare (BEMFAM). The society was founded in 1965 at the Fifteenth Meeting of Obstetrics and Gynecology and affiliated with the IPPF two years later. Its founders were largely male doctors but included economists and other social scientists. In addition to building a national network of clinics, BEMFAM's early efforts included biomedical and social research and the organization of seminars and courses aimed at doctors, politicians, journalists, and other strategically located professionals. It also spearheaded efforts to press the Brazilian military government to adopt a national family planning program. The government occasionally gestured toward doing so but ultimately never did. It did, however, issue a decree in 1971 declaring BEMFAM a "public utility," implying tax-exempt status, and by 1988 the group had signed almost two thousand contracts with state and municipal governments to provide family planning services, which were offered throughout the country but heavily concentrated in the poor northeast region (Sobrinho 1993). The early funding for BEMFAM came primarily from the Ford Foundation and the IPPF. In 1971 these accounted for 15 and 85 percent of its funding respectively.[1]

For its opponents, including feminists, BEMFAM's articulation with foreign donors and close advocacy work with the military government aligned it with an imperialist project of population control and the authoritarian status quo, both read through the Manichean lens of Cold War geopolitics. They routinely cast BEMFAM as an agent of foreign powers and harshly condemned it for conducting "mass sterilizations" and indiscriminately distributing birth control pills and IUDs, with little information or follow-up. Without discounting all of these charges, it is worth noting that BEMFAM did not conduct sterilizations in its clinics, in part to avoid political controversy, although it subsequently trained doctors in sterilization procedures through its agreements with university teaching hospitals (Rodrigues 1984).

Rafael de la Dehesa

In addition to BEMFAM, a broad network of private clinics, many of which did perform sterilizations, formed the Brazilian Association of Family Planning Entities in 1981, a network that included over 140 organizations by 1987.[2]

The question of sterilization abuse in particular first erupted on the national stage when reports broke in 1966 that the Brazilian government had requested US aid to look into the creation of a family planning program (immediately denied by the government); early the following year, US Peace Corps volunteers and Protestant missionaries were reported to be conducting campaigns of mass sterilization in the eastern Amazon region. The reports prompted outcries by Catholic bishops and opposition lawmakers, student protests in three states, and visits to the region by government ministers, as well as scattered statements of support for family planning by a handful of doctors and government officials (Pessoa 1967). The scandal eventually led to a congressional inquiry commission, which called twenty-five witnesses, all men, to testify. Testimony at the hearings and news reports suggest some doctors and nurses associated with missionary outposts in the region were inserting IUDs, which was repeatedly framed as a campaign of mass sterilization. The commission, however, never issued a final report, derailed by the promulgation of Institutional Act 5 in December 1968, a draconian decree that shut down Congress, heralding the ascension of the most hard-line sectors of the military government.

Two points are worth noting about these early debates for the precedents they set and their echoes in later feminist mobilization. First, they underscore the early salience of the discourse of mass sterilization, which even extended to other contraceptive methods. Sterilization became a symbolically laden sign around which debates often pivoted. This was in part because it was able to mobilize various constituencies by condensing various meanings for different groups, standing for imperialism, racism, violations of national sovereignty, and violations of natural motherhood, as well as, in later years, for women's autonomy.

The second is the controversy provoked specifically by technologies of governmentality structured by transnational networks, particularly revolving around the role of international agencies and private actors in the Cold War project of population control. The historian Matthew Connelly (2006, 201) has underscored the central and strategic role of networks for the global population control movement, which "decentralized authority and promoted informal coordination" through networks "as a deliberate strategy" to insulate actions from public scrutiny. Such dynamics were clearly at play in Brazil. A 1976 cable from the US embassy in Brasilia, for instance, recommended that in light of the controversies provoked by family planning within the Brazilian government and society, the US government should "discreetly continue support for BEMFAM through international organizations such as the IPPF."[3] Reporting on a meeting with the secretary of special health programs of the Brazilian Health Ministry in 1978, another embassy cable noted the Brazilian official's recommendation that a possible $3 million disbursement by the Population Council "be channeled through international health organizations . . . to reduce [the] possibility of negative political repercussions in Brazil."[4] The examples underscore the opaque channels of funding, created to blur lines of accountability, and the strategic use of networks, by both Brazilian and foreign actors, not just to channel resources and assign responsibilities but to insulate projects from nationalist backlash.

Finally, while BEMFAM and other advocates of family planning had made significant inroads promoting birth control before the resurgence of feminism, the Brazilian government remained divided and hesitant in relation to this project. This in part reflected a pronatalist stance long held by Brazilian political elites and embraced at the time by sectors of the military, rooted in a perceived geopolitical imperative to populate vast empty tracts of land, particularly in the Amazon region, for national security and economic development. Brazil had too few people, not too many: a position also echoed by sectors of the revolutionary left. It also reflected the government's trepidation about the political heat surrounding the issue and specific concern over opposition by the Catholic Church.

Over the course of the 1970s and 1980s, the government flirted periodically with adopting a vertical family planning program on the model envisioned by the international population establishment but never did so. At the Bucharest Population Conference in 1974, it moved away from official pronatalism, while aligning itself with the position of so-called Third World countries, which pushed back against First World governments' advocacy of population targets and the use of incentives and disincentives to promote birth control. Brazilian delegates at the conference announced a new "Brazilian Demographic Policy," asserting that family planning is a right of couples and a matter of national sovereignty but also that the state was obligated to make methods and information available across class lines. The UN declaration of 1975 as International Women's Year sparked the establishment of feminist organizations in Brazil, ushering in a new chapter in this story.

Rafael de la Dehesa

FEMINISTS ENTER THE NETWORK ECOLOGY

In 1978 activists with the Circle of Brazilian Women, an organization of Brazilian political exiles in Paris, sent the editors of *Brasil Mulher* (Brazil woman), the first newspaper of a resurgent feminist movement, an analysis of its first ten issues. Both founded in 1975, the Circle and Brasil Mulher Society, which published the newspaper, were among the first organizations of a resurgent—diasporic—Brazilian feminist movement. The Circle was founded with the goal of "maintaining a permanent relationship" with the women's movement in Brazil, learning "what might be generalizable" from the international and French feminist movements, and establishing ties with other organizations of Latin American women in exile.[5] In some sense, then, the organizations also constituted two new nodes in the evolving transnational feminist networks.

Analyzing the newspaper's coverage of birth control, the Circle activists observed that the topic generally appeared "through the campaign against the imposition of contraceptives from above and in a compulsory way" and against BEMFAM. While applauding this focus, the analysis nonetheless noted a lack of coherence in the paper's editorial position on birth control itself, which occasionally slipped into the more pronatalist stances then defended by sectors of the left. They pointed, for instance, to an article in the paper's fourth issue, entitled "We Are Still Being Born." The article situated early reports that the Brazilian Health Ministry might begin studying family planning and charges that BEMFAM was indiscriminately distributing birth control pills and conducting a campaign of mass sterilization within a global project of population control. It ended, however, with a quotation by the Argentine leftist intellectual Enrique Dussel affirming that "Latin American children will continue being born, demanding their natural right to a place in the sun." Likening this position to that of France's fledgling pro-life movement, Circle activists attributed such inconsistencies to divisions within the newspaper's editorial team on matters like abortion, which reflected underlying disagreements over basic questions about the role of feminism and the relationship between so-called specific struggles (including feminism) and the general (class) struggle.[6]

As suggested by this analysis, many of the women involved in both groups also participated in clandestine leftist organizations mobilizing against the Brazilian military government, which were also transnationally articulated in part through diasporic contacts with political exiles (Leite 2003). The Brazilian left was broadly united in its stance against population control, understanding it as an extension of imperialism and an effort to get rid of poverty by getting rid of the poor. Some sectors, however, echoed right-wing nationalist precepts contending that Brazil needed more people, not less, for the sake of national security and economic development (Sobrinho 1993). The ambiguities in the newspaper's editorial position identified by the Circle thus reflected some of the dilemmas of activists' dual militancy in two movements and two overlapping transnational networks. They also suggest the multidirectional nature of sidestreaming within network ecologies, its potential to constrain as well as expand movements' political horizons, and its direct influence on early feminist debates on reproductive politics.

Over the next two decades, the changing contours of this network ecology would shape feminist mobilization around sterilization abuse, family planning, and women's health in important ways. In the late 1970s, a large, heterogeneous array of civil society actors, including feminists, were united against the military dictatorship and its supporters. A national expression of global Cold War geopolitics, this central division shaped social movement activism and the nature and salience of transnational linkages in Brazil in specific ways. It was manifest, for instance, in the centrality of Marxism across multiple movements, the ever-present debate concerning the relationship between the general and specific struggles, the role of political exiles in articulating transnational linkages, and the construction or occupation of shared spaces of contention. These broadly shared ideational and organizational structures reverberated in reproductive politics as well, fostering certain coalitional and oppositional formations while precluding others and in some cases making for some fairly strange bedfellows.

Global changes in the Catholic Church, for instance, had specific national reverberations in Brazil, with direct implications for the politics of family planning. At one level, a Latin American movement of liberation theology, inspired by the Second Vatican Council, found one of its strongest national expressions in Brazil. As progressive sectors gained ascendance within the Brazilian church, it became a leading voice opposing military rule and created thousands of Christian base communities, which channeled activists into various social movements, including feminism and numerous so-called feminine organizations of working-class women demanding health care, housing, and other basic services. The church's institutional position within the larger network ecology thus gave it both significant leverage among progressive sectors and enough political autonomy and legitimacy to influence the dictatorship. Concurrently, papal encyclicals recognized a role for governments in addressing problems deriving from "accelerated population growth" so long as they conformed with "moral law" (*Populorum Progressio* 1967) and sanctioned the use of "natural" birth control methods within a paradigm of "responsible parenthood" (*Humanae Vitae* 1968).[7]

During the 1970s, the Brazilian Catholic Church adopted the language of responsible parenthood (as did other actors, like BEMFAM, in its largely unsuccessful overtures to the church), and Catholic activists began disseminating information on "natural" methods, obtained through contacts in Australia and the United States.[8] The Brazilian church both facilitated and constrained early feminist debates on reproduction, again reflecting its peculiar position within the network ecology. For example, the progressive Archdiocese of São Paulo cosponsored (with the UN Information Office in Brazil) the Meeting to Diagnose the Paulista Woman, the first major feminist conference of a resurgent movement, organized in 1975 for International Women's Year. The roundtable on women's health at the conference featured critics of the global project of population control, a point on which feminists, the left, and the Catholic Church agreed.[9] At the same time, the progressive alliance with the Catholic Church constrained early feminist engagement with the question of abortion, with the first public protest on the issue occurring in 1980, after police raided a clandestine clinic outside Rio de Janeiro (*Jornal da Rede* 1992). Moreover, the church's position allowed it to exercise unusual influence on government initiatives in family planning and women's health, as I elaborate in the following.

Alongside and overlapping these actors, another transnational movement found unique expression in Brazil, in ways that would both shape the substance of the feminist movement's health-care demands and facilitate their mainstreaming or incorporation by state health-care bureaucracies. From the 1960s, a broad network of Latin American social scientists and health-care professionals mobilizing around the banner of "social medicine" began challenging the individualizing and biologizing tendencies of mainstream epidemiology by drawing on social scientific approaches, particularly historical materialism, to shed light on the social determination of health and health disparities. From an institutional foothold in the Human Resources Development Department of the Pan-American Health Organization, advocates of the paradigm promoted research, seminars, scholarships, publications, and other forms of institution building throughout the region (De la Dehesa 2019).

The *movimento sanitario*, Brazil's progressive health-care reform movement, stood out among the national instantiations of this broader regional network for its size and influence, finding expression in several academic departments and successfully pressing for recognition of the right to health care and the creation of the country's universal public health-care system in the 1988 Constitution. In Brazil, as in the larger regional network, questions about the relative priority of the general and specific struggles again gained traction, often translating into an emphasis on universal health care and class inequalities and a tendency to dismiss sector-specific demands like women's health as secondary. The Brazilian movement, however, also stood out for its early engagement with feminism. Dual militants, feminist *sanitaristas*, many of whom also participated in clandestine Marxist organizations, were most directly responsible for this. But it also reflected the particularities of the network's embeddedness and institutionalization in the national polity, which found a unique expression as a social movement organization in the Brazilian Center for Health Research (Centro Brasileiro de Estudos de Saúde [CEBES]). Founded in 1976, CEBES reproduced the left's model of party cells, establishing a network of "nuclei," or discussion groups, throughout the country, with the explicit goal of bridging the academy, unions, popular movements, women's organizations, and other social movements, thus unifying struggles across institutional domains.

The issue of population control gained particular traction in bridging sanitaristas and feminists, in part because it resonated with the former's critique of imperialism and concern with how geopolitical asymmetries shaped health care in conditions of dependent development. At its National Assembly of Delegates in 1980, CEBES defined population policy as one of three key priorities, calling on its nuclei to engage in research, denunciations, and mobilization around the issue (*Saúde em Debate* 1980). Feminist sanitaristas in São Paulo created the CEBES Women's Studies Group, and several other nuclei created family planning commissions to address the issue. In addition to reinforcing a shared critique of population control and of the activities of family planning organizations like BEMFAM, the sidestreaming between these movements also produced a shared insistence on the need for comprehensive women's health care in the context of a universal health-care system and a related repudiation of vertical family planning programs decoupled from a comprehensive approach.

Beyond reinforcing shared perspectives and demands, sanitaristas were also institutionally well positioned to facilitate their mainstreaming into health-care bureaucracies. The movimento sanitario embraced a strategy of occupying "gaps" (*brechas*) in the state's health sector, which began in states and municipalities won by the opposition and extended to the federal Health Ministry. Feminist sanitaristas in the ministry's Maternal and Child

Rafael de la Dehesa

Health Division designed and administered the feminist movement's most important policy initiative of the 1980s, the Program of Integral Attention to Women's Health (PAISM). Strongly influenced by the precepts of social medicine, PAISM contemplated comprehensive attention to women's health in all phases of the life course, including access to and information about contraceptives (including pills, barrier methods, and "natural" methods). The program's implementation would fall far short of expectations, constrained by underfunding and political neglect, but it remained a key reference for the feminist movement, which made its effective implementation a top health-care priority.[10]

Two points help situate PAISM within the changing contours of the larger network ecology. First, the 1980s and 1990s saw a more general mainstreaming of the feminist movement (and others) in the country. This was reflected both in the creation of government bureaucracies like women's rights councils, first in some states and then at the federal level in 1985, and in the NGOization of social movement organizations, involving a professionalization of activism increasingly reliant on activist claims to expertise. This mainstreaming occurred against the backdrop of the country's piecemeal transition to formal democracy, which fostered a gradual reorientation among activists from stark opposition to the state toward engagement with public policy. It also reflected changing relations between feminists and international donors, including key players of the population establishment, which gradually embraced the feminist language of reproductive rights and increased feminist NGOs' access to funding. The case of PAISM itself is telling in this regard. It was initially rejected by many feminist organizations as "*controlismo* disguised as feminism," given its origins in a military dictatorship (Leon 1984). But the feminist team in the Health Ministry met with feminist groups throughout the country and contracted some to produce education materials and train health-care professionals. In 1984 the feminist doctor Maria José Araújo criticized some feminists' "systematic rejection of government health-care programs" as politically "backward," framing PAISM as a hard-fought victory against the government's more "controlist" impulses. The following year, the feminist Inês Castilho (1985) argued that PAISM emerged "in the gaps of the authoritarian system," noted the role of feminist groups in its implementation, and argued that the movement's fight now was not to oppose the program but to push for its effective implementation.

Second, the health minister's announcement of PAISM in 1983 occurred during his testimony before a congressional inquiry commission created to look into "problems related to population growth in Brazil," which in some ways crystallized the opposing coalitions of transnationally networked actors that would continue to confront each other in the legislature and executive bureaucracies until passage of the Family Planning Law of 1996. The commission was created by the Parliamentary Population and Development Group, a caucus of neo-Malthusian lawmakers, disproportionately on the right, initially brought together at a seminar organized by BEMFAM, which held permanent consultative status with the group. The group was created in the spirit of the Colombo Declaration issued at the International Conference of Parliamentarians on Population and Development in 1979. In 1982 it hosted a regional conference in Brasilia that gave rise to an inter-American network, one of four regional networks of parliamentarians to grow out of the Colombo conference. The conclusions of the congressional inquiry commission included a bill that would create a vertical National Family Planning and Population Council outside of the Health Ministry, with the goal of harmonizing population growth with economic development.[11] That this proposal was presented in the same context as the health minister's announcement of PAISM speaks to the contradictions within the state machinery, where different sectors of civil society were constructing competing alliances.

Also worth noting in this context is the position of the Catholic Church. The National Council of Brazilian Bishops (CNBB) held several meetings with the Health Ministry team that designed PAISM, as its secretary-general acknowledged in his testimony at the congressional inquiry. Through these efforts, the church pressed successfully for the inclusion of "natural" family planning methods in PAISM and the exclusion of others, including IUDs, which it considered abortifacient (Sobrinho 1993). The ministry also signed agreements with the Confederation of Natural Family Planning Centers, initially created within the São Paulo Archdiocese but subsequently splitting to become an NGO affiliated with the World Organisation of Ovulation Method Billings. Despite this influence, the church criticized the program for underemphasizing natural methods. At its Twenty-Second Assembly in 1984, the CNBB issued a statement titled "In Favor of the Family and in Defense of Life," which lambasted BEMFAM, denounced outside pressures to limit births by organizations like the World Bank and IPPF, and ascribed to PAISM "identical objectives."[12] More broadly, the 1980s saw a strengthening of conservative sectors within the church, prompted by the gradual return to formal democratic politics, feminists' initial efforts to liberalize abortion, and Pope John Paul II's concerted attack on liberation theology. The bipolar network ecology that shaped the terms of reproductive politics in the 1970s,

Rafael de la Dehesa

pitting neo-Malthusians aligned with the military against an opposition that included feminists and the Catholic Church, thus gradually gave way to a tripolar arrangement, with BEMFAM, feminists, and pro-life activists forging competing alliances within the state. This constellation of forces would characterize debates around the Constitution of 1988, which included a right to family planning, as well as the Family Planning Law of 1996.

Against the shifting contours of this network ecology, feminist attention to sterilization abuse found new expressions, such as funded research, as well as renewed urgency after national surveys revealed a significant increase in sterilizations and a rapid decline in fertility rates.[13] A striking dimension of feminists' mobilization around the issue in the 1980s and 1990s was how they grappled with the fact that many working-class women and women of color who underwent sterilization actively sought it, countering their image as passive victims of imperialist and eugenic projects, widely circulated nationally and transnationally in the context of Cold War geopolitics. Noting many poor women's strategic recourse to eugenic sterilization boards in North Carolina, the feminist historian Johanna Schoen (2005) has argued that the same technology can enhance or restrict different women's reproductive control, depending on the options available to them and the larger sociopolitical context. Moreover, while poor women and women of color have been more vulnerable to coercive interventions, the dichotomy between coercion and choice does not map neatly across racial and class lines, just as the fact that many might actively seek a technology does not preclude the possibility that larger racist and classist projects might also be at play (79). These debates gained traction in Brazil as feminist demands were mainstreamed precisely because the operationalization of critiques as public policy meant treading a difficult boundary between "justifiable protection from abuse and unjustifiable paternalism" (Petchesky 1979, 29).

In the northeastern city of Recife, SOS Corpo, the first feminist NGO focused on women's health, conducted a research study in 1982 of "voluntary female sterilization," the first of a series of projects funded by the Ford Foundation. In a report of their findings, activists explained that they broached such a controversial topic because their experiences working directly with women revealed important lacunae in political debates on the topic, most important, the absence of women who had themselves been sterilized. Why, they asked, given the method's illegality and widespread public condemnation, did most women prefer it over other more easily accessible and reversible methods (Corrêa 1982, 6–7)? Much of the study drew on interviews with sixty-two largely working-class women, ages seventeen to forty-seven. Of these, forty-six had been sterilized, including a mother and daughter, ages thirty-seven and seventeen. Two reported not having wanted the procedure, both from rural areas. The rest spoke of their "battle" to obtain it, and all but two who had not undergone the procedure expressed a desire to do so. Asked why they opted for sterilization, the most common answer involved economic factors. While middle-class women responded, "I did not want more children," those of the urban periphery often responded, "I could not have more children," referring to external constraints (Corrêa 1989, 36). The study positioned these decisions as the outcome of pathways sharply constrained by gendered and economic structures, which led women to choose sterilization as a reproductive strategy and produced it as a cultural norm.

Few sites in the network ecology crystallized the tensions between establishing measures to ensure individual reproductive autonomy and protecting populations from aggregate-scale biopolitical interventions more than those created or occupied by black feminist organizations. While black women had participated in the concurrent resurgence of the country's feminist and black movements in the late 1970s, black women activists—many of whom had participated in either or both of these movements—established a number of autonomous organizations throughout the country in the 1980s and 1990s, responding to the common marginalization of their concerns within these larger movements. Interviews with several black women's health activists suggest that formal articulations with counterparts in other countries and international donors came some years after the movement's emergence, reflecting and reinforcing a relative lack of resources. Early transnational connections took the form of ideational identification with a larger Afro-diasporic counterpublic, as reflected, for instance, in the Winnie Mandela Tribunal, organized by black feminists in 1988 to mark the centenary of the country's abolition of slavery and to put its actual contributions to black emancipation on trial (Gilroy 1995). While sterilization abuse was broadly condemned by feminists overall, the issue became a central catalyst in the development of the country's black feminist movement, which both increased its political salience and highlighted its racist dimensions (Damasco 2009). Certain incidents brought these dimensions to the fore in the national debate. In 1986, for example, the Center for Research and Assistance in Human Reproduction, a private clinic in Salvador, Bahia, launched an advertising campaign that included a billboard featuring a black child holding a switchblade under the banner "Manufacturing Defect."[14]

Black feminists, like feminists overall, were divided about how to respond to the rising sterilization rates in the country. In the late 1980s, activists with the Health Program of Geledés, a black feminist NGO in São Paulo, worked with Workers' Party congressman Eduardo Jorge, a leader of the movimento sanitario, to craft a bill that would regulate the procedure. Between 1990 and 1992, black women's health activists in the Rio-based Center for the Articulation of Marginalized Populations launched the Forum against the Mass Sterilization of the Black Woman, which organized events around the country. Its leader, the physician and women's health activist Jurema Werneck, understood efforts to regulate the procedure as a concession to racism and sought instead to change the "culture of sterilization" that made so many poor women and women of color seek it.[15] Broadly, debates revolved not just around whether to regulate or criminalize the procedure but around what regulations could protect both individuals' reproductive autonomy and groups' collective vulnerability to abuse.

Along parallel lines, black feminist as well as other feminist organizations spearheaded campaigns that prompted congressional inquiry commissions into "mass sterilization" by three state assemblies (Rio de Janeiro, Espírito Santo, and Goiás) and the Salvador City Council. In 1991 an inquiry was called in the federal Congress, overseen by the Workers' Party deputy Benedita da Silva, the first black woman elected to Congress. One complication that black feminists encountered in their charges of genocide was that available survey data showed higher rates of sterilization among white and middle-class women than among black and low-income women, suggesting that the procedure's widespread dissemination was due less to direct coercion than to social and cultural structures that normalized it as a reproductive strategy. The commission's final report also noted the notorious difficulties in obtaining accurate statistics on race in the country (presumably given the fluidity of racial categories and many Afro-Brazilians' disidentification with blackness). More broadly, the report concluded that "the institutions conducting fertility control in Brazil . . . [were implementing] policies of demographic control conceived by foreign governments and international organizations," in violation of national sovereignty, and that, against the backdrop of the government's failure to implement PAISM, these institutions relied on its failure to exercise oversight (Comissão Parlamentar Mista de Inquérito 1993, 116).

Ultimately, the federal commission produced the bill that would form the basis for the country's Family Planning Law of 1996. That law and its implementing regulations instituted several requirements designed to ensure informed consent, including a minimum age of twenty-five; at least two living children; a sixty-day waiting period after the initial request; state counseling on the procedure's implications and alternatives; a forty-two-day waiting period after childbirth, except in medically prescribed circumstances; and, through an amendment by a conservative lawmaker, the consent of the spouse or partner.

CONCLUSION

Writing about the (trans)national politics surrounding sterilization abuse in Puerto Rico—widely debated in transnational networks as a paradigmatic case of coercive campaigns—the feminist historian Laura Briggs (2003b) has underscored the complex problems of translation in a transnational field marked by geopolitical imbalances and the ways in which multiple nationalisms haunted these debates. Without denying the violence that characterized the United States' colonial relationship with the island, Briggs contends that most Puerto Rican women exercised agency in seeking the procedure and that there is little evidence of a "forced sterilization campaign" by a "repressive state apparatus" (2003b, 159). Rather, she argues, US-based feminists projected US-based politics onto the island, imagining idealized victims who lacked agency and needed rescuing, and in doing so sidestepped potential alliances with Puerto Rican feminists, including some working with the local IPPF affiliate. They thereby inadvertently aligned themselves with pronatalist projects advanced by conservative sectors like the Catholic Church. Drawing on Iris Lopez's (1993) notion of "constrained choice" to counter the image of a passive victim, Briggs calls for subtler analyses that pay close attention to the local embeddedness and implications of transnational practices (2003b, 159).

In Brazil, as in Puerto Rico, there is little evidence of a coercive campaign imposed by the state. Rather, the massive proliferation of sterilization can perhaps best be understood in terms of constrained choice, with women's agency often delimited by socioeconomic inequities, patriarchal gender norms, and a lack of access to safe, reliable alternatives. Yet here, unlike in Puerto Rico, sterilization abuse as a topic became central to the local feminist agenda. Its political salience in part reflected a repudiation of the role of transnational networks in implementing birth control programs in the country, against the backdrop of a state that formally adopted feminist precepts but did little to implement them. Sterilization also became a bridge that linked various national actors that were articulated with transnational networks, fostering shifting oppositional and coalitional relations among them against the backdrop of national and transnational political transformations. This chapter has offered the concept of network ecologies in order to shed light on the complex and polyvalent ways that transnational networks become embedded in national contexts.

ACKNOWLEDGMENTS

I would like to thank the editors of this volume, Ashwini Tambe and Millie Thayer, for organizing the conversations that led to its publication and for their feedback on versions of this chapter. Thanks also to Francesca Degiuli, Jean Halley, and Hosu Kim for their feedback on early drafts. Finally, I would like to thank the many people who contributed to this research project with their time and resources, in particular Sonia Corrêa, Ana Maria Costa, and Carmen Barroso for the many insights they provided me in thinking through this history.

NOTES

1 Thomas H. Naylor, "Brazil: The Population Situation 1971," Ford Foundation Collection, box 356, folder 008447, Rockefeller Archive Center, Sleepy Hollow, New York.
2 Integrated Maternal and Child Care Research and Development Center (CPAIMC) and Brazilian Association of Family Planning Entitities (ABEPF), "Family Planning in Brazil: It's Time to Invest!," July 1987, Centro de Documentação-BEMFAM, Rio de Janeiro.
3 US embassy, Brasilia, to secretary of state, Washington, DC, subject: Implications of Worldwide Population Growth for United States Security and Overseas Interests, March 11, 1976, http://www.wikileaks.org/plusd/cables/1976BRASIL02153_b.html.
4 US embassy, Brasilia, to secretary of state, Washington, DC, subject: Population-Discussions with a Ministry of Health Official, April 11, 1978, https://wikileaks.org/plusd/cables/1978BRASIL02904_d.html.
5 L. & G., "O nosso Círculo, ou tudo começou em 75," *Este é o Número Zero/Zero/Zero—como vai se chamar a nossa publicação???*, May 1978, 1–8, Archivio Storico del Movimento Operaio Brasiliano (ASMOB), box 10.03.30.7, Centro de Documentação e Memória da Universidade Estadual Paulista (CEDEM/UNESP), São Paulo.
6 Sub-Grupo Imprensa Feminista/Círculo de Mulheres Brasileiras, "Como 'Brasil Mulher' vê a questão do controle de natalidade e que propõe," April 1978, ASMOB, box 10.03.30.7, CEDEM/UNESP; and "Continuamos Nascendo," *Brasil Mulher* 1, no. 4 (1976): 6, CEDEM/UNESP.

7 Paul VI. *Populorum Progressio*, encyclical letter, March 26, 1967, Vatican Website, http://www.vatican.va/content/paul-vi/en/encyclicals/documents/hf _p-vi_enc_26031967_populorum.html. Paul VI, *Humanae Vitae*, encyclical letter, July 25, 1968, Vatican Website, http://www.vatican.va/content/paul-vi /en/encyclicals/documents/hf_p-vi_enc_25071968_humanae-vitae.html.

8 Sister Maria José Torres, "Histórico sumário do método da ovulação (Billings) no Brasil," unpublished report, July 28, 1982, doc. 19530, Centro de Documentação e Informação-Conselho Nacional dos Bispos do Brasil (CDI-CNBB), Brasilia.

9 Centro de Informações do Exercito, "I Encontro para Diagnóstico da Mulher Paulista," Secret Report by the Brazilian Military Intelligence Service, November 18, 1975, Acervos dos Órgãos de Informação do Regime Militar-SNI, doc. A0877256-1975, National Archives, Brasilia.

10 Ana Maria Costa, "O PAISM: Uma política de assistência integral à saúde da mulher a ser resgatada," 1992, Comissão de Cidadania e Reprodução, São Paulo, Conselho Nacional dos Direitos da Mulher (CNDM) Collection, Code 210, box 93, doc. 10000002392, National Archives, Brasilia.

11 Ata da 255a Sessão, em 5 de dezembro de 1984, 2a Sessão Legislativa Ordinária, da 47a Legislatura, *Diário do Congresso Nacional*, sec. 2 (December 1984): 5019–31.

12 CNBB, "Em prol da familia e em defesa da vida," statement approved at the Twenty-Second CNBB General Assembly, Itaicí, São Paulo, April 25–May 4, 1984, doc. 17526, CNBB-CDI, Brasilia.

13 By 1984, sterilization had become the most common contraceptive method, used by 27 percent of married or partnered women of reproductive age. The fertility rate fell from an average of 5.8 children per woman in 1970 to 3.5 in 1984 (BEMFAM 1987).

14 Conselho Estadual da Condição Feminina-Comissão para Assuntos da Mulher Negra, *Mulher negra: Dossiê sobre a discriminação racial* (São Paulo: CECF, December 1986), Federal and State Government Collection, box 4, doc. 6069, CEDM/UNESP.

15 Jurema Werneck, in discussion with author, Rio de Janeiro, May 31, 2012.

INTERROGATING CORPORATE POWER

Part III

7

Transnational Childhoods

Linking Global Production, Local Consumption, and Feminist Resistance

LAURA L. LOVETT

THE LITERATURE on transnational childhood typically combines the topics of children and migration. Beginning with the discussion of transnational childhoods by anthropologists Marjorie Orellana, Barrie Thorne, Anna Chee, and Wan Shun Eva Lam (2001) nearly twenty years ago, the focus has been on the way in which children are moved through, across, or around national borders. These studies describe what it means for children to participate in processes of cross-national migration and how they are affected by parents' movement for work (Horton 2008). In these narratives, children are on the move: they are themselves transnational. Where scholars have considered the artifacts of childhood, they have seen toys as substitutes for parental presence, especially when discussing the translocation of parents, with toys standing in for a vision of increased opportunity. As described by one Salvadoran migrant mother, "Yes, their life is better here because they have their toys, shoes, their little notebooks, and we have enough money" (quoted in Horton 2008, 934). While these scholarly conversations represent important contributions to our understanding of transnational childhood, focusing on children's material culture offers a new perspective on what it means to be transnational. The globalization of children's material culture shapes childhood in ways that render children transnational subjects of global corporations without children crossing any borders at all. Children's toys, books, and educational materials, I argue, form a material node in a network of "transnational connectivities" that link patterns of global production, local consumption, feminist resistance, and children's acts of making meaning and identity (Grewal 2005). Feminist claims about these toys often push back against an intensified gender binary used to market toys to children; they often contextualize their efforts as part of a larger campaign for gender equity in education. I support my analysis of the place of children's toys using studies of changing patterns of gendered toys in Brazil and elsewhere over the past twenty-five years.

My goal in this chapter is to demonstrate the relevance of transnational feminism to issues arising in connection with the production and reception of gendered stereotypes in the materials of childhood. In their *American Quarterly* article, Laura Briggs, Gladys McCormack, and J. T. Way suggest that transnationalism "can do for the nation what gender did for sexed bodies: provide the conceptual acid that denaturalizes all their deployments, compelling us to acknowledge that the nation, like sex, is a thing contested, interrupted, and always shot through with contradiction" (2008, 627). The same can be said of childhood: the tools of transnational feminist analysis can help us denaturalize the deployment of childhood, allowing us to understand it as a thing, often an idealization, that is "contested, interrupted, and always shot through with contradiction." This contestation is readily apparent, I claim, in the material nexus occupied by children's toys and other materials of childhood.

Toys have always represented aspirational models, from the codification of dollhouses, first designed to help nobility "play" at managing a household filled with servants and space, to Elsa, the Disney snow-queen doll meant to model sisterly concern for ever-shrinking families. These objects, though, communicate in increasingly gender-specific modes what a girl and a boy should want and be. Connected to multifaceted, multimedia corporate marketing campaigns, they draw children into an ever-narrowing vision of what childhood should be. But if the power of the idea of the "normal" child can help to rationalize globalization of toy production, what does the importation of the artifacts of childhood do to localized ideas of gender roles? And what role do children play in navigating and challenging these ideas?

As increasingly globalized objects for consumption, toys are emblematic of corporate interests, while often embodying cultural values and stereotypes held by the manufacturer regarding gender, race, and ability. That said, feminist critiques of toys are also specific: they exemplify transnational feminisms' rejection of assumed universal ideals of gender and gender roles (Tambe 2010). We have to realize that ideals of childhood are profoundly contingent and local, even as dominant groups have typically promoted their standards of childhood and child rearing as the norm or standard.[1]

BEYOND "LOST CHILDHOODS"

Just as transnational feminists rightly criticize some early Western and northern feminists for projecting a universal idea or ideal of womanhood, children are also being subjected to a universalizing idea or ideal of childhood globally. The assumption of a Western ideal of white, middle-class childhood leads to a perceived "loss of childhood" by those who do not meet this vision. For example, poor children are thought to have a "lost childhood" because they had to work to help support their family or did not have the opportunity for leisure and play because they were caring for younger siblings. Because leisure and play are assumed to be normal for children, their absence is read as a loss (Stephens 1995; Fass 2007).

Just as transnational feminism questions the universalization of women and gender espoused by some forms of liberal feminism, scholarly analysis of global childhood allows us to plainly see that a romanticized Eurocentric, middle-class ideal of childhood cannot be assumed to be universal. On the one hand, this rejection of universal ideals of childhood was achieved by insightful comparative analysis that documented changes in childhood and its idealization over time and from one local context to another.[2] On the other hand, these ideals of childhood have also been criticized for ignoring children's agency and instead focusing on the attitudes of parents and experts. Children themselves are not passive consumers of culture, and their experience and the ways they make sense of it vary radically across time and region. That said, finding records of children's agency can be a formidable challenge, especially among groups that may not leave written records or whose records and testimony may not have been valued by archivists and historians in the past.

Framing children as consumers is one particular way of acknowledging their agency, but that agency is given value in terms of their contributions to global capitalism as first consumers and later producers. In the United States, marketing to children began in earnest in the nineteenth century through children's magazines (Ringle 2015). Toys became associated with status by children and parents alike, and by the twentieth century, as children had more say in their consumption habits, advertising and its venues became much more child focused (Schor 2004; Cross 1997). Purchasing preference is a consumerist form of agency that is limited by the choices that manufacturers present. Industry-sponsored focus groups and play sessions offer a more direct route for children's input, but the least constrained form of children's agency is probably the myriad of ways in which they take a toy and make it their own: changing it, playing with it, and fitting it into their lives and their experiences. This range of children's agency with regard to their toys, books, and material surroundings resists any universal understanding of how a toy or object is received by a child. Transnational feminist arguments against the imposition of gender and racial stereotypes typically focus on resisting manufacturers' efforts to impose uniformity in cultural objects across the globe, but children also play a role in creating distinct and varied meanings for the materials in their lives.

GENDER AND THE MATERIALS OF CHILDHOOD

Scholars have explored, in depth, the global circulation of ideas of childhood, especially the notion that childhood should be devoted to education and play (Mintz 2004, 16). Indeed, the normalized notion of play and the freedom from responsibilities that it represents, along with education and its promise of class mobility, are often mentioned as a motivation for parents to migrate, in search of the "norms" of health, safety, and prosperity that the idealized child represents for their own family (Horton 2008). Despite the strong association of childhood with play, efforts at universalizing understandings of childhood, such as the United Nations Convention on the Rights of the Child (UNCRC), do not enshrine it. Drawn up in 1989, the UNCRC did not explicitly guarantee the right to play for signatory nations' children. Article 27, for instance, urges the signatory states parties to support parents in their primary responsibility "to secure, within their abilities and financial capacities, the conditions of living necessary for the child's development" by offering "material assistance and support programmes, particularly with regard to nutrition, clothing and housing" (United Nations 1989). In other words, it does not treat children's right to play as a universal primary responsibility of all parents across class locations. The closest the UNCRC comes to engaging with child-centered material objects is in its encouragement to state parties to produce and disseminate "children's books" when it recognizes the role of the mass media in promoting social, spiritual, and moral well-being. The gendered nature of children's material culture is also not acknowledged in this claim for developmental necessities. The

Laura L. Lovett

need for gender equality enters in the article on education, where the UNCRC states that the direction of the child's education should be "the preparation of the child for responsible life in a free society, in the spirit of understanding, peace, tolerance, equality of sexes, and friendship among all peoples, ethnic, national and religious groups and persons of indigenous origin."

Four years after the UNCRC was ratified in the United Nations, the North American Free Trade Agreement (NAFTA) also was adopted. The impact of NAFTA on children's toys in Mexico was profound (Bacon 2004). In informal interviews, Mexican mothers commented that, following 1994, Mexican toy stores became "just like toy stores in the US." The aisles were gender segregated, and almost none of the toys were designed and produced by Mexican toy makers. In fact, one of the only toy makers in Mexico to survive the transition under NAFTA is Mi Alegria—a company that in 1956 started making cosmetics that were safe for children and then branched out into scientific and educational toys.[3] Even companies that held licenses from the global toy producers Mattel and Hasbro to produce plastic toys based on popular TV shows, such as the Transformers, found themselves undercut by the new tariff structure, which made it very difficult for them to compete with foreign manufacturers (Golden 1992).

Mexican toy makers did of course produce some gender-specific toys before NAFTA. In fact, a quick glance at Mi Alegria shows gender-specific lines of toys. But when NAFTA dropped tariffs on toy imports, the Mexican toy industry association lost 80 of its 265 members in just one year. One major toy manufacturer, Plasticos Igo, cut almost 60 percent of its workforce. As local toy makers went out of business, the kinds of toys offered in Mexico became globalized and became subject to the importation of gender norms set by global corporations. The American toy company Hasbro, for instance, opened its first Latin American office in Mexico in 1991, then expanded to Chile in 1996, and then to Brazil, Colombia, and Peru after 2006 (Mann 2015). As the two largest countries in the region, Mexico and Brazil were the principal markets for Hasbro. In both countries, the company manufactured some toys locally, but most were imported from Asia. In the fierce competition for the growing toy market in Latin America, Hasbro worked to integrate its toys with media by producing its own TV series, such as *My Little Pony*, and seeking lucrative movie tie-in arrangements with the Transformers series and Marvel Studios. Significantly, they also targeted traditional local toy companies with strong brand recognition in order to push them out of the Latin American market (Mann 2015). The manufacture of "children's transnational culture," as Inderpal Grewal (2005, 97) calls it, was achieved by this process of competitive exclusion and the rise of transnational toy manufacturers that control manufacturing, marketing, and relevant mass media. Grewal's examination of the global production of Barbie dolls by Mattel speaks directly to the communication of gendered stereotypes, but similar stereotyped messages are present with other transnational producers.

In Brazil a number of researchers have been tracking changes in toys, their marketing, and their representations of gender roles (Sarat, Campos, and Macedo 2016; Biella, Almeida, and Gonzalez 2010; Kropeniscki and Perurena 2017). For instance, Fernanda Battagli Kropeniscki and Fátima Cristina Vieira Perurena's study offers a detailed comparison of how toys were represented in a Brazilian toy store company catalog from 2009 to 2017. (They do not name the toy company, but the company gave them access to their complete records.) They note that toys are often gender segregated by color (pink for girls, blue and other colors for boys) and activity (girls are depicted with domestic toys, while boys are depicted with cars and tools). Yet between 2009 and 2015, they noticed a shift in the pattern of representation in the catalog. In 2009 domestic environments were associated with girls and had pink and white colors. Race cars and war scenarios were offered only to boys. Thus, the toys differentiated play for boys and for girls. In 2015 the home environment depicted in advertising gained new colors (not just pink), and more boys were depicted in domestic settings. She infers that the color, not the domestic setting, was perceived as a barrier to interest by boys.

The shift in boys' relationship to domestic work that Kropeniscki and Perurena found in the Brazilian toy catalog suggests to them a move beyond gender binaries but only a slight one. They see these toys as proposing to boys that they assist in domestic work but that the domestic sphere still belongs to girls. In their words, "toys portray selected realities, and these realities are marked by gender relations. In this way, colors, environments and varied situations can refer us to the feminine or masculine" (979). Changing to a "unisex" color scheme in the 2015 ad for the toy cooking set, Top Kitchen, serves, then, as an invitation to boys to help in the kitchen. In their words, "in a capitalist society marked by consumption, a toy factory must (re)produce what matters to its consuming public. In this way, the observed changes in production and supply of toys walk at slow steps" (979). Of course, this kind of analysis does not touch on how children actually use these toys. Their use and interpretation are not passive but often disruptive as children appropriate toys for new and imaginative uses.

Laura L. Lovett

Because I was interested in how these toys were arranged in stores, I visited a number of PBKids stores in Rio de Janeiro and Florianópolis, Brazil, in 2017. The stores were strongly gender segregated, with cars and Legos in one aisle and princess dolls and kitchens in another. Top Kitchen was there and definitely stood out in a wall of pink, purple, and white plastic kitchen gear. These particular lines of toys are, however, the exception in PBKids. Indeed, what was most striking in the stores I visited was the dominance of media figures and brands from the United States. While some of these are licensed to Brazilian manufacturers, most of the toys in these large stores bore the stamp of Disney, Pixar, or Marvel Comics or were produced by US toy giant Mattel (of Barbie and Hot Wheels fame). Here was a very North American idealized gender system embodied in the layout and content of a Brazilian toy store.

That said, one toy stuck out: the Boneca Bebê doll from Coleção Adunni. It was a pink ballerina baby, but its features, color, and packaging were distinctive. Boneca Bebê was shaped like a baby and had a dark complexion and a red box with lettering in rich primary colors. Interestingly, this doll was a vehicle to promote social, educational, and economic empowerment for Black women in Brazil through the Baobá Fund, a Kellogg Foundation fund designed to promote racial equality in Brazil. Invoking "bodies and memories" as the only goods available to the "'naked migrants' forcibly brought to the Americas as enslaved men and women" (Édouard Glissant, quoted in Pereira, Correia de Oliveira, and Silva de Lima 2015, 5), the fund proposes the doll for its potential to reflect the image of the child back to him or her. They also have a line of black Barbie-like dolls, which are at once transnational and local: Coleção Adunni is producing a distinctively Brazilian baby, on the one hand, and co-opting the globally recognized form of the Barbie doll, on the other.

TOYS AND FEMINIST ACTION

Toys as vehicles for political activism have a long feminist history. In the United States, children, childcare, and children's toys and books were significant issues in the 1970s. For instance, Letty Cottin Pogrebin, a founding editor of *Ms.*, created a special section of the magazine for "free children" that featured stories without sexist stereotyping and articles focused on nonsexist parenting. One of her first contributions was an article titled "Toys for Free Children" (1974). Before offering a list of recommended toys, Pogrebin explained why parents needed to take toys seriously. She understood toys as powerful influences on children's "character, personality, and temperament" (48). Toys mattered because they could "inspire occupational choice, unleash artistic talent, and leave an emotional imprint for life" (48).

The idea that toys could instill lessons was relatively new in the 1970s. The marketing of "educational toys" to parents in the United States really only began in the interwar era when Holgate, later acquired by Milton Bradley, hired Norman Rockwell's brother, Julius, as their main designer. Nursery schools, where children played to learn, were still a relatively elite phenomenon, beginning in the 1920s, but through the 1930s and 1940s, they moved into middle-class culture. Objects like Carolyn Pratt's unit blocks, designed to foster "creative pedagogy," then moved from schools to middle-class playrooms.

The actions of teachers and parents in supplying objects that allowed for creative play imbued the objects themselves with a central place in child development and socialization. Play, at least for middle- and upper-class white children, was understood to be both important and influential. Revaluing toys with the language of freedom and equality may have addressed inequities based on gender, but it did not recognize the economic inequities underlying the assumption that all children would have access to the latest educational or creative toy line from Milton Bradley. Toys were recognized as a vehicle for sex-role socialization, but they also assumed a middle-class ideal of childhood.

In an attempt to forge a national feminist agenda in the early 1970s, the Women's Action Alliance (WAA) solicited opinions on what issues mattered most to American feminists. They received over five thousand letters from parents across the United States asking for parenting advice: "How do we keep young children from developing the rigidities of sex-role stereotyping? How do we help little boys realize that love, affection, and nurturing are indeed part of the proper role of a man? How do we help little girls realize that the world is theirs to have and to hold? How do we help them in their earliest years make choices that will not one day limit their choices?" (Abram 1978, 17). In response, the WAA created the Non-sexist Child Development project (NSCD) in 1972. Citing evidence that children as young as three years old had already learned sex-role stereotyping, NSCD director Barbara Sprung decided to focus the organization on preschool children and their socialization. Sprung had been an elementary schoolteacher for eight years. As the director of NSCD, she would help parents, teachers, and school administrators become aware of sex-role stereotyping and of ways to address it. Sprung began her work with a review of the scholarly literature and moved on to evaluate classroom materials. Children's toys, for instance, were considered in terms of the degree of sex and racial stereotyping found in each.

The WAA's NSCD was only one of many similar US efforts. Locally, parents opened nonsexist childcare centers, and some teachers designed their own nonsexist and nonracist curricula. Nationally, the National Foundation for the Improvement of Education undertook a massive study of biased images in elementary school textbooks in 1974. With support from the Rockefeller Family Fund, this was one of many efforts to reevaluate textbooks. Others included the Dick and Jane as Victims project organized by the Women on Words and Images group in Princeton, New Jersey (Women on Words and Images 1972; Weitzman and Rizzo 1974; Paris 2011).

In Brazil, scholars point to the adoption in 1984 of UN Resolution 34/180 mandating gender equity as a turning point for advocacy for gender equality in children's educational materials and then children's material culture (Schwartzman 1988). This resolution mandated the "elimination of any stereotyped concept of male and female roles in all the levels and in all forms of education, by stimulating mixed education and other types of education that contribute to achieving this objective and, in particular, through modification of school books and programs and adaptation of teaching methods" (Barbosa and Andrade 2017). In the wake of this resolution, various national education plans and curricular frameworks in Brazil began including considerations of gender equality (Soares et al. 1995).

Fúlvia Rosemberg, Neide Cardoso de Moura, and Paulo Vinícius Baptista Silva (2009) locate the roots of Brazilian resistance to gendered stereotypes earlier, in the feminist movement of the 1970s. Rosemberg's (1969) doctoral thesis had confronted the issue under the influence of French feminists such as Simone de Beauvoir. She brought her work back to Brazil and in the 1970s began a systematic study of the representation of the sexes and of stereotyping in children's literature and textbooks (Rosemberg 1975). Rosemberg tracked the academic literature on this subject in the United States and around the world. In her assessment, "As occurred in the United States the condemnation of sexism in textbooks in Europe, Latin America, and the Caribbean, Africa and Asia has been accompanied by a series of recommendations and actions for overcoming it: Public opinion awareness-building, changes in legislation, competition and prizes for non-sexist books, self-regulation codes for publishing houses, the formation of teachers and producers of text books, in addition to the countless publications, seminars, and meetings that have been held" (Rosemberg, de Moura, and Silva 2009, 8). In Brazil, Rosemberg and her colleagues document significant efforts to reveal sexist stereotypes and shape educational policy beginning in the 1970s and 1980s (Rosemberg and Piza 1995). Yet, as Fábia Cristina Mendes Barbosa and Helisangela Andrade (2017) point out, in Brazil "we still do not have nonsexist education, because school is sexist and reproduces machismo."

Outside of the academy, Brazilian feminists tied their efforts to create nonsexist education, nonsexist toys, and a nonsexist children's culture directly to the often-violent consequences of a machismo culture (Cowan 2017). The Committee for Latin America and the Caribbean for the Defense of Women's Rights (CLADEM) emerged from the 1985 UN Conference on Women in Nairobi, when a group of women recognized that a regional approach could be powerful. An important part of their agenda was nonsexist education, but, in their words, they "aim[ed] for a school that practices respect for diversity, that deconstructs the ideological bases of the violence suffered by women of all ages, indigenous and African-American populations, the disabled and those who chose a sexuality different from that of the prevailing patterns" (CLADEM n.d.). One of the feminist groups with strong Brazilian participation that allied with CLADEM was the Network of Popular Education among Women (REPEM), which shared their goal of nonsexist education. In 1990 REPEM launched a campaign for "nonsexist human education." Part of this campaign was the declaration of June 21 as a day of action for nonsexist education (De Aza Mejía n.d.; see also Núñez n.d.). This regional organization with a transnational vision launched a public campaign against sexist stereotypes aimed at children. Like US feminists, REPEM saw their efforts aimed at children as having the potential to transform society. In the words of Cecilia Millán (n.d.), "If the gender prejudice and the power relations that entail and protect that prejudice are not attacked or eradicated, no form of inclusion of populations marginalized or excluded by their color, choice of culture and sexual experience will lead to a real transformation of our societies." Unlike feminist actions in the United States, however, efforts by REPEM and CLADEM in Latin America were more widespread and longer lasting.

At a more popular level, Brazilian blogs calling for nonsexist toys also recognize the impact of the gender binaries communicated in many toys. Nina Lemos (2016) and others picked up on some trends in other countries in their advocacy of nonsexist toys. They pointed to GoldieBlox in the United States—an engineering toy aimed at encouraging girls' creativity. They also highlighted Top Toy from Sweden, which decided in 2012 to promote only toys that could be nonsexist. Interestingly, pages from the Swedish Top Toy catalog then ended up on the pages of Brazilian bloggers. As Mariana

Granato Barbosa put it, "If the understanding of society, symbols and meanings occurs through play, what are we showing the children when we restrict little playhouses, food, and dolls only to the girls?" (Barbosa 2013).

These conversations among Brazilian bloggers mirror the emergence and increased media attention given to the gendered assumptions inherent in the increasingly "pinkified" landscape allocated to girls. Consider the PINKSTINKS campaign in England and Germany and similar protests in Sweden. Founded by twin sisters in England, PINKSTINKS took inspiration in part from the efforts of thirteen-year-old Philipe Johansson and classmate Ebba Silvert in Sweden, who campaigned against the Christmas Toys "R" Us catalog, noting that boys were presented as active and girls as passive. They reported the American toy retailer to Sweden's advertising ombudsperson who agreed with the children, declaring that the Toys "R" Us catalog "discriminates based on gender and counteracts positive social behavior, lifestyles, and attitudes," issuing a public reprimand of the company (PINKSTINKS 2010). The first campaign of PINKSTINKS took on a favorite English educational toy company called the Early Learning Center. The catalog grouped toys by gender with "passive, beauty-centred products" targeting girls. In their words, in Early Learning Center stores, "the swathes of pastel pink all along one side clearly signpost to a child what's for them and what isn't. Girls go one way, boys another. . . . We don't believe this is real choice—more an illusion of choice" (PINKSTINKS 2010). Within weeks, the "Early Learning Emergency," as PINKSTINKS called it, had been covered by media in more than forty countries. Their website had over fifty thousand hits, and their social media feed was attracting thousands of followers (PINKSTINKS 2018). Among them was a sixteen-year-old from Brazil named Beatriz, who wrote:

> I'm Brazilian and I've just discovered your website by reading an article of a Brazilian news website. I have to say: the statistics have scared me to death about our generation's future. . . . Even considering that my country doesn't have such consuming habits in general due to its secondary place in global economy and to its huge wealth concentration, we can still notice in here how harmful media can be. Then, I found out good actions as this young student's (and also yours!) are happening now and I felt happy and, somehow, hopeful. Many people can say, as I've read in this comments list, that pink is just a color. But we have to remember that it's more than that: it's a symbol. (Felix 2009)

The transnational appeal of PINKSTINKS makes sense given the history of nonsexist educational campaigns in other continents, such as Latin America.

Yet while Beatriz is correct about the symbolic importance of pink and other gender signifiers, what they mean to Beatriz in Brazil is not what they mean to the founders of PINKSTINKS in England. While they all recognize that gender stereotypes limit girls' options, the nature of those options and the realities of consumption are very different in Brazil and Europe, as Beatriz points out.

CONCLUSION

The toy industry has been subject to the same processes of globalization as other industries. Chains of production, distribution, and consumption intensified by trade agreements such as NAFTA have spread the power of US toy manufacturers. As a vehicle for the communication of gender stereotypes, these material objects of childhood are also sites of transnational feminist concern. The increased feminist awareness that children's toys and books are sites of transnational corporate imperialism has also fostered regional strategies for contesting gender roles and expectations. Activism about these issues has become increasingly transnational, as the examples of Brazilian educational campaigns and PINKSTINKS show. Even as the meanings of gendered toys vary across location, such networks of connected strategies demonstrate increasingly powerful ways of confronting harmful stereotypes.

ACKNOWLEDGMENTS

I am grateful to the audience at the Women's World Conference in Florianópolis, Brazil, for their comments as well as to Ashwini Tambe and Millie Thayer for their editorial care and insight.

NOTES

1 See Steven Mintz's *Huck's Raft: A History of American Childhood* (2004) for a discussion of myths of childhood promoted in the United States.
2 Karen Sanchez-Eppler's "Playing at Class" (2000) articulates the ways in which working-class child laborers in the United States helped create the idea of middle- and upper-class children's play, even as they worked to make the textiles that clothed more and more middle-class children.
3 Mi Alegria Toys, Mexico, accessed July 20, 2017, http://www.mialegria.com.mx.

8

Nike's Search for Third World Potential

The Tensions between Corporate Funding and Feminist Futures

KATHRYN MOELLER

The Girl Effect, n.
The unique potential of 250 million adolescent girls to end
poverty for themselves and the world.

—Nike Foundation (2012)

IN THE EARLY 1990s, Nike, Inc., the world's largest sporting goods and apparel manufacturer, became the global target of antisweatshop and antiglobalization movements (Locke 2002). Their criticism focused on the corporation's well-documented abusive practices against its predominantly young, uneducated, poor, female labor force in the Global South.[1] Responding to tarnishing accusations, including media exposés on child labor, cofounder and then CEO Phil H. Knight publicly stated at the National Press Club in Washington, DC, in May 1998 that "Nike product has become synonymous with slave wages, forced overtime, and arbitrary abuse" (Cushman 1998). Despite Knight's promises two decades ago to transform the corporation's practices, accusations of abusive labor problems in Nike's contract factories persist. Nevertheless, since its moment of crisis, the corporation has focused on remaking itself as a socially responsible entity.

On March 8, 2005—International Women's Day—Nike, Inc., recast its corporate foundation to focus exclusively on "improving the lives and well-being of adolescent girls." As Knight wrote in the press release, the Nike Foundation's investments in the "human capital" of adolescent girls "complements Nike, Inc.'s efforts around improvements in our fundamental business practices" (Nike Foundation 2005). The company linked its new efforts to the United Nations' Millennium Development Goals on poverty alleviation and gender equality.

The Nike Foundation officially launched the Girl Effect, its corporate philanthropic brand, approximately three years later, on May 27, 2008, with financial support from the NoVo Foundation. The campaign conferred on adolescent girls who are poor, of color, and living in the Global South the potential to end poverty in the new millennium. When adolescent girls are educated and empowered, the campaign argued, the ripple effect is reduced fertility, less poverty, greater economic growth, lower population growth, slower spread of HIV/AIDS, and greater conservation of environmental resources. From this perspective, adolescent girls are human capital investments akin to natural, physical, technological, or other kinds of resource investments.

Between 2005 and 2015, the corporation and its foundation invested together in the Girl Effect through institutional partnerships with other private foundations, such as the NoVo Foundation; nongovernmental organizations (NGOs), such as CARE and Grameen Bank; bilateral and multilateral agencies, such as the United Kingdom's Department for International Development and the World Bank; and global forums, such as the World Economic Forum and the Clinton Global Initiative. As the brand's reach extended far beyond the headquarters of the corporate foundation, the Girl Effect functioned as a site of competing and often-contradictory interests. Its power and legitimacy derived from the authentic desires and grassroots demands of marginalized girls and women seeking access to rights from which they have historically been excluded: gender-sensitive schooling; effective job-training opportunities; secure, fairly compensated employment; affordable health care; safe living conditions; and increased economic security. Yet, in addressing this inequality, the Girl Effect took an instrumental approach, branding adolescent girls as a means to development rather than as ends in and of themselves.

In this chapter I analyze how Nike, Inc., and the Nike Foundation constructed adolescent girls as a development population category with the "unique potential" to end poverty. While I focus on one corporation and its foundation, they are part of a movement of corporations investing in poor girls and women in the Global South as instruments of development. Some of the corporations involved in this area over time include Becton Dickinson; Booz and Co.; Chevron Corporation; Cisco Systems, Inc.; Coca-Cola Company; Ernst and Young Global Limited; Exxon Mobil Corporation; Gap, Inc.; General Electric Company; Goldman Sachs Group, Inc.; Gucci; Intel Corporation; Johnson and Johnson; J. P. Morgan Chase & Co.; Microsoft Corporation; Nike, Inc.; Standard Chartered PLC; Starbucks Corporation; Stella Artois; and Walmart Inc., among others.

To illuminate this broader phenomenon, I employ an ethnographic lens to examine one of the Nike Foundation's NGO grantees in Brazil—an NGO I call the Alliance for Development (AFD), whose Program for Young Women (Programa pelas jovens mulheres [PEIM]) searched for adolescent girls with "unique potential"—through an analysis of the AFD's efforts to recruit one hundred adolescent girls to join a session of its educational program. This search for adolescent girls provides a lived and embodied way of understanding how the category of the adolescent girl was constructed through the Girl Effect and how the brand's development discourse played out on the ground.

Through my analysis I argue that the search for adolescent girls was predicated on finding adolescent girls with an imagined "Third World potential" to end poverty. The logic of the Girl Effect positioned particular adolescent girls—those racialized, classed, and situated geographically as "Third World girls"—as disproportionately responsible for ending poverty for themselves and their families, communities, nations, and the world. The logic attempted to push back the timing of childbearing and marriage to unleash girls' economic potential. This intimate relationship between heterosexual reproduction and economics enabled the Girl Effect's returns—real or imagined—from the scale of the individual girl to the world. Thus, contrary to the Nike Foundation's claims of promoting gender equity, the Girl Effect has perpetuated traditionally inequitable roles of social reproduction while claiming to transform them (Ananya Roy 2010b; Chant 2006). In addition, the philanthropic campaign enabled Nike, Inc., to effectively disarticulate poverty from the structural conditions that produce it and to separate its investments in adolescent girls from girls' and women's demands for fair corporate labor practices and a just global economy.

NOTES ON METHOD

This chapter is part of a larger, multiyear study analyzing how and why transnational corporations based in the United States and their foundations are investing in girls' education. Although I conducted participant observation and interviews at three NGOs in Brazil (from 2009 to 2010), my analysis in this chapter focuses on data I collected at only one of the Nike Foundation's grantees, an international NGO in Rio de Janeiro.[2] I also draw on data I collected through interviews and participant observation with the Nike Foundation's management team and its program managers in Beaverton, Oregon, in addition to interviews with former Nike Foundation employees and consultants. In addition, I draw on data from public and internal documents I gathered through internet research and visits to the Nike Foundation headquarters.

According to its grant contract with the Nike Foundation, the AFD was required to educate 1,400 adolescent girls in Brazil between 2008 and 2011. Before the relationship with the foundation, the NGO had worked with both young women and young men. Nevertheless, since adolescent girls were the Nike's Foundation's target population, the NGO adopted adolescent girls as its focus before applying for funding. The AFD's program aimed to "empower" girls to enter the formal labor market or pursue entrepreneurial activities. The primary coursework of the program focused on developing skills for becoming an administrative assistant or an entrepreneur. Other areas of study included basic computer and mathematics skills, writing and reading, and legal, gender, and human rights education. The program was largely unsuccessful in finding the participants jobs either before or after graduation, and, when successful, the program channeled the participants into insecure, often-temporary, low-wage employment in businesses such as telecommunications centers, supermarkets, and bus companies. There were few exceptions.

The program was part of the Nike Foundation's joint philanthropic portfolio with the NoVo Foundation, called "She's an Economic Powerhouse: Economic Empowerment Models for Girls." The foundation launched the portfolio in October 2007. As articulated in the request for proposals (RFP), the portfolio, which is no longer operating, was based on the following conceptualization of adolescent girls: "We see girls as economic powerhouses. She's powerful today as the backbone of her family's economic and social health. She could be even more powerful tomorrow, if her role as an economic actor is shifted. The potential impact of this approach will complement ideals of gender equity and basic human rights. That's what this set of RFPs is all about" (Nike Foundation 2007). The portfolio sought to increase the power of girls—as future women—to end poverty: "We want to see this power increase. But that growth relies on an unspoken truth: unless more of the 500 million adolescent girls living in the developing world today make safe passage to productive womanhood tomorrow, this means of ending poverty will plateau." The portfolio included grantees operating in diverse sociocultural and political-economic contexts, such as Brazil, Paraguay, the Dominican Republic, Kenya, Burundi, Uganda, and Mongolia.

INSTRUMENTAL INVESTMENTS

The discourse of empowering adolescent girls as a means to end poverty did not begin with Nike, Inc. Rather, it has a long, contested history.[3] For the past three decades, as gender mainstreaming took hold in traditional development institutions, the empowerment of girls and women has become a primary goal of development programs and policies—a product of the convergence of liberal development and liberal feminism (Kabeer 2003). As a result, girls have been positioned as key "instruments" for alleviating poverty, slowing population increase, and generating economic growth (Jackson 1996, 490). With this logic, empowering girls and women purportedly provides higher rates of return than do development investments in other areas, such as technology, infrastructure, or other populations.[4]

This has resulted in what Ananya Roy (2010a) describes as the large-scale "feminization of policy." The phrase highlights "the ways in which development operates through women-oriented policies that serve to maintain traditional gender roles of social reproduction" even as they promote nontraditional pathways such as entrepreneurship (548). These policies ultimately contribute to what Sylvia Chant identifies as the "feminization of responsibility and obligation" on multiple scales (Chant 2006, 206). Through this process, these burdens have fallen on the shoulders of the "Millennial Woman, the iconic figure of millennial development" (Ananya Roy 2010b, 70).

This subject position of the millennial woman is different from—yet related to—the construction of the Third World woman in the past three decades of development. In contrast, as articulated by Chandra Talpade Mohanty (1984), the Third World difference that defines the subject position of the Third World girl constructs her as both an object of pity and the answer. She occupies a precarious location in which she is simultaneously the potential savior of development and its universal victim, in need of saving. The productivity of this basic contradiction motivates her investors.

The NGO's efforts to recruit one hundred adolescent girls spanned the summer months from the end of November 2009 through the beginning of March 2010. The terrain I traversed with the AFD program staff covered an expansive, sprawling area of Rio de Janeiro's periphery. On some days, Susanna, a senior staff member, and I spent our time in the surrounding community, walking through the quiet, dusty streets.[5] We hung program posters in the windows of beauty parlors and internet cafés. We left flyers on desks and tacked posters to the bulletin boards of other local NGOs.

In February, during the week before carnival, we visited a nearby neighborhood association in the late afternoon. A poster from the first session of the program hung on the closed door of the president's office. It depicted an orange soccer ball filled with a yellow flower and read, "A vitória começa com elas" (Victory begins with them; using the feminine form of *them*).[6] The faces of three young, brown girls with quiet eyes and long expressions hovered in the bottom corner of the poster, whereas an older, white girl chasing a soccer ball in an athletic T-shirt and shorts, sporting cleats, shin guards, and tall socks was positioned along the poster's edge.

The president, a middle-aged woman, greeted us. When we sat down, we joined an older woman from the neighborhood. After a brief conversation, Susanna explained that the program was beginning a new session. She asked the president if she knew of any young women from their neighborhood who might be interested or eligible. The president asked which age groups we were recruiting. Susanna responded, "Between sixteen and twenty-four years old." The president explained in a matter-of-fact tone, "I know lots of young women, but they are all pregnant," using popular slang for describing a pregnant woman. Directing her question to the president and the older woman, Susanna asked, "Are there a lot of pregnant young women?" The president and the older woman nodded their heads in disappointment. The president expressed how pregnancy ruins these young women's lives. It eliminates opportunities, she said, explaining that no one would hire them while they were pregnant. I anticipated that Susanna would seek to include the pregnant young women in the recruitment, because several young mothers were in the first session of the program. However, she did not.

Before we left, the older woman asked with a sarcastic laugh, "Do you have a program for adults?" Susanna responded, "No, just young women." The woman continued, "I am unemployed." Susanna asked, "What type of work do you do?" Looking down, the woman replied, "Cook." She paused

Kathryn Moeller

for a moment, then stated with more confidence, "I am a cook." Noticing the woman's discomfort, Susanna explained, "I ask because I might know of an opening." As the conversation ended, Susanna handed the president a new poster and a set of small informational flyers. She asked if she could take down the old poster on the door. After realizing it was stuck, almost glued to the glass, the president said that she would place the new one over it.

On other days, we traveled to more distant communities. On the first of March, the rains had already begun. Summer was ending. We hoped it would be the last day of recruitment. Despite the low numbers of recruits, the program was scheduled to begin in early March. As rain inundated the streets early in the morning, four of us from the program arrived at a public high school in a community approximately thirty minutes away by bus from the NGO's office. Our group included Susanna; Gabriella, a new employee; Vanessa, a fifteen-year-old intern and former program participant; and me. For six hours, we climbed up and down the school's stairways, entering more than sixteen classrooms. We interrupted academic lessons and provided teachers with unanticipated coffee breaks. In each classroom we stood in a line before rows of young women and men seated at their desks in narrow yet deep rooms. Susanna and Gabriella introduced the program as Vanessa and I walked around the classrooms passing out small flyers to interested young women. "SPORT—QUALIFICATION—WORK" was written in Portuguese on the flyers in bold letters. A description of the desired participant was printed below, also in bold letters: "Female sex, 16–24 years old, likes sports, and interested in entering the labor market or becoming an entrepreneur."

In each classroom Susanna would introduce the program to the young people. During one introduction, she explained, "The course objective is preparation for the labor market. . . . We work to develop abilities that the labor market looks for, like teamwork, discipline, respect." She described the commitment, explaining to them, "The program has two main courses: technical administration and entrepreneurship. It is a five-month-long, intensive course, Monday through Friday, from eight to one or one to five." The young people's eyes grew wide when they learned of the course's intensity. She further explained:

Our program is completely free. Many times, you see a program that says it's free, but then when you arrive there, you have to pay for the materials. We don't charge you even one real because our funder, the Nike Foundation, already paid for you to participate. The Nike Foundation supports us for this program. You will receive a program T-shirt, the materials, and a very simple, small snack. But the program requires a lot of you—a lot of dedication and discipline. It may not pay off in the short or medium term, but in the long term, it will pay off. Right, teacher?

She leaned over to seek the teacher's reassurance. The teacher responded, "Yes."

As I handed out flyers in the back of one of the classrooms, a young Afro-Brazilian man shyly asked me if a program also existed for men. I explained the program was currently only for young women. I asked him, "Do you want to participate?" He responded, "Yes." I handed him a flyer and told him to call the program the following year, when it might serve young men as well. Addressing this dilemma, Susanna told the young men in the room not to be disappointed. "The organization will have another program for young men and women in the future. But right now, it is only offering a course for women." Taking advantage of the young men's attention, she told them, "If you have a sister, a girlfriend, or a neighbor who fits the profile, you should take a flyer for her."

By the end of the long day, we had distributed all of the materials we brought with us, including a small strip of paper with information for the group interview the following day. The next day, we waited anxiously at the office for those we had invited to interview. Only two young women came.

CATEGORICAL COMPLICATIONS IN THE GIRL EFFECT

After months of searching for adolescent girls, they eluded us even as we anxiously pursued them. One hundred adolescent girls were neither found nor educated during the session I observed. The program officially began in a celebration of International Women's Day on March 8, 2010, with seventy participants, even though this group did not consist of entirely the kind of young women the NGO was looking for. Moreover, after the first day, the young women who had been recruited immediately began to leave the program for various reasons, including a need to work, inability to pay for transportation, and health problems. By March 20 the program was already down to sixty-four participants. The leaders of the NGO explained to me that future sessions would compensate for the insufficient numbers in this group.

In spite of the NGO's anxiety regarding its recruitment of an insufficient number of adolescent girls, the length and location of the search were not factors in the low number of recruits, because there were adolescent girls nearby and the search had lasted three months. The search for adolescent girls was a linear trajectory with an imagined beginning (the category of the adolescent girl) and a fictitious end (the unleashing of the Girl Effect). Our encounters in the search provide entrée to examining the maneuvers involved in the material production of the category of the adolescent girl in the Girl Effect.

To understand this process, I draw on David Valentine's (2007) methodological approach to understanding the origins, meanings, and institutionalization of population categories. As Valentine notes, categories and the values attached to them are never neutral. Language is constitutive of the power relations operating in the discursive production of categories. By considering what he identifies as "categorical complications" or, more specifically, who was included in and excluded from our search for adolescent girls, I hope to elucidate the development discourse of the Girl Effect brand as the Nike Foundation and its partners sought to intervene in particular adolescent girls' lives, molding them into desirable developmental subjects.

The categorical complications I identify occurred as the ideas, money, and other resources shaping this program moved within, across, between, and among unequal social actors and institutions in such seemingly disparate places as Beaverton, Oregon, and Rio de Janeiro, Brazil. Many of these actors were unfamiliar and often ultimately unknowable to one another. Many of them will never be aware that they are imagined within, excluded from, or participating in the production of the category of the adolescent girl. The categorical complications were created among profound relations of difference, yet they were ultimately constitutive of the category.

The complications emerged as the universalized category of the adolescent girl was institutionalized in a particular time and place through the search. The official profile of the adolescent girls we were looking for was written in Portuguese on the program's flyers and posters: "Female sex, 16–24 years old, likes sports, and interested in entering the labor market or becoming an entrepreneur." These generic characteristics reflected the Nike Foundation's mobilization of the universalized category. Yet, while they were officially looking for this profile, a range of nonofficial characteristics influenced recruitment, as I show in the following. These were less tangible and more conditional, and they emerged from the NGO's idea of who constituted the population target in terms of race, class position, education level, employment status, and fertility. These nonofficial characteristics were, in part, a result of pressure—real or perceived—to achieve successful program outcomes. This pressure imbued the everyday of the program and created an ongoing aura of anxiety, particularly around recruitment. Consciously or unconsciously, the pressure influenced which participants the program selected.

Despite the official color blindness of the Nike Foundation's broader deployment of the category adolescent girl, the search for recruits was a racialized process, as depicted on the recruitment poster. On one level, the search mapped onto the "racial formation" of this Brazilian city, where the uneven spatial distribution of opportunity occurs along racial and class lines (Omi and Winant 1994). The search for adolescent girls took place only in and around favelas, areas of the city where the majority of residents are Afro-Brazilian, mixed race, and/or darker skinned. With a few exceptions, the young women in the first two sessions of the program identified in the NGO's survey as Afro-Brazilian or mixed race. They differed from the young women in the nearby white, middle- and upper-class neighborhoods, where residents have better access to opportunity, particularly high-quality private primary and secondary education.

On a discursive level, the official color blindness of the search and the broader mobilization of the race-neutral adolescent girl corresponded to Brazilian and US color-blind discourses in which race talk and racial differences are muted despite everyday racial discrimination and broader structural racialization (Caldwell 2007; Reichmann 1999; Twine 1998). As Susanna once explained to me, "We focus on gender, not race." Although gender was the official focus of the program, in reality, the race of the young women could not be separated from their class positioning, the conditions of poverty in which they lived, and their geographic location. Therefore, the program was neither race neutral in the search nor cognizant of the racialized dynamics through which it functioned.

In relation to class, because the broader goal of the Girl Effect was to end poverty, the young women needed to be poor, yet not too poor. On two occasions, Susanna told me about the daughter of a street recycler who had left the first session of the program after only a few weeks. Susanna surmised that the young woman's low-class status meant she had little in common with the other participants. At the same time, if a young woman's family earned even a small amount over the federal monthly minimum wage, she was considered to have too many resources at her disposal. In another example, the employer of a young woman's father paid for her private school tuition. Susanna was concerned that the young woman's access to the additional resource of a private school education gave her a significant advantage over the other young women.

From an educational perspective, the young women needed to be in high school, to be willing to return to high school, or to have graduated from high school. If they were pursuing an education or training degree beyond high school, they were considered overqualified. An unemployed twenty-four-year-old with a nursing degree, for example, was turned away from the program, as was her friend who was already enrolled in a professional program in oil and gas, a burgeoning field in Brazil at the time. As numbers mattered more than age, young women ages fourteen and fifteen were admitted, despite their limited employability under Brazilian labor law. Because the program focused on employability, the young women the program sought were generally unemployed, unless their employment was informal, very low skilled, or within their family.

As the preceding description of the search illustrates, the program also did not recruit pregnant young women even though staff knew otherwise-qualified young women were in the surrounding communities and mothers had successfully completed the first session of the program. The program considered it too late to intervene in the life of a pregnant adolescent. She had already lost her potential to end poverty, or, in other terms, perhaps she was too reproductive to still be considered productive. The rationale for excluding older female adults was similar. They were imagined to no longer hold the social potential to end poverty.

The program also assumed young men lacked the social potential to end poverty since girls and women were presumed responsible for the education, health, safety, and economic well-being of their children and communities. Yet numerous young men or their parents approached me to express interest in the program either during recruitment or at the program site. For example, a mother came to the program staff to ask if they would accept her stepson, and on another occasion, a young man and I discussed his interest in the program as he waited for his female friend during her interview. Neither of these young men had an equivalent educational opportunity in the community. However, as the search revealed, this program and the other program in the Economic Empowerment Portfolio of Nike, Inc., in Brazil accepted only adolescent girls, even though each of the NGOs had previously worked with young men and women and would later return to working with both after their grant funding ended. Although the Nike Foundation funded a limited number of other programs targeting boys and young men—on questions of gender-based violence and HIV/AIDS—through its Men and Boys Portfolio during this same period, this funding was the exception to the foundation's broader focus.

The categorical complications illuminated through the search are based on the race, class position, education level, employment status, and fertility of the adolescent girls for whom the NGO was searching. The complications reflect how the supposedly universal adolescent girl deployed in the Girl Effect program masked the particular girl that Nike Foundation's programs actually targeted. In spite of the ostensible neutrality of her official profile in the program's promotional materials, the foundation—and, in this case, the NGO—sought her distinct Third World girl potential to end poverty. If girls lacked this potential, then they were not recruited—despite the NGO's desperate need to find enough participants and the genuine diversity of educational and economic needs and desires in the community.

CORPORATE FUNDING FOR FEMINIST FUTURES?

The search for adolescent girls in Brazil has served as an ethnographic entrée into understanding the category's constitutive nature within the Girl Effect. It reveals which adolescent girls the Nike Foundation was seeking and why, which returns me to the premise of this chapter. Particular subjects were excluded from the educational program because they were perceived as lacking the necessary social utility for investment. More specifically, they did not hold the Third World potential imagined by the Nike Foundation. Yet the focus on adolescent girls' Third World potential did not persist beyond the NGO's grant contract with the Nike Foundation, which ended in 2012. Adolescent girls disappeared as the target of its programming. It had strategically employed the category to secure funding; after it did not receive renewed funding, the organization returned to its prior focus on young women and young men. This demonstrated that the category itself was ephemeral.

The NGO's strategic, temporary employment of the adolescent girl simultaneously reveals the influence of corporate funding on NGO practices *and* the contingent, rather than persistent, power that corporations have over NGO practices and, correspondingly, the lives, educations, and futures of girls and women. That the category was eclipsed demonstrates how these corporate efforts are deeply tied to financial resources and accompanying forms of authoritative knowledge. They are therefore neither stable nor enduring, particularly after the corporation is no longer funding its on-the-ground partners. The study consequently reveals the fragility of corporate efforts at the subjectification of particular girls and women.

As Nike, Inc., and the Nike Foundation disengaged from their focus on adolescent girls in 2015, an increasing number of corporations were entering

Kathryn Moeller

the field on local, national, regional, and transnational scales.[7] Like Nike, many of these corporations have overwhelmingly pursued the "business case" for girls' and women's empowerment, which has translated, in most cases, into a narrow economic focus detached from a women's rights agenda. These corporations have tended to avoid the language of women's rights, and human rights more broadly, given potential contradictions with their own business practices. Instead, they have framed girls and women as "resources" for poverty alleviation and development, the language and meaning of which are often contested by women's rights and feminist organizations who resent this framing.

Yet some of these companies have realized the complexities of working with girls and women on the ground and are challenging this instrumental manner of engagement. Rather than plowing forward with their economic agendas and limited knowledge of the issues facing girls and women, a number of corporations are moving toward a more holistic approach where they seek the expertise of more progressive transnational feminist and women's organizations that have long worked with girls and women. This is evident in the relationships between a small group of corporations (including Pepsi-Co, C&A, and Symantec) and progressive, transnational women's rights and feminist organizations that previously rejected corporate funding yet are now cautiously engaging corporations to capture this funding stream and to advocate for more progressive feminist understandings of girls' and women's well-being and futures.

In August 2015 the Win-Win Coalition was launched to support these "cross-sector partnerships" after almost two years of efforts by these women's and feminist organizations, including the Association of Women in Development, the Global Fund for Women, Mama Cash, and Fundo Elas; their "bridge builder" allies that move between the women's rights and corporate sectors; and a small group of companies.[8] How these new types of partnerships are negotiated, and to whose benefit, is critical to understanding how this phenomenon will play out in the future.

With time, this most recent moment of transnational corporate investment in girls and women will reveal the possibilities, tensions, and contradictions of these awkward engagements, as the relationships among philanthropic benevolence, corporate profit, and feminism are articulated with gender, sexuality, race, and poverty across diverse institutions in uneven geographies. The women's rights and feminist organizations that engage in these corporate partnerships may have to negotiate the often-conflicting, if not explicitly antagonistic, agendas of their corporate donors and grassroots grantees, many of whom live with and work against exploitative corporate labor and environmental, consumer, and militaristic practices in their communities and countries.

Continuing to examine this phenomenon is important for understanding how the ongoing, yet subtly transforming processes of the feminization of capitalism are shaping the terrain of feminist struggle against social, cultural, political, and economic exploitation, particularly as progressive, transnational feminist and women's organizations are seeking funding and the ability to influence how these investments in girls and women are structured, and for whom.

What does it mean for the hegemony of corporate capitalism when feminist and women's organizations long involved in holding corporations accountable and transparent are now partnering with them? Is this another example of a "corporate effect" where corporations need not only mainstream NGOs and liberal feminist organizations but also progressive feminist and women's organizations to legitimize their corporate power by neutralizing critique against them and allowing them to extend their reach into new frontiers?

Or are feminist and women's organizations defining the terms of engagement and perhaps even creating partnerships that move "beyond the business case," as Suzanne Bergeron and Stephen Healy (2013) describe, toward a more just conceptualization of gender, development, and the global economy? As explained to me by one feminist activist who had long criticized feminist engagement in corporate spaces, these are attempts to command a "seat at the table rather than under it." If this is possible, what is gained, and what is lost, in this strategic maneuver?

Throughout this study my interlocutors across diverse locations in the development regime have consistently called for increased transparency and accountability for corporations in their relationships with girls and women as laborers in their factories, agricultural fields, and retail stores as well as the purported beneficiaries of their philanthropic and socially responsible endeavors. Yet, in these complicated transnational relationships, to whom and for what are these corporations responsible? And who and what can hold them accountable for their effects on girls' and women's lives and futures as well as on labor, the environment, and communities around the world? As progressive, transnational feminist and women's organizations become increasingly important actors in this phenomenon, critical feminist scholars and activists must contend with whether, how, and to what extent corporate capital can be used for progressive feminist purposes, and whether these actors can, in turn, hold corporations accountable to the girls and women their capital supposedly benefits and shape, if not transform, the hegemonic discourse on the Third World potential of girls and women. Or, as evidenced thus far, will corporate capital continue to remake itself, incorporating progressive feminist claims into its new hegemony, as it shapes the terrain of struggle in its own image and further entrenches relations of exploitation that put poor, racialized girls and women in increasingly precarious positions as the frontiers of capitalism expand?

ACKNOWLEDGMENTS

My sincerest gratitude to Millie Thayer and Ashwini Tambe for organizing this group of scholars to interrogate the trajectories of transnational feminism. They are exemplary feminist mentors and scholars. I am grateful to the reviewers and editors of Duke University Press. The research in this chapter was supported by grants from the National Science Foundation, the Fulbright-Hays Program, and the National Academy of Education/Spencer Foundation.

NOTES

Portions of this chapter were previously published as "Searching for Adolescent Girls in Brazil: The Transnational Politics of Poverty in 'The Girl Effect,'" *Feminist Studies* 40, no. 3 (2014): 575–601.

1 In its corporate responsibility report for the fiscal year 2005–6, Nike, Inc., estimated that 80 percent of its workers were women ages eighteen to twenty-four who were "typically poorly educated, living against a precarious backdrop of poverty and insecurity, within emerging economies" (Nike, Inc. 2006, 16).

2 I exercised caution during the fieldwork and in writing this study in order to protect the individuals and institutions that I studied. At the time of my fieldwork, the Nike Foundation had two male employees, and the grantee NGO had only one male employee. Both institutions had few employees of color. Therefore, I have decided to gender all participants in my study as female and have chosen not to specify the race of the participants to reduce the likelihood of their identification, even though such omission limits aspects of the analysis.

3 The Modern Girl around the World Research Group (2008) has documented the earlier colonial and national histories of how girls were marketed to within capitalism.

4 For corresponding analysis of this discourse, which appeared after the development of my analysis, see Michelle Murphy's "The Girl: Mergers of Feminism and Finance in Neoliberal Times" (2012–13).

5 In accordance with the protection of human subjects, all individuals in my study are given pseudonyms.

6 All translations are my own.

7 These final paragraphs of the chapter are drawn from Kathryn Moeller, *The Gender Effect: Capitalism, Feminism, and the Corporate Politics of Development* (2018), 206–9.

8 In 2016, Win-Win Coalition became Win-Win Strategies, a nonprofit social enterprise, and then merged with Women Win, a Dutch-based NGO. Win-Win Coalition, accessed July 13, 2018, http://www.winwincoalition.org.

INTRACTABLE

Part IV   # DILEMMAS

9

Reproductive Justice and the Contradictions of International Surrogacy Claims by Gay Men in Australia

NANCY A. NAPLES & MARY BERNSTEIN

IN THIS CHAPTER we consider the configuration of international commercial surrogacy, state regulation of reproduction, and reproductive rights discourse to illustrate the value of intersectional analysis for transnational feminist praxis. By broadening the framework of intersectionality beyond identity-based framing and extending the structural approach to reflect the analytic exemplified by Kimberlé Crenshaw (1989) and other intersectional and transnational feminist analysts (see, for example, Carastathis 2016; Collins and Bilge 2016; Grewal and Kaplan 2001), we bring into view the structural dimensions of power embedded in economic, political, cultural, and colonial structures and discursive practices that shape and reproduce inequalities (Naples 2016). Given a context in which sexual minorities (specifically, gay male couples in wealthy settler countries like Australia) and postcolonial subjects in Southeast Asia (specifically, in this case study, India) face divergent challenges to their reproductive rights, we analyze how the silences in movement claims reveal gendered, racialized, colonialist, and class-based assumptions.

Intersectional feminist praxis includes a commitment to acknowledging and honoring differences, especially in terms of power dynamics, while working toward solidarity for radical social change with a framing that broadens the goals to embrace diverse investments (Mohanty 2003; Naples 2016). In practice, the needs and preferred political strategies held by diverse actors, even when they share long-term goals, often come into conflict. In this case, gay male couples' reproductive claims for the legalization of international commercial surrogacy in Australia may conflict with the reproductive rights of less privileged surrogates performing this reproductive labor in other parts of the world.

HISTORICAL CONTEXT

Surrogacy has a long history that predates the development of new reproductive technologies. Some authors note that surrogacy is mentioned in the Bible and has been linked to slavery since that time. For example, legal scholar Anita L. Allen (1991) points out that "before the American civil war, virtually all Black southern mothers were . . . surrogate mothers. Slave women knowingly gave birth to children with the understanding that those children would be owned by others" (quoted in Lewis 2018, 218). It is problematic to define enslaved women as surrogates since what they experienced is better defined as rape and child abduction, even when the women knew that their children would be taken. However, the structural inequality and exploitation typical of their time continue to shape contemporary practices in certain contexts.

Contemporary policy distinguishes between altruistic and commercial surrogacy. Altruistic surrogacy has been more accepted in practice, policy, and popular culture than commercial surrogacy, which involves payment beyond the costs of the pregnancy incurred by the surrogate.[1] There is no way to track the number of cases where a family member or friend might have offered to carry a child for another woman without the use of a legal contract. One of the first legal surrogacy contracts in the United States was drawn up in 1976 by the lawyer Noel Keane. In this case, the surrogate did not receive payment. Keane negotiated hundreds of additional contracts, including the famous case of Baby M, described later on.

The earliest contracts relate to so-called traditional surrogacy, where the surrogate is the genetic mother. The new technology of in vitro fertilization (IVF), where a woman's eggs are retrieved and fertilized outside the womb, then reimplanted into the birth mother, facilitated the possibility of nongenetic, or gestational, surrogacy. The first known birth through IVF occurred in London in 1978. In this case, the biological mother, Lesley Brown, had not been able to conceive owing to blocked fallopian tubes. In this case, the baby, Louise Brown, was genetically related to the birth mother. The development of IVF enhanced the possibility of gestational surrogacy, in which the birth mother has no genetic connection to the child. A successful birth from gestational surrogacy was reported in 1985.

Medical and legal scholars have debated the ethics of surrogacy from the late 1970s onward. Contemporary debates over the legitimacy of surrogacy and women's exploitation heated up with the high-profile legal case of Baby M, born in 1986 to Mary Beth Whitehead, a working-class mother of two. Following the birth, Whitehead contested the surrogacy contract and sought to retain her legal parental status. The court first affirmed the contract, but the Supreme Court of New Jersey overturned the ruling and asserted that the surrogacy contract was illegal. Despite this, the Court awarded custody to the contracting sperm donor William Stern and his wife, with the argument that it was "in the best interest of the child." Sophie Lewis reports that "in response to the drawn-out litigation and Supreme Court appeal that ensued, crowds demonstrated, and an activist antisurrogacy coalition was born" (2018, 218–19). However, "a mass moral reaction was *not* triggered" following the court ruling in the *Johnson v. Calvert* case, in which the claim for parental status of an African American surrogate mother, Anna Johnson, was denied and the contract upheld (Lewis 2017, 213).

While Whitehead was the genetic mother of the child to whom she gave birth, Johnson was not genetically related to the child. In weighing the validity of the contract, the judges faced the question of who should be considered the legitimate or legal parent for determining custody. In the first case, Whitehead was granted parental status, although the Sterns were able to retain custody. In the second case, based on the logic of genetics, Johnson was not granted legal recognition. Race was also a factor in the second case, although race was not raised by the judge. However, as Allen notes, "For the first time in history, an African-American woman had given birth to a child exclusively of European and Philippine ancestry" (1991, 19). As a Black surrogate mother, Johnson was constructed in the judge's argument as an "opportunistic, dishonest" person who "had signed the contract voluntarily" (25–26). In contrast, Whitehead was constructed as a much more sympathetic figure. In this instance, it is difficult to tease apart the impact of the genetic logics from the racist logics (see also Rothman 2005).

As more prospective parents turned to surrogacy as a solution to infertility or other medical limitations, courts, states, and countries were increasingly involved in adjudicating the legality of altruistic and commercial surrogacy. Many jurisdictions ruled against the legality of commercial surrogacy and required disclosure and, in many cases, legal recognition of donors—or recognized only the birth mother as the legitimate mother. Consequently, many prospective parents in the Global North who could afford the expense turned to commercial surrogacy beyond their national borders. This turn mirrors the class privilege of prospective parents who sought intercountry adoption to achieve parenthood. Until the early 2000s, intercountry adoption was "the primary non-biological way to create a family, particularly for those who perceived it as a method to adopt a healthy infant/young child" (Rotabi et al. 2017, 64). According to Karen Rotabi and colleagues, the 1993 Hague Convention on Protection of Children and Co-operation in Respect of Intercountry Adoption led to a decrease in intercountry adoptions, although it took some time to see the effects of this convention. Rotabi and colleagues report that the number of intercountry adoptions reached a high of forty-five thousand in 2004 and declined by over 70 percent by the mid-2000s, while commercial international surrogacy increased substantially during that time.

The global expansion of commercial surrogacy was reflected in the 2000s in the increased demand for international surrogacy services in Australia, where commercial surrogacy was not legal and donors needed to be identified on birth certificates (see, for example, Cuthbert and Fronek 2014). In an Australian Broadcasting Network radio interview on January 21, 2011, family law specialist and former registrar of the Family Court of Australia Paul Boers reports that the number of people engaging in surrogacy arrangements had increased greatly since 2006, although commercial surrogacy continues to be illegal in most territories and states in Australia. He explains that although there were no adequate statistics on the extent to which couples in Australia were having children through surrogacy arrangements by 2011, commercial surrogacy was "far more typical than people think it is" (Australian Broadcasting Network 2011). In fact, the advocacy group Surrogacy Australia reported that "the number of Australian babies born to overseas surrogate mothers leapt from 97 in 2009 to 296" in 2012 (Vaughn 2013).

However, over these years, because of a number of high-profile cases in which the intended birth parents did not choose to adopt the child or the birth mother challenged the contract for a variety of reasons, countries where commercial surrogacy was legal and largely unregulated closed their borders. For example, the Thai government ruled against the practice following the case of Baby Gammy, a twin with Down syndrome born to a Thai surrogate whose Australian intending heterosexual parents returned to Australia with only the healthy twin (Tillett 2015).

Despite their race and class privilege, gay men and other single or non-married adults seeking surrogacy services continue to occupy spaces outside the heteronormative context in which parenting is expected to occur and have increasingly been prevented from accessing surrogacy in countries that were previously open to them, even though married heterosexual parents could still access these reproductive services in India. Single and unmarried prospective parents were the next to be denied access to international surrogacy in former sites in countries like India. However, as of 2015, only Indian citizens could access commercial surrogacy in India. There are important contradictions in the claims of gay men for access to international commercial surrogacy, although legal challenges have reduced access for others as well. In the following we examine these contradictions in the context of feminist debates over reproductive rights and reproductive justice.

SHIFTING FROM REPRODUCTIVE RIGHTS
TO REPRODUCTIVE JUSTICE

Zakiya Luna and Kristin Luker present a contrast between reproductive rights as a "law-focused" approach and reproductive justice as "a social justice-aimed movement that emphasizes intersecting social identities (e.g., gender, race, and class) and community-developed solutions to structural inequalities" (2013, 327). Reflecting on the limits of the rights framework, which is based on constructions of choice and privacy, activists generated a more radical movement claim of reproductive justice that contests this narrow focus. In doing so, they link "sexuality, health, and human rights and social justice movements by examining the larger context of the health and well-being of women's family and community" (Ross et al. 2017, 23).

As has been the case with many feminist insights developed through movement praxis (for example, intersectional analysis was a feature of Black feminist praxis long before it was given a name by Crenshaw 1989), many reproductive rights activists from around the world were critical of the rights framework before *reproductive justice* was coined as a term and approached their organizing through intersectional constructions of social justice. The challenge to the rights framework was especially evident in reproductive rights activism among Black, Latina, Indigenous, and Asian feminists in

North America and Europe and feminists from the Global South, although the construct of reproductive justice did not take hold as a movement frame until the 1990s (Petchesky 2003).

In a 1994 report for the Global South transnational organization DAWN (Development Alternatives for a New Era), Sonia Corrêa and Rebecca Lynn Reichmann noted that "today's Southern feminist perspective on reproductive rights is modifying the earlier framework by analyzing how political, cultural, ethnic and racial factors interact with fertility" (1994, 14). Women activists from the Global South were effective in redirecting discussions of development to center concern for women and girls at the 1994 UN Meeting on Population and Development in Cairo. Their radical reframing "placed individual dignity and human rights, including the right to plan one's family, at the very heart of development" (United Nations Population Fund n.d., n.p.). Although not framed in terms of reproductive justice, this articulation of an understanding of the intersection between development practices and reproductive rights shifted attention from a single-issue and individual-choice approach to one that attended to the intersectional complexity of the lives of women and girls. By 2014 the intersectional framework had been taken up by important policy actors such as South Africa's minister of social development, who drew on reproductive justice in a speech to the UN General Assembly in 2014 "to explicitly embrace LGBTQ rights" in reproductive policy (Ross et al. 2017, 27). Efforts to "queer" reproductive justice include acknowledging the ways in which LGBTQ people are also subject to sexual abuse and denial of access to adoption and reproductive technologies.

New reproductive technologies unsettle the normative family ethic (Abramovitz 2017) and gendered expectations about who can parent and under what conditions (Markens 2007), while also contributing to the reproduction of class and race privilege. Surrogacy, in particular, calls into question the presumed essentialism of women's maternal identity (Ragoné 1994). Policies on donor insemination and egg implantation and on access to fertility services by single and unmarried couples have obvious implications for lesbians and gay men, especially in countries like Australia, where same-sex couples did not have equal status with heterosexual couples until November 15, 2017. Before that date, same-sex couples' legal rights were recognized only through a nonmarital form of de facto relationship status.[2] Parental rights have also been contested in Australia, especially as they relate to the legal status of sperm donors, second-parent adoption, and surrogacy (Millbank 2011).

Kimala Price (2017) examines "the search for common ground" between LGBTQ movement activists and reproductive justice activists in some local

Nancy A. Naples & Mary Bernstein

contexts like Oakland, California, as well as in national organizations like the US National Gay and Lesbian Task Force (72). In a statement generated by the Causes in Common program of the LGBTQ Community Center of New York City, reproductive justice was expanded to include "the right to form relationships and families of one's choosing—and to have those relationships legally recognized and supported" (81). Price concludes that "an intersectional approach to coalition politics allows us to see how bodily integrity and autonomy unite these two movements" (84). However, putting a radical collaborative vision into practice also reveals contradictions that limit the possibility of achieving these broad movement goals, as revealed in the case of queer claims for the legalization of international surrogacy. In the next section, we outline the methodology for the analysis of these reproductive tensions and then examine the contradictions between the reproductive rights claims of gay male activists and commercial international surrogacy.

REPRODUCTIVE RIGHTS, QUEER ACTIVISM, AND METHODOLOGY

We situate reproductive claims-making strategies at the intersection of local processes and political, economic, and cultural globalization while recognizing the myriad ways that place shapes gendered constructions and experiences of sexuality and reproduction. We highlight when and how localized social movement claims depend on and serve to reproduce inequalities that run counter to social justice frames. Drawing on Nancy Naples's (2003) materialist feminist discourse analysis, we understand movement frames as constituted in discourses that organize and are structured by "ruling relations" that land in "everyday life" (D. Smith 1990). Movement frames are drawn from wider discourses either as a way to resonate in a broader societal context (such as the human rights frame) or as a way to separate from or stand against a dominant discourse (such as antiracism or anticolonialism). Analysis of silences in discourse reveals the taken-for-granted dimensions of the social movement claims, which, in this case, mask the relations of ruling that contour the claims for the legalization of international commercial surrogacy. As already noted, we conceptualize these processes not only as discursive politics but also in terms of the intersection of economic, political, cultural, and colonial structures and practices.

Our data are drawn from three different primary sources. The first is in-depth interviews with LGBTQ activists and scholars in Australia conducted over the course of two extended field trips in 2008 and 2010 (M. Bernstein and Naples 2010, 2015). While in Australia we interviewed lesbians, gay men, legislators, and activists located in all but one region of the country (the Northern Territory). For this chapter, of the fifty-two interviews we conducted, we draw on fifteen interviews in which the topic of surrogacy was discussed in some depth.

The second set of primary data are derived from the websites and publications of LGBTQ rights organizations and organizations established to advocate for or support surrogacy arrangements. Most of the latter organizations, at the time of this volume's publication, focused on providing information on the process of accessing international surrogacy.

A third set of data are drawn from articles on surrogacy published in the following Australian newspapers: the *Age*, the *Australian*, the *Daily Telegraph*, the *Courier-Mail*, the *Herald Sun*, the *Sunday Morning Herald*, and the *West Australian*. The first mention of surrogacy was in 1985 in the *Daily Telegraph*. Across the newspapers, most of the coverage about the legal context for surrogacy duplicated human interest stories about particular couples and sensational cases such as Baby Gammy. We searched for the following terms: "surrogacy," "domestic surrogacy," and "international surrogacy" and the countries most mentioned at the time of the interviews (2008–10) as destinations for international surrogacy on Australian surrogacy websites. We also searched for mention of Australian activism on behalf of domestic and international surrogacy. We supplemented the primary data with secondary data on international surrogacy by scholars working in India who conducted ethnographic research and in-depth interviews. Finally, we also conducted broad internet searches to identify coverage of surrogacy around the world with a focus on India and Australia.

Following the transcription of interviews and downloading of relevant newspaper articles and organizational materials identified on the various websites into the qualitative software NVivo, the analysis began with a thematic content analysis to identify the ways in which surrogacy was covered and the extent to which different forms of surrogacy were discussed. We subsequently conducted a materialist feminist discourse analysis of these constructions attending to any silences and contradictions in the interviews, representations on websites, and media coverage.

SEEKING SURROGACY SERVICES IN INDIA AND BEYOND

Commercial surrogacy is illegal in most countries. In some national contexts where it is legal, there is a diversity of state court decisions. In the US in some states like California, one of the destinations mentioned for Australian

Nancy A. Naples & Mary Bernstein

couples seeking access to commercial surrogacy, courts ruled to uphold contracts for both altruistic and commercial surrogacy, while courts in other states took different positions (Perrett 2011). In other jurisdictions, like the United Kingdom, when a surrogacy contract is challenged (for example, the surrogate mother decides that she does not want to give the child to the intending parent), the courts will support the surrogate mother's claim.

The cost of international commercial surrogacy also varies, with the most expensive arrangements found in the United States. Before international commercial surrogacy was banned for foreigners in 2015 in India, many Australians turned to India, where the costs were relatively low and there was little regulation. According to Amrita Pande, who conducted in-depth research on surrogacy practices in India, the Indian surrogacy industry followed a "liberal market model" similar to that "in California, where surrogacy births are primarily managed by private, commercial agencies that screen, match, and regulate agreements according to their own criteria and without state interference" (2010b, 972–73).

Commercial surrogacy was legalized in India in 2004. At that time, India was one of the few countries in the world that had legalized commercial surrogacy. Owing to the 2012 changes in visa requirements in India, which limited travel to the country for surrogacy services to heterosexual couples who had been married for at least two years, gay male couples turned to Thailand, where, as was previously the case in India, surrogacy clinics and surrogacy contracts were not regulated (Whittaker 2009). The public outcry over the Baby Gammy case led the Thai parliament to prohibit international and same-sex commercial surrogacy in 2015. After the prohibition in Thailand, Australians interested in international surrogacy turned to Cambodia, Nepal, Georgia, Russia, Ukraine, and Mexico, but there as well same-sex couples and, in most cases, single or unmarried adults were quickly denied access. Despite their class privilege, gay men and other single and, in some cases, nonmarried heterosexual couples seeking surrogacy services continue to occupy spaces outside the heteronormative context in which parenting is expected to occur.

In this context, Australian scholars Damien W. Riggs and Clemence Due discuss what they term "reproductive vulnerability," namely, "vulnerability arising from being located outside of the norm" (2013, 956). They explain that "whilst reproduction is indeed a hallmark of contemporary citizenship, the cultural capital arising from this is still differentiated by mode of reproduction, with reproductive heterosex remaining the norm against which other modes are compared" (956). They conclude that "reproductive vulnerability causes people to seek reproductive alternatives, and therefore reproductive travel is driven not only by a lack of services within a person's country of residence, but also by a desire to overcome a perceived vulnerability" (956). Riggs and Due's analysis of the complex dynamics of claims to transnational commercial surrogacy presents a queer reading of what Twine (2011) and others call "stratified reproduction." Drawing on an intersectional reproductive justice framework, Twine analyzes inequalities associated with the surrogacy industry through this construct, which, she explains, was first defined by Shellee Colen to "mean that physical and social reproductive tasks are accomplished differentially according to inequalities that are based on hierarchies of class, race, ethnicity, gender, [and] place in a global economy" (1995, 78; quoted in Twine 2011, 3). Riggs and Due (2013) recognize the different vulnerabilities of both gay men and the women who serve as surrogates. They define the vulnerability of the women serving as surrogates "both in terms of the commodification of women's bodies (that is, that the capability of women's bodies for reproduction renders them vulnerable to practices such as surrogacy), as well as inequalities in terms of outcomes and choice between the privileged and the disadvantaged, leading to the potential for exploitation" (959). This stratified system that positions some actors as more vulnerable than others is clearly evident when we examine the legal basis for access to reproductive technologies, adoption, and surrogacy in Australia.

REPRODUCTIVE RIGHTS AND SURROGACY

Access to reproductive technologies and adoption for single women and same-sex couples in Australia varies across the country and is less supported than relationship recognition for same-sex couples. In recognition of the uneven legislative landscape and inequalities shaping the lives of lesbians and gay men in Australia, the Australian Human Rights and Equal Opportunity Commission (renamed the Human Rights Commission in 2008) began an inquiry that culminated in a report titled "Same-Sex: Same Entitlements." It was published in 2007 just before the Labor Party was elected to power. When the Labor Party assumed power under Prime Minister Kevin Rudd, the recommendations of the report, which included changes in eighty-five different laws and policies, were implemented, thus creating a more level legal context for same-sex couples. As a result of this extensive law reform, as of July 1, 2009, same-sex couples were essentially defined as equal to different-sex couples under the law in financial and work-related entitlements and benefits such as superannuation (or social security), health, eldercare, employment,

Nancy A. Naples & Mary Bernstein

and taxation. The changes included recognition of parental rights for some same-sex couples (primarily those who already had children), but the report did not address adoption or surrogacy.

While the commonwealth or federal government in Australia has the power to legislate relationship recognition and marriage, the states and territories are charged with legislative power in the area of adoption and reproductive technology. Same-sex couples seeking reproductive and parental rights faced numerous obstacles in Australia in the early 2000s. For example, gay men reported difficulty in adopting children, even those they had fostered for many years. Not until July 2013 did the Tasmanian Upper House pass a bill that would allow same-sex couples to adopt. As recently as 2016, same-sex couples did not have formal rights to adopt in Victoria (Tomazin 2016). Adoption by same-sex couples became legal in the Northern Territory only in 2018.

In 2010 New South Wales passed the Surrogacy Act to regulate surrogacy. It set procedures for establishing parentage in the case of altruistic surrogacy, prohibited advertising for a surrogate, and stipulated that those found to have paid a surrogate either in Australia or abroad could face up to two years in jail and fines of over $100,000. Tasmania decriminalized altruistic surrogacy in 2012 and included access to surrogacy for same-sex and single adults. When we reviewed the transcripts of our interviews with activists in Australia in 2008 and 2010, there was clearly a difference of opinion on surrogacy. However, all those we interviewed emphasized the complexity and lack of clarity of Australian law regarding international commercial surrogacy.[3] In considering what would be needed to address surrogacy in the future, legal scholar Jenni Millbank argued in her interview, "I support parentage transfer in surrogacy, but I just don't think that it is okay [to] deprive [the surrogate mother] of parentage before they've given birth or at the point of birth." Millbank's response captures the tension between reproductive rights claims for surrogacy and reproductive justice that incorporates the rights of women serving as surrogates. She was one of the few activists and scholars we interviewed who put the rights of surrogate mothers directly in the frame. When they do appear in the narratives, surrogate women's motivations to participate in international commercial surrogacy were often discussed through the rhetoric of choice and the economic benefits that surrogacy provides.

Driving both the complexity of the debate over international commercial surrogacy and the parental desires of gay men is the biogenetic and normative construction of family and parentage. In a study of gay men in

Victoria about motivations to seek parentage through commercial surrogacy, Deborah Dempsey found "that when gay male couples form families through commercial or altruistic surrogacy, a range of symbols and metaphors conventional to heteronormative nuclear family formation are in play in this ostensibly unconventional context" (2013, 37). For gay men, the goal of having a biologically related child fuels their willingness to invest time and financial resources to access transnational commercial surrogacy. The desire to create a family with biological links to one or more of the intending parents runs up against definitions of legal parenthood defined by many nation-states that privilege the parental rights of the birth mother regardless of biogenetic relatedness.

INTERNATIONAL COMMERCIAL SURROGACY AND REPRODUCTIVE JUSTICE

Missing from the Australian debate on surrogacy was a discussion of the rights of the women who would be carrying a fetus for another individual or couple. With the exception of the point made by Millbank in our 2010 interview, none of our informants mentioned the rights of the surrogate mother in their construction of sexual citizenship. In the broader discussion of surrogacy, three themes dominate: the women are making a "free choice" to serve as surrogates, the money they receive for the services is well beyond the income they could receive from any other kind of labor, and, as mothers themselves, they appreciate giving the gift of a child to another family (Riggs and Due 2013; Fixmer-Oraiz 2013).

From a reproductive justice perspective, it is important to put the notion of free choice into the broader context of these women's lives. Sayantani Dasgupta and Shamita Das Dasgupta report that many of the women they interviewed felt they had no real choice in serving as a surrogate mother. They quote one woman who explains that, in her view, "this work is not ethical—it's just something we have to do to survive" (2010, 140–41). The process by which Indian women are drawn into surrogacy is fraught with coercive pressures. Pande describes the recruitment strategies that are designed to prey on the women's economic needs and gendered identities. Recruiters solicit women in poor communities by going door-to-door explaining the payment the potential surrogate would receive for the reproductive service and tying it to the benefits of their own families. Pande's analysis foregrounds the intersection of gender, class, and nation in shaping surrogate mothers' decision-making. It also draws attention to the context in which they enter into a contractual relationship with the intending parents.

In another study of transnational surrogacy in India that included interviews with infertility professionals, intending parents, and Indian surrogate mothers, Sharmila Rudrappa and Caitlyn Collins identify two "moral frames" used by "market actors" to justify their engagement in transnational surrogacy: "(1) surrogacy liberates and empowers Indian women from patriarchal control; and (2) surrogacy furthers reproductive rights" (2015, 937). Not surprisingly, they also find that infertility doctors and Indian surrogacy agencies "posit an image of working-class Indian women as poor mothers who are victims of their culture, dependent on men in their families and inextricably tied to their familial and kinship networks" (948). They conclude that "by framing commercial surrogacy as compassionate consumerism, couples adopt a moral identity that allows them to navigate around threats of racism (Deeb-Sossa 2007), classism, or sexism. Yet . . . the ability to navigate around these threats is shaped by moral frames that rely upon racist, classist, and sexist tropes about Third World working-class women" (954). Attention to the intersection of gender, class, race, and colonialism sheds light on the multiple systems of oppression that coconstruct the unequal terrain on which international surrogacy contracts are made and enforced. Citing Chandra Talpade Mohanty (2003), Anne Donchin (2010) points out that "colonialization is a common rationalization for seeing subject people as inferior, fit only for the most menial labor," and that a "fertility tourist who use[s] this means to justify hiring a nonwhite woman to gestate a child for her perpetuates this kind of colonialist mindset" (329). Furthermore, she notes that although the desire to have a child that looks like you and "the preference for a racially matched child may seem natural, . . . [it] harbors a persistent bias that has underlying eugenic overtones" (329).

The racial differences between the birth mother and the child also provide another layer to "ownership" when viewed through an intersectional analytic perspective. The power of "color" to serve as a proxy for deservingness of motherhood has had a long history in Australia and beyond (see, for example, Maddison 2007; Neill 2003; A. Smith 2007). Although not necessarily framing this around the trope of deservingness, surrogate mothers also point to their genetic and racialized differences from the child they give birth to in order to distance themselves emotionally in the course of giving up the child to the intending parents (Smerdon 2008).

Riggs and Due (2010) are two of the few scholars who have addressed the contradictions of Australian gay men's claims for surrogacy. They point out that "the work of carrying and birthing a child carries with it unique stresses and expectations that are often not adequately recognized" by gay men. They note that many gay men who turn to surrogates to help them become parents rarely consider the contract from the point of view of the women performing this challenging reproductive labor. Riggs and Due also foreground "the race privilege that white gay men evoke when they undertake surrogacy arrangements in India, and the specific constructions of the maternal and women's bodies that this produces."

While some of the intending parents do recognize the inequalities, they all too often conclude that the money they pay and the satisfaction the women feel at giving the gift of a child to another family put their concerns to rest (Riggs and Due 2013). As Natalie Fixmer-Oraiz asserts, "Romantic dismissals of reproductive stratification and hierarchy enable westerners to envision commercial surrogacy as a form of philanthropy, a discourse eerily reminiscent of a kind of 'western benevolence' critical to colonial projects" (2013, 145). Since, as Twine points out, "international commercial surrogacy is embedded in a transnational capitalist market that is structured by racial, ethnic, class and gender inequities and by competing nation-state regulatory regimes" (2011, 4), shifting the practice to a domestic reproductive political economy will not eliminate the structural racial, ethnic, and class inequalities within the commercial reproductive marketplace.

INTERROGATING THE DYNAMICS OF AGENCY IN THE GENDERED SURROGACY CONTRACT

Gay men seeking surrogacy services to achieve parenthood certainly queer the heteronormative paradigm. Yet class-based colonial processes further inscribe power dynamics in the surrogacy contract. That the women who enter into these contracts are fully aware of the terms of the contract is further belied by the limited extent to which the contract is translated. One major concern is whether the women understand the medical risks and the regulation of their bodies before signing a contract, especially the requirement of a cesarean section birth (Fixmer-Oraiz 2013; Gupta 2012). In the context of the surrogacy contract, the birth mother must agree to surveillance over her body and her everyday activities in order to comply with the contract (Pande 2010b). For example, surrogates for the Hope Maternity Clinic in Anand, India, were expected to stay in rooms above the clinic where every aspect of their daily lives was regulated (Pande 2010b, 982; see also Pande 2014).

Nancy A. Naples & Mary Bernstein

It would be a mistake to view the surrogate mothers in India as without agency, however. Pande (2010b, 985) analyzes how the hostels in which many of the surrogate mothers in India are required to stay during fertilization and pregnancy serve as a site of resistance where women share their concerns and may develop modes of resistance to the disciplining and commodifying aspects of their reproductive work. One example she gives is the collective resistance to the amount of pay given to recruiters for identifying surrogates, thus lowering the surrogates' wages. Daisy Deomampo's (2013) in-depth study of the experiences of surrogate mothers who were not living in clinics during the pregnancy as well as of the agents who recruited them further contextualizes the agency of the surrogate mothers and complicates our understanding of the role of the surrogate agent. Many of the recruiters were former surrogate mothers. In their role, they often administered hormone injections and "serve[d] as a mediator and advisor for women and their families" (179). In addition, as Deomampo explains, few of the surrogates "described themselves as 'desperate' for the money," and "several depicted a solidly middle-class lifestyle" that enabled them "to capitalize on and negotiate their social positions" as surrogates (177). Although Deomampo's findings contrast with Pande's, both studies highlight the intersectional transnational insight offered by Vida Panitch (2013a): "The exploitation lens Occidentalizes surrogacy by conceptualizing the practice in universal terms, thereby eclipsing the particularities of the global surrogate's lived experience" (329). While Indian women who participate in the international commercial surrogacy industry are more economically vulnerable than the middle-class gay men who purchase their reproductive labor, their agency must also be recognized and analyzed in the local context in which their economic choices are made.

Panitch (2013b) considers what social and economic conditions would be needed to facilitate Indian surrogate mothers' engagement as full citizens in contract surrogacy negotiations. In her analysis of the limits of contracting for surrogacy services in the context of unequal power, Panitch argues that "positive reproductive rights can therefore be justified only up to the point at which they interfere with the negative reproductive rights of others" (285). In other words, the parental rights claims of First World citizens should not outweigh the negative reproductive rights of women who—owing to unequal economic, social, and political conditions—may be unable to enter into surrogacy contracts free from coercion.

Obviously, many ethical, political, cultural, and economic dilemmas must be considered in generating a socially just reproductive rights claim for international surrogacy. For example, what are the contracting couple's or the nation-state's responsibilities if the surrogate experiences ongoing health problems associated with the birth or disruptions in her family relations that may contribute to economic hardship or emotional stress? At the time of this research, these concerns were rarely incorporated into the claims-making strategies and debates over access to surrogacy among activists in Australia. Deomampo and Pande both emphasize the power imbalances as well as the complexities of international commercial surrogacy. And, as Deomampo concludes, "because the social processes from which agency emerges limits it, resistance, as it recuperates power, does not necessarily challenge structural inequalities" (2013, 184). The intersectional reproductive justice approach considers "women's agency [in the context of] a broader system of relational power and privilege that shapes transnational commodified markets in bodies, babies, and reproductive labor" (Jolly 2016, 173).

CLOSING BORDERS, SHIFTING CLAIMS

The context in which transnational surrogacy takes place is changing rapidly, as is the global economy more generally. The current economic crisis of capitalism, fueling more poverty, unemployment, and economic displacement, is contributing to an increase in economically vulnerable populations (Naples 2018). The uneven dynamics shaping transnational surrogacy practices include the legalization of commercial surrogacy in some locations and its criminalization in other places. There are also stark local and national differences in the extent to which states regulate clinics and the surrogacy contract, the attribution of parenthood at birth, the amount a surrogate can be paid, the services that can be paid for, the surrogate's health, and the citizenship status of the child born to a surrogate mother who is intended for a couple from another country.

As borders closed for gay men seeking to access international commercial surrogacy and the costs of remaining venues, such as the United States, were out of reach for many, the call for legalization of domestic commercial surrogacy became more prevalent across gay rights and Australian surrogacy sites. This shift also followed the legalization of same-sex marriage and the passage of laws permitting altruistic surrogacy in all Australian states and territories (except the Northern Territory) over the past decade. While individual activists and policy makers were already speaking in favor of legalizing domestic commercial surrogacy before the early 2010s, as our research

Nancy A. Naples & Mary Bernstein

revealed, more general calls did not become visible until the rapid sequence of border closings abroad occurred.

Newspaper coverage about the shift in claims making became especially prominent beginning in 2016. For example, the *Gay Star News* published an article titled "Gay Dads in Australia Call for Government to Legalize Commercial Surrogacy" (Chubb 2016) that featured an interview with activist and lawyer Rodney Chiang-Cruise, who cofathers a child born to a US surrogate, and another gay couple who also had a successful experience with surrogacy in the United States. At the time, the Australian government was reviewing surrogacy laws following "a spate of surrogacy 'horror stories' in developing countries." Chiang-Cruise invoked a narrative shared by many activists and some legislators: that the legalization of commercial surrogacy in Australia would lead to fewer Australians going "overseas to countries with less rigorous surrogacy regimes." He emphasized that Australia could provide a better-regulated environment that followed best practices as established in the United States. He explained that "best practices compensates women who are informed and want to take control of their financial future." Chiang-Cruise added that "the most common argument against commercial surrogacy—that it opens the door to exploitation—is a curious one. In altruistic surrogacy everyone gets paid—the doctors, the lawyers, the courts—except the surrogate, who is actually the person doing the work! It is, in my view, disingenuous for people to deny a woman the right to be compensated for acting as a surrogate in these circumstances, while everyone else gets paid."

The general shift in public attitudes and legal grounds in Australia has opened up spaces for increased access to parental rights for LGBTQ individuals. For example, the first LGBTQ fertility center, the Rainbow Fertility center, opened in Brisbane in 2016. The changing conditions for reproductive access can be read as another success for the gay rights movement. However, as Lewis explains in her case study of Italy, a radical approach to "Reproductive Justice envisioned a rejection of biogenetic, 'nuclear' familiality altogether" (2018, 220).

Other prominent voices also spoke out in favor of legalizing commercial surrogacy with the goal of protecting all parties implicated in surrogacy arrangements. For example, in a 2019 post on the website of the International Fertility Law Group, the group's founder, attorney Richard Vaughn (2013), reports that the chief federal court magistrate John Pascoe recommended legalization of "commercial surrogacy to stop the exploitation of women overseas and to ensure that agreements are properly regulated to protect children, surrogates and commissioning parents." Vaughn explains that Pascoe's approach replicated the system currently adopted in California, which relies on contracts that "clearly define the legal status of the child as well as the responsibilities of all parties to the agreement."

CONCLUSION

Our study of surrogacy claims began when we spoke to LGBTQ activists about movement strategies and coalition building among activists in Australia. In a context where it was difficult for gay men and lesbians to gain legal recognition as couples (Bernstein and Naples 2010) and parents and to access reproductive technologies to help achieve parenthood, we were intrigued to find that advocates were not, for the most part, calling for the legalization of commercial surrogacy in their country along with their other reproductive claims. The heterosexism and homophobia that had shaped adoption and parenting law in Australia were directly implicated in both the movement politics and the practical decisions that gay men made in order to fulfill their parental desires. However, their claims often reproduced inequalities that were opposed to the social justice frames through which their own claims were made. While efforts were underway to challenge limits on access to adoption, IVF, and altruistic surrogacy, claims for commercial surrogacy focused on international solutions rather than the legalization of domestic commercial surrogacy. Rather than viewing gay rights claims to the expansion of marriage and parenting as either normalizing or transgressive (Bernstein and Taylor 2013), we attend to the contradictions of these claims as they simultaneously destabilize and reinscribe traditional constructions of family and parenthood.

Heteronormativity, homonormativity, patriarchal dynamics, colonialism, racism, and the internalized societal demands for biological progeny all shape the cross-border politics of international surrogacy. Both Indian surrogates and commissioning parents are caught within these complex intersectional and transnational processes. However, the class, gender, and colonial power imbalance clearly privileges consumers of international commercial surrogacy over the surrogates. We have interrogated this conflicting and contradictory political claim through intersectional transnational feminist analysis that examines the material and discursive world in which the claims making is situated. By foregrounding the political, economic, and social context of the women who are providing reproductive labor for Western and wealthy individuals and couples, as well as rendering visible what is taken for granted in gay men's reproductive claims, a productive dialogue can pro-

Nancy A. Naples & Mary Bernstein

ceed that draws on both intersectional and transnational feminist praxis. As noted by Jyotsna Agnihotri Gupta, "Transnational feminist analyses and practices require an acknowledgement of the fact that one's privileges in the world-system are always linked to another woman's oppression or exploitation" (2006, 34, quoted in Kroløkke and Pant 2012, 237). This insight is vital for achieving reproductive justice in both transnational and national contexts. As claims for commercial surrogacy shift from an international to a domestic political economy, the neoliberal, racial, class, and gendered inequalities remain.

Adopting a reproductive justice framework requires recognizing and challenging "neoliberal 'equality' politics" (Duggan 2003, xii) and normativity in all its complicated forms. It further requires reflexivity about whose justice is served through different formulations of social justice. While the framework does broaden beyond the rights approach, it does not automatically remove the relations of ruling evident in the diverse economic and political claims-making contexts. Whether or not a reproductive justice framework advances, tempers, or reframes claims for legalizing commercial surrogacy in Australia remains to be seen. However, failure to consider the reproductive justice issues raised by expanding sexual citizenship for gay men in Australia and in other Western countries, informed by intersectional transnational feminist praxis, serves to further enhance neoliberal and colonialist power relations.

ACKNOWLEDGMENTS

We would like to thank the University of Adelaide for its support through a Distinguished Scholar Award. A portion of this research was supported by a University of Connecticut Research Foundation Large Faculty Grant and a grant from the National Science Foundation (SES-0848048). Any opinions, findings, and conclusions or recommendations expressed in this material are those of the authors and do not necessarily reflect the views of the National Science Foundation.

The authors also wish to thank M. J. Taylor for research and editorial assistance.

NOTES

This chapter draws on two unpublished papers, "Sexual Citizenship, Reproductive Rights, and Surrogacy in Transnational Context: Creating a Dialogue between Feminist and Queer Theories," presented at the *8th International*

Meetings Against Homophobia, Koas-GL, Ankara, Turkey, May 18, 2013, as well as "Intersectional Transnational Organizing and Shifting Border Politics" by Nancy A. Naples, which was presented in the workshop on "Whither Transnational Feminism?" at the Women's Worlds Conference, Florianópolis, Brazil, August 30, 2017.

1 As in other jurisdictions where altruistic surrogacy is legal, most jurisdictions in Australia allow for only the "reasonable expenses" of the birth mother to be compensated. Reasonable expenses include those related to getting pregnant, carrying the child to term, and giving birth to the child. Court costs related to establishing parentage should be covered by the intended parents. However, surrogacy contracts are not enforceable, so if the surrogate mother decides she wants to keep the child, the courts can uphold her decision despite the contract she signed before the birth of the child.

2 According to the Family Court of Australia (2016), "A de facto relationship is defined in Section 4AA of the *Family Law Act 1975*. The law requires that you and your former partner, who may be of the same or opposite sex, had a relationship as a couple living together on a genuine domestic basis. However, your relationship is not a de facto relationship if you were legally married to one another or if you are related by family."

3 In 2015 altruistic surrogacy was legal in all states for heterosexual couples and for gay couples who resided in Queensland, Victoria, and New South Wales. In January 2018 the West Australian government called for a review that could result in a change in the current law that prohibits same-sex couples in West Australia from accessing surrogacy (O'Leary 2018). Altruistic surrogacy for heterosexual couples is now permitted in all jurisdictions except the Northern Territory.

Nancy A. Naples & Mary Bernstein

10

Wombs in India

Revisiting Commercial Surrogacy

AMRITA PANDE

FIELD NOTE 1 HOPE MATERNITY CLINIC, INDIA, OCTOBER 2007

A long room is lined with nine iron cots with barely enough space to
walk in between. There is nothing else in the room. Each of the beds has
a pregnant woman resting on it. I walk up to the last cot, where Yashoda,
a twenty-eight-year old widow, is resting after a surgery. She has been
hired as a surrogate, a gestational mother, by a single man from Spain
and is pregnant with triplets. On the client's insistence, one of the fetuses
has been surgically removed. She starts telling me her story—about her
husband's death, her mentally challenged daughter, and her in-laws abandoning "the widow who dared to become pregnant for some foreigner."
When she breaks down in the middle and starts crying, the gestational
mother on the third bed gets up and completes her story. By the end of
the conversation, eight of the nine are sitting around the bed, talking and
listening. All agree that Yashoda need not feel guilty; she has done nothing
immoral. Munni adds, "Go and tell your in-laws, 'At least I am not sleeping with anyone.'"

FIELD NOTE 2 NEW HOPE FERTILITY CLINIC, INDIA, APRIL 2016

I am at the brand-new fertility clinic—a three-story glass-and-steel building in the middle of fields. There are no people on the main floor, except
the staff of the clinic. Very unlike the bustling, chaotic, and slightly grubby

clinic and hostels that existed in this same city a decade ago. The basement is the domain of "gestational mothers"—their home for the next nine months. There are twelve rooms with ten beds in each, almost all occupied by women in various stages of pregnancy. Some are sitting, but most are lying down watching a cartoon play on loop on the television. There is a feel of everything working in slow motion, of mundanity and intense boredom. Aarati seems to speak for them all when she says, "I don't even know whether I will get paid anymore. The government has told the doctor that this [surrogacy] is wrong. I don't know if it's right or wrong for them. I thought it is right for me."

NEARLY A DECADE AGO, while still in the midst of my doctoral fieldwork in India, I published a paper titled "'At Least I Am Not Sleeping with Anyone': Resisting the Stigma of Commercial Surrogacy in India," in the journal *Feminist Studies* (Pande 2010a). My intention in that essay was to extend the literature on commercial surrogacy beyond the Global North or Euro-American contexts by looking at what was then the "unique case of India." In the essay, and in many of my works thereafter, I argued that despite warnings by radical feminists that surrogacy is akin to baby farms where poor Black women are breeding white babies, there is much more to debate (Pande 2010b, 2014). Surrogacy, I argued, has parallels with many other forms of reproductive and/or gendered labor available for women in the Global South. By identifying commercial surrogacy as a new form of labor, it is possible to arrive at a much more nuanced analysis than one based solely on morality. If we are able to understand how gestational mothers experience and define their act in this new form of labor, we can move beyond a universalistic moralizing position and develop some knowledge of the complex realities of women's experience of commercial surrogacy. In the 2010 essay, I argued that women who work as gestational surrogates or gestational mothers in India are engaged in a form of dirty or stigmatized labor and that these women perform considerable emotional work to manage the stigma. I classified this as not merely remedial work done to counter the stigma attached to surrogacy but an everyday form of resistance by the gestational mothers to subvert the hegemonic discourses that construct their role within the surrogacy process, as well as the relationships forged within it, as "disposable."

In this chapter I revisit this argument to clarify ideas that were implicit in my analysis a decade ago and to further develop the theoretical framework I outlined then. In gestational surrogacy, attributes like caste, religion, skin

Amrita Pande

color, and race are assumed to be of little relevance. Gestational mothers are understood as "just the vessel" or the "oven" or "carrier," where the health of the womb matters far more than the attributes of the carrier. This might explain why surrogacy scholarship (including some of my previous works) has paid surprisingly little attention to how caste, religion, and race, as structures of inequality, shape the global fertility market. Although race and racial stratifications are observed to be stark within transnational surrogacy, these were, until recently, mostly invisible in the analysis itself. In this chapter I bring attention to these missing pieces to argue that while these structures are fundamental in making India the "mother destination" of surrogacy and are convenient mechanisms for imposing discipline at clinics and surrogacy hostels, they also shape the strategies of subversion employed by the gestational mothers themselves. Finally, I use current feminist debates around transnational commercial surrogacy to reflect on our understanding of transnational feminist solidarity and transnational feminist praxis.

SURROGACY THEN AND NOW

The practice of surrogacy has long troubled people. Some are repulsed by the commodification of mothering and pregnancy—of what they argue are "acts of love," with "priceless" children increasingly entering the market. For instance, dystopic imageries of reproductive brothels, baby machines, and baby farms have been associated with this industry long before it reached its current proportions. Others are troubled by the surrogacy industry's potential to be utterly exploitative of women, especially Black women. In recent years this anxiety has reached panic levels after surrogacy and the related industry spread to the Global South. Intended parents, usually from the Global North, get labeled "reproductive tourists," using their privileges to fulfill their "right to a child" born by poor women in the Global South. The media reports cases where intended parents "abandon" their newborn or allegedly sell their babies born out of surrogacy; they even exposed a case where an intending father had a history of child abuse (Ackland 2014).

Although the United States remains the top global destination for commercial surrogacy, India emerged as a key site in the 2000s. Clients from countries where surrogacy is either illegal or restricted (such as Japan, Australia, Taiwan, Kuwait, and the United Kingdom) have for decades hired women in the United States to bear babies for them. However, while the total cost of such transnational packages is roughly US$100,000 in the United States, in India such packages were available for less than half that price. But what made India an attractive destination was not just the sheer economics of it. A critical factor drawing international clients to India was that the power dynamics explicitly favored the clients, making surrogacy in India a convenient bargain for the clients. For instance, a major attraction for clients hiring gestational mothers at the clinic I studied intensively, and the one that has caught much of the media attention, was the surrogacy hostels where women were kept under constant surveillance during their pregnancy—their food, medicines, and daily activities were monitored by the medical staff. While fertility clinics exist in every Indian city, this is one of the only clinics where the doctors, nurses, and brokers played an active role in recruiting and surveilling these women. In 2019 the clinic announced that it had delivered a total of 1,424 babies through surrogacy.

When I started my ethnographic research on surrogacy in India in 2006, this industry was booming in a legal vacuum, with minimum state interference and few laws regulating the procedures, the contract, or the surrogate-client relationship. Fertility clinics in India not only operated without state interference but often benefited from the neoliberal state, which was an enthusiastic advocate of medical tourism. As a consequence, intended parents were able to take advantage of the client-friendly policies of private clinics and hospitals, where doctors were willing to offer options and services that are banned or heavily regulated in other parts of the world. But this has changed dramatically since 2015, when an affidavit was placed before the Supreme Court of India that in a nutshell declared that the Indian government "does not support commercial surrogacy" and that the scope of surrogacy would now be limited to "needy Indian married couples only" (Najar 2015). In March 2020, the Indian parliament approved these clauses as the Surrogacy (Regulation) Bill 2020. As of November 2020, the Bill is yet to be passed as a law.

In banning transnational commercial surrogacy, the Indian government seems to be arguing that restricting the clientele to couples the government deems legitimate—namely, heterosexual married couples from India—will erase the underlying problems with surrogacy. Some media reports indicated that the practice of surrogacy, the "surrogacy scandals" (Pande 2017), and the negative media publicity abroad might have become a source of embarrassment (Najar 2015) and a detriment to "Brand India" (Rotabi and Bromfield 2017). While scholars and activists around the world have hailed the ban and the protectionist stance of the government (Stop Surrogacy Now 2015), others have seen it as counterproductive and indicative of the conservative heteronormative ethics of the current government and its emphasis on Hindu nationalism (Pande 2020; Rudrappa 2016). Although the exact impact of these new restrictions is not yet clear, the immediate effects can be seen in clinics like Hope Fertility Clinic.

DIRTY AND DISPOSABLE GESTATIONAL MOTHERS

I told my parents that I am doing this. I told them if you can help me,
fine. But don't be a hindrance in what I am doing. If I was doing something wrong you could stop me, hit me, anything, but this is not wrong.
At least I am not like some other women who have [sexual] relations
for money, just because they are so desperate. This is what I told them.

—Dipali, single mother of two with intended
parents from South Africa, 2007

In her book *Disposable Women and Other Myths of Global Capitalism*, Melissa Wright (2006) provides a powerful analysis of the "myth of disposability" of women workers in global factories. She argues that the inherent "paradox" of this myth "provides it with organizational structure": the Third World woman is assumed to be easily substitutable and yet is simultaneously believed to possess the exact qualities (dexterity and patience) that make her invaluable. This "internal contradiction" makes this myth a "socially useful lie" that can be used to "influence social behavior on the basis that power is naturalized, apolitical and beyond human intervention" (4). This myth works as an effective disciplinary mechanism by defining the behavior expected from disposable women.

The myths of gestational mothers as dirty and disposable worked as convenient and complementary disciplinary mechanisms. At any point in time, the number of clients waiting to be assigned a gestational mother at Hope Fertility Clinic was greater than the number of available gestational mothers. In essence, by the logics of supply and demand, the gestational mothers were far from disposable. This reality made it even more critical that the clinic, the medical professionals, and the hostel staff convincingly establish the disposability of the women. This tactic of "inventing disposability" worked in tandem with the constant yet contradictory use of the "surrogate-prostitute" analogy. Although surrogacy is an ethical quagmire in almost all countries, a critical reason for the huge amount of stigma surrounding surrogacy is that many Indians equate surrogacy with sex work. This is partly due to a lack of information and partly due to misinformation. Many people are just not aware of the assisted reproduction technologies (ARTS) that separate pregnancy from sexual intercourse. Popular media, especially the handful of Bollywood movies that have equated surrogacy with sex work, influence other people. Whatever the source of (mis)information, the result was that the surrogate-prostitute analogy became particularly convenient for the clinic staff. Although, at the time of recruitment, the gestational mothers were assured that their role would not involve any "immoral acts" like having sex with clients, the clinic and hostel staff often compared the "bad" gestational mother (one who was business minded and negotiated her contract) to a prostitute. The process of commercial gestational surrogacy in India, in general, and the rules of the clinic, in particular, reiterated the dirtiness and disposability of gestational mothers. The gestational mothers were told that their role in the pregnancy was to serve only as a vessel—they would have no genetic connection with the child, and the child would be taken away from them immediately after delivery.

In the 2010 essay in *Feminist Studies*, I outlined the strategies employed by the gestational mothers themselves to subvert these discourses of dirtiness and disposability. Some women emphasized their special attributes that made couples choose them over the other gestational mothers. A striking example was that of Pushpa. Pushpa had delivered a baby for an Indian couple and was pregnant for the second time in two years—this time for a nonresident Indian couple from the United States. Pushpa felt proud that the intended parents had insisted that she carry their baby and not any other woman: "A couple came from America during the delivery of my first baby. They said that they don't care how long they have to wait—I can rest for one or two years, as much as I want, but they only want me to carry their baby. Mrs. Shroff—the woman—she is also a Brahman [upper caste]. Maybe that's why she liked me, because I am clean. But almost everyone who comes here for a surrogate wants me. Doctor madam says to me, '*Why can't you get me ten or fifteen more Pushpas!*'" In my more recent interactions with Pushpa, she continued to emphasize her special qualities, namely, her fair skin and high caste. Divya was equally proud of her own special qualities. In 2007, when surrogacy was still in its infancy, Divya narrated how she rejected her first potential clients: "There was a couple from Delhi that we were introduced to first. But we somehow didn't like them. . . . We took a risk, but we said no to them. Doctor Khanderia was surprised because it's usually the couples who reject surrogates."

Her risk paid off, and in 2007 a couple from California hired Divya. When I met Divya again in 2010, she confirmed that the intended mother, Anne, wanted her to become a gestational mother for their next baby as well: "Anne [the intended mother from California] wants two more children, and in December she will get another surrogate. Of course she wanted me, but I have already had two cesarean babies. I know how sad she is feeling that this time she will have to just *get one of these other girls* to be her surrogate" (emphasis added). Like Pushpa, Divya was an exception at many levels, and her story was unusual. I am aware of no other instances when a gestational mother refused a client. Divya was a high-caste Hindu, and the only gestational mother with a college education. This, she felt, made her more special than "the other girls." Divya and Pushpa are exceptions in their high-caste Hindu status, something they celebrate and use to their advantage. I use these two narratives to open up discussions on some of the understudied aspects of this industry: How do caste and skin color shape the surrogacy industry in India?

CASTE AND RELIGION: THE MISSING VARIABLES IN SURROGACY STUDIES

In the past decade, the growing scholarship on transnational reproduction has queried the multiple forms of power embedded in the surrogacy industry (Deomampo 2016; Inhorn 2015; Nahman 2013; Pande 2014; E. Roberts 2012; Rudrappa 2015; Speier 2016; Whittaker and Speier 2010). The differential access to reproductive technologies by economic class is a focus of many of these studies. Only a handful of scholars have observed stratifications across race, and even fewer have made religion and caste the focus of their research. For instance, in her work on surrogacy, feminist philosopher Amrita Banerjee (2013) speaks of a "transnational reproductive caste system," which manifests as structural violence within the fertility industry. Although I find Banerjee's conceptualization of structural violence fitting in its description of the surrogacy industry as it exists today, the allusion to a caste system remains underanalyzed, with more connections needed between the caste system and the surrogacy industry in India. Daisy Deomampo (2016) is one of the few surrogacy scholars to highlight the visible invisibility of caste in discussions around surrogacy. In her ethnographic work with surrogacy clinics, she finds that caste becomes a concern (for the intended parents) only in relation to the baby's nutrition and health. In most other works on surrogacy in India, religion and caste have not been a focus, which is particularly surprising given that these continue to be salient organizing factors of social life in India. Caste has become especially potent within the current political climate of Hindu nationalism and fervent communal politics, where even the dietary choices of minority communities have become a criminal offense likely to be punished by mob lynching. Despite the current obsessive focus on the pollution and purity of certain bodies, the immensely intimate practice of gestational surrogacy, tied to the bodies of gestational mothers, is analyzed independent of religion and caste.

Religion and God, science and technology, and assisted conception may not intuitively go together but can seldom be kept apart. Social scientists across the world, especially ethnographers, have observed deep entanglements between religion and assisted conception (Bharadwaj 2006; Inhorn 2015; F. Roberts 2012). This entanglement assumes a fascinating form in contemporary India, where the current government attempts to rewrite history and shape policies on the basis of a mythical Hindu past, what scholars have labeled the "biopolitics of Hindu nationalism" (Subramaniam 2019). In a 2014 speech, for instance, the Indian prime minister, Narendra Modi, claimed that genetic science existed in ancient India. Modi cited excerpts from Hindu epic mythologies and mixed fantasy with reality as he said, "We all read about *Karna* in the *Mahabharata*. If we think a little more, we realize that the Mahabharata says Karna was not born from his mother's womb. This means that genetic science was present at that time. That is why Karna could be born outside his mother's womb. . . . We worship Lord *Ganesha* [a Hindu god who is half man, half elephant]. There must have been some plastic surgeon at that time who got an elephant's head on the body of a human being and began the practice of plastic surgery" (Rahman 2014). However ludicrous this statement might sound, it captures the essence of Hindutva, the brand of Hindu nationalism promoted by the Modi government—where religion, science, and neoliberal capital can meld together. It is not surprising, then, that the government's vehement support of the surrogacy ban and Hindu protectionism of its women from foreign clients can sit comfortably with an enthusiastic promotion of a neoliberal privatized market in health care.

In the case of India, any discussion on religion and assisted conception has to begin with Hindutva and Hinduism, in part because it is the majority religion. But the popularity of characters from Hindu epics and mythology cuts across religions; irrespective of their religion, people evoke narratives from Hindu mythology to make sense of surrogacy. Hinduism is widely accepted as being far more flexible about assisted conception than Christianity, Judaism, and Islam.[1] In fact, as indicated by Modi's speech, the variety of ancient Hindu parables that focus on assisted conception is quite remarkable. There are numerous detailed discussions on "strategies of heirship"

Amrita Pande

in the Hindu epic *Mahabharata*, many of which involve creative ways of procreation (Sutherland 1990). Surrogacy, in various guises, appears to be a popular theme in Hindu mythology, especially in tales involving the demon king Kansa. According to the epic *Bhagavata Purana*, Kansa was intent on killing all of his sister's children because of a prediction that he would die at the hands of her eighth son. Kansa threw his sister, Devaki, and her husband, Vasudeva, into prison and proceeded to kill their first six children. Lord Vishnu heard his disciple Vasudeva's prayers and miraculously transferred the seventh embryo from Devaki's womb to the womb of Rohini (Vasudeva's second wife). Rohini gave birth to the baby and secretly raised the child. But the gestational mother Rohini is not as celebrated as the other mother in the same tale—Yashoda. Vasudeva's eighth child, Krishna, predicted to meet the same fate as his first six siblings, was secretly exchanged for a cowherd's daughter. Lord Krishna was brought up by the cowherd's wife, Yashoda, and most stories surrounding Lord Krishna in his infant years are about the loving bond shared between him and his surrogate or foster mother, Yashoda. This mother-son interaction is a popular theme in media representations of Indian mythology as well as in Hindu devotional songs and prayers. Innumerable devotional songs have been dedicated to establishing Yashoda's loyal motherhood, in which Yashoda bathes and dresses the child, cooks for him, feeds him, tells him stories, and rocks him to sleep (Krishnan 1990).

Not surprisingly, the gestational mothers themselves regularly invoked this particular mother-son relationship. These mythological characters allowed the women at the clinic I studied to reimagine kinship ties with the baby and resist the medical construction of gestational mothers as dirty and disposable mothers. As the gestational mother Parvati argued, surrogacy is not new to Hindus: "I personally feel it's nothing strange to us Hindus, it's in our religion. It's something like what Yashoda ma did for Lord Krishna. And Krishna loved his Yashoda ma, didn't he? Do you ever hear stories of Devaki, his real mother?"

In my previous work, I have discussed in more detail this strategy of normalizing surrogacy by using idioms from Hindu mythology (Pande 2014). In *Wombs in Labor* (2014), I devoted an entire chapter to religion and argued that writing about religion in this region of India, where extreme forms of Hindu nationalism have wreaked havoc in the past decade, was exceptionally difficult. While I accepted that the lingering effect of the brutal and systematic carnage of a minority community was still palpable in the environment, I discussed the surrogacy hostel as a haven where all religions coexisted and argued that the narratives of the divine, when used by actors involved in surrogacy at the clinic, had little to do with organized religion. For the gestational mothers at the clinic and hostel, what I labeled the "everyday divine" took precedence over organized religion (Pande 2014, 118). The process of surrogacy and the doctor herself were deified, while religious endogamy and prescriptions were underplayed. But despite this assertion that the everyday of the clinic and hostel was not entirely determined by the reality outside, the connections cannot be ignored. The everyday divinities in the hostel and clinic were as much a reflection of Hindu majoritarianism as of the world outside the clinic.

In my decade of studying the clinic in India, I encountered no respondent who would be classified as "Dalit" or untouchable. Although not all gestational mothers were upper-caste Brahmins like Pushpa, the ones who declared their "special qualities" with striking confidence belonged to other Hindu upper castes. In terms of religion, while there was a fairly diverse group of Hindu, Muslim, and Christian gestational mothers, all women, irrespective of their religion, were expected to pray to Hindu gods like Lord Krishna in the small Hindu temple placed inside the hostel. The clinic had a prayer hour for the gestational mothers, and during my ethnographic journey, much of my interaction happened around this temple. The temple had a small collection of Hindu idols, and the walls were plastered with bright pictures of many more Hindu gods and goddesses. Muslim and Christian gestational mothers were routinely found there with heads bowed and hands clasped in prayer, much like their Hindu colleagues. In 2008, after participating in such a prayer hour, I asked Tina, a Christian, why she participated in a Hindu praying session. She laughed it off and explained, "We [Tina and her husband] are from a Christian community. All our neighbors are Christians, and we all go to church every Sunday. But here [for gestational mothers], things are different. These are our two gods: Lord Krishna [a Hindu god] and Doctor *Devi* [Doctor Goddess]." For Tina, a practicing Christian, Christianity was on hold at the hostel. While she was at the hostel, the doctor as well as the god (Lord Krishna) worshipped by the doctor and by her colleagues needed to take precedence over Christianity. The gestational mothers belonging to minority communities—Islam and Christianity—most actively evoked the alternative forms of the everyday divine. Although many of these respondents were unsure about their religion's position on surrogacy, they intuitively predicted that it would be prohibited. Razia summarized it perfectly when she announced, "I don't want to know what the Quran says about this. Isn't it better this way?"

Amrita Pande

The conversations around Hindu gods, the ample presence and guidance of Hinduism around them, acted as reassurance that surrogacy was normal and that the prescriptions of other religions (apart from Hinduism) did not matter. Gestational mothers within the hostel reaffirmed this in their everyday by praying in the Hindu temple and forging sisterly ties with other gestational mothers, irrespective of caste and religion. Such sisterly ties across differences of caste and religion were forged with the intended mothers as well. Caste and religion manifested in complex ways in the choice of a gestational mother as well as in the relationships forged between gestational and intended mothers.

Apart from stressing their own special qualities, as Pushpa and Divya did, gestational mothers often resisted the commercial and contractual nature of their relationship by establishing or imagining a relationship with the intended mother. While all gestational mothers recognized the immense class difference between themselves and the intended mothers, their narratives sometimes constructed relations that seemingly transcended all differences of race, class, caste, and religion. While transnational ties across racial lines were rare, something I discuss in more detail in the next section, there were numerous examples of sisterly ties among those of South Asian origin across caste and religion. For instance, Salma, a Muslim surrogate, shared an intimate relationship with the intended mother Preeti, a Hindu nonresident Indian from South Africa. Salma talked fondly of Preeti: "She is not a Muslim, yet she wanted to keep *roza* [a fast that Muslims keep during their festive season] on my behalf because I can't keep it when I am pregnant. Our relationship is not dependent on our beliefs. We feel a much stronger bond. Sisters don't need to be from the same mother, right? We are like sisters—just one Muslim and one Christian. I think she is Christian. I haven't asked. But I know she is not from India."

Ironically, in a similar conversation with Preeti, she confessed that she had, in fact, been searching for a high-caste Hindu gestational mother, but none was available: "I was actually looking for someone who is a Hindu— from a good culture and preferably a Brahman [upper-caste Hindu]. Hasn't it scientifically been proven that what a woman does when she is pregnant affects the child? So if a surrogate does *pooja* [a Hindu form of prayer] when she is pregnant, the baby can hear her and be blessed by the prayer. But at that time no other surrogate, except Salma, was available." Preeti wanted a religion and caste match with her surrogate so that the fetus could hear Hindu prayers in the womb. In her work with surrogacy clinics in India,

Deomampo (2016) notices a similar conflation and biologization of caste and religion by her respondents, especially when gauging the suitability of surrogates. Higher-caste Hindu women were also desired because they were assumed to have better physical fitness for childbearing and awareness of nutrition and health.

The intended parents' desire for high-caste Hindu gestational mothers was often left unfulfilled; much as Preeti had to forge connections with her Muslim surrogate, other parents had to submit to the law of supply and demand. Dr. Khanderia, the main doctor and manager of the clinic, explained to me, "See, the couples can't afford to be picky. At the moment the demand for surrogates is greater than the supply, and I think it will remain that way. There are more than three hundred intended parents on the waiting list. Only one or two couples have said they are not happy with the surrogate we have given them—the way she looks or her caste and religion. Our philosophy is 'take what you get,' and if you don't like what you are getting, [she shrugs] too bad for you." Despite the doctor's apparent indifference to and commercial interpretation of the relationships emerging out of surrogacy, gestational mothers firmly believed in the sanctity of the bonds they forged with intended mothers across caste and religion and sometimes across borders of nationality and race.

RACE AND TRANSNATIONAL SURROGACY

In *Brown Bodies, White Babies: The Politics of Cross-Racial Surrogacy*, Laura Harrison argues that twenty-first-century "post genomic science" and race-based medical treatments have "revitalized, rather than undermined, the use of racial categories to stand in for biological difference" (2016, 135). Within the ART industry, specifically, race is commoditized and packaged as traits that can be purchased. But while for gamete provision the commodification of race is explicit and written into the recruitment of donors and differential payment for specific gametes, the importance of race works differently within gestational surrogacy. Eggs are commonly portrayed as "white," "black," "Asian," or even "Jewish," and some intended parents go to great lengths to ensure a genetic or racial match with the donors to ensure that the desired racial characteristics are successfully transmitted to the next generation. Since genes work as a code for race, religion, and ethnicity, the relationship between the gestational mother and the fetus is assumed to be fundamentally different from that between an egg provider and the offspring. As Harrison notes, in cross-racial surrogacy, "the raced body of the surrogate can be read as a text that marks her liminality both socially and legally; when a surrogate's skin color reflects the lack of genetic tie between herself and the child, this serves as evidence of the authentic connection between the child and the biological parents" (181).

Scholars have argued that this "racial distancing" between the gestational mother and the child makes the Indian fertility market an attractive destination for white fertility travelers and "may make hiring a woman to gestate, give birth to, and give up a child psychologically comfortable. It is a post-industrial form of master-servant privilege" (Ikemoto 2009, 308). While other scholars and popular media talk of race as a similar and convenient mechanism used to "other" the surrogate-fetus tie (Harrison 2016), very few of my respondents—the medical staff, the intended parents, or the gestational mothers—mentioned the stark racial difference between the gestational mother and the baby or between the two mothers. Gestational mothers' desperate poverty and physical distance from the intended parents and the child's intended home, rather than race, were used to emphasize distancing and legitimize the separation.

This silence around race, however, is revealing. For this chapter and a larger project, I systematically revisited my original transcriptions and field notes with relevant codes and noticed a pattern discernible even within this silence around racial difference. While racial differences may not be a regular topic of discussion, the *whiteness* of the intended parents becomes a key factor in naturalizing the skewed power relations within surrogacy. Much as there is an implicit ranking of gestational mothers' desirability by caste and religion, there is a clear ranking of gestational mothers according to the whiteness of the clients hiring them. "American," a proxy term used by nurses and gestational mothers for any white foreigner, is at the top of that ranking. This ranking is illustrated in the housing privileges at the hostel. From 2006 to 2014, gestational mothers were housed in a cramped hostel close to the clinic. Here the women hired by foreigners had visible benefits, for instance, being allotted the "luxury" rooms. The term *foreign* excluded anyone of Indian origin; only gestational mothers hired by "real foreigners" (or "white" clients) were assigned the luxury rooms.[2] There were stark differences between the general and the luxury rooms. While the general rooms had minimal furniture—eight to ten iron cots, a shared bathroom, and barely any comforts—the luxury rooms were equipped with a color television, air conditioner, and attached bath. Neeti, a nurse at the clinic, justified the ranking thus: "We have to do at least this much for our foreign clients. In any case these surrogates deserve this. They are at the last stage and have successfully kept the pregnancy." When I interrupted her to ask why all gestational mothers in the last trimester were not rewarded in a similar fashion, Neeti shrugged and said, "Right from the start the ones hired by foreign couples have it better—whether it be tips, cell phones, or small gifts. In any case they all have to go back and stay in their own homes where, forget AC, some don't even have fans! The girls [gestational mothers] know all this, and they don't complain. They are happy with whatever they get. As a matter of fact, some feel more isolated in these [luxury] rooms."

According to Neeti, the luxury rooms were a reward reserved for a select few, those hired by white clients, and the other, less privileged gestational mothers accepted this hierarchy. However, some gestational mothers were far less docile and accepting that some received such selected privileges; they complained vociferously about not being assigned to white clients. Tina, hired by an Indian settled in Dubai, complained about unfair privileges: "Doctor Madam usually assigns the 'foreigners' to the neediest surrogate. Say, your son has tuberculosis, or your husband has a kidney problem. She makes sure you get a foreign client who pays you at least rupees 2 lakhs ($5,000). But needs are relative—I may not have a sick husband, but I have starving children. Why should I get stuck with a stingy Indian family?" Most of the gestational mothers echoed Tina's sentiments—being assigned a white client was akin to winning the surrogacy lottery. Apart from Tina's unambiguous ranking of clients, what is also striking in her narrative is the doctor's role in matchmaking, which allegedly is not purely medical. Here, too, the whiteness of intended parents works efficiently in naturalizing the fundamental inequalities within cross-racial surrogacy. By assigning needy women to white foreigners, the doctor reaffirms a *savior* narrative implicit in cross-racial transnational surrogacy as well as the inequities in the relationship between the gestational mother and the client.

Across the world, women involved in surrogacy have reportedly used narratives of altruism, gift giving, sisterhood, and mission to naturalize and decommodify surrogacy services and downplay the contractual nature of their relationship with each other (Ragoné 1994; Harrison 2016). For instance, gestational mothers are often construed as "angels" giving another mother the priceless gift of a child. For white intended parents hiring an Indian gestational surrogate, however, the gifting metaphor gets reversed. The intended mother becomes the gift giver, akin to a missionary helping with a worthy cause. Anne, an intended mother from the United States, had hired two gestational mothers in two years. Anne was quick to assure me that her decision to come to India was not a financial one: "It's not because of the cost difference. I already spent a lot at home. People travel to the US to get a surrogate, and here I am traveling out of it into some place as far as India. My friends think I am very brave to be traveling to this country. I mean, if you take one look at the streets outside, you would know why. But we decided on India because we thought women here would be more conservative—drug- and alcohol-free."

While Anne recognized the advantages of hiring a presumably drug-free, conservative woman, she also emphasized the "bravery" of her decision. She added, "What makes me happy about my decision is that the life of my surrogate would change with the money. Without our help her family would not be able to get out of the situation they are in, not even in a million years." The desire to contribute to a worthy cause was echoed by Judy, another intended mother from the United States: "Most importantly, we realized that for surrogates here the amount we pay would be a life-altering one, while in the US it's just some extra money. What really helped us take this decision was that we knew our surrogate wouldn't spend the money for drugs or a flat-screen TV. She would be using it to feed her family, build her own house. It would feel good to make such a change in someone's life. I am not religious, but this seemed almost like God's work, call it a worthy cause . . . a mission." What is intriguing is that both Anne and Judy construct the Indian woman and her family not only as desperately poor but also as worthy poor. Unlike their counterparts in the United States, who allegedly would use the money for drugs and other frivolous consumption, the Indian gestational mother is expected to use the money productively. While most intended mothers I spoke to were willing to acknowledge the range of benefits of hiring a gestational mother in India, from easy laws to maximum control, they reiterated that these benefits were secondary. Their primary motivation, the clients insisted, was to transform the life of a family living in desperate poverty. Hiring a gestational mother from a distant Third World nation was visualized as another form of development aid, with the hiring couple playing the role of saviors battling all odds to help the needy.

Scholarship on transnational adoption has indicated that adopting parents often invoke similar narratives, in which the desire to adopt children is constructed as a form of international aid (Cartwright 2005; Briggs 2003a; Volkman 2005). Ideologies of rescue, care, and compassion are rampant in accounts given by people involved in transnational adoptions. Curiously, even in the absence of an abandoned child in need of being rescued, transnational clients of reproductive services gave similar accounts of "moral adoption." The mission and charity narrative fits perfectly with the myth of disposability analyzed earlier in this chapter. In spite of the various advantages for the clients hiring gestational mothers in India, the pay rates remain the lowest in the world, partly because the women are framed not as desired mothers but as desperate and needy figures. The picture of a needy woman legitimizes the low pay, and the framing of this transaction as a worthy cause equates the payment to a donation—informal and/or voluntary. When used in the context of transnational surrogacy in India, these narratives further highlight and often reify the inequalities based on class, race, and nationality between the buyers and sellers of surrogacy in India.

SURROGACY AND TRANSNATIONAL FEMINISMS: SOLIDARITY AND PRAXIS

Women around the world are helping other women. I just think that's beautiful. I think that's a beautiful thing.

—Oprah Winfrey, 2007

Affective bonds, sisterhood, and altruism are popular metaphors within surrogacy debates. These are gendered and complex metaphors that need further unpacking. In much of the popular media portrayals of cross-border surrogacy, for instance, discussions start with the acute pain and desperation of infertility, the focus almost always being the heart-wrenching maternal longing of the intended mother. The race of the intended mother, in these popular portrayals, is always white, once again making black people and black bodies invisible within discourses of infertility and assisted reproduction (D. Roberts 2011). Elsewhere, I have discussed the inherent whiteness of ARTs, which normalizes the invisibility of black women in the entire discussion of ARTs (Pande 2021). Such an individualized and affective telling of infertility tends to "normalize motherhood as the fulfillment of white, class-privileged womanhood; and refuse critical analyses of infertility as an issue of social justice" (Fixmer-Oraiz 2013, 146).

While infertility is portrayed as an ultimate personal failure (on the part of a white, typically class-privileged woman), the remedy becomes an arduous journey of infertility treatment, ending, for some, in India. In such popular portrayals, as the reporter crosses borders, the discussion switches gears from the pain of infertility to the acute poverty of the gestational mother and her family. The gestational mothers in India are described in predictable tropes—as illiterate yet enterprising women, battling desperate poverty and, often, drunken husbands but *choosing* surrogacy as a way to

Amrita Pande

better their life chances. The story once again becomes individualized—one desperate woman helping another. In essence, commercial surrogacy, with its exploitative potential, is given legitimacy by the affect, choice, and altruism in this narrative.

The work of several feminist academics and activists is a rich antidote to this sensationalized portrayal of surrogacy as a win-win situation. As with other issues that revolve around reproduction and sexuality, for instance, sex work and pornography, feminists are divided on the issue of surrogacy and have debated this issue in complex and nuanced ways. While some are convinced that surrogacy is an extreme example of human trafficking and patriarchal exploitation and needs to be stopped at any cost, others have advocated for cross-national feminist dialogue and harm reduction. Although these differences cannot simply be categorized as Western feminisms versus the rest, the most vociferous call for stopping surrogacy has come from Western feminist lobbies.[3]

Despite the power of this lobby, its narrative has not gone unquestioned. Philosopher Alison Bailey notably comments on the "distorting effects" and "moral discursive colonialism" of the Western media and Western feminist thought on this topic. According to Bailey (2011), Western feminists' normative responses—which rely on feminist interpretations of liberal, Marxist/socialist, and radical political values to make moral judgments about surrogacy—are problematic: "Extending Western moral frameworks to Indian surrogacy work raises the specter of discursive colonialism along with concerns about how Western intellectual traditions distort, erase, and misread non-Western subjects' lived experiences" (716). Information on surrogacy, Bailey believes, is selective and limited, as well as tainted by Orientalist and colonial understandings of Third World women as in constant need of rescue and liberation. How much can Western feminists really understand the lived reality of surrogates in India, given the vast distance between them—distance that is not just physical but also created by class, language, and culture? Feminists, whether coming from the West or situated in the West, have paid attention to Bailey's call for such "epistemic honesty" in their understanding of the logics of commercial surrogacy in India.

The rich and growing ethnographic scholarship on surrogacy, as well as the interdisciplinary nature of the debates on surrogacy, across multiple locations, may well be a response to the call for reflexivity and honesty. Much less attention, however, has been paid to how this epistemic honesty can deepen transnational feminist solidarity and transnational feminist praxis. Over the years, the need to recognize the diversity, situatedness, and multiplicity of experiences has been pushing feminists away from the concept of global sisterhood toward the notion of transnational feminisms. While the concept of global sisterhood allegedly glosses over the differences between women, transnational feminisms may have the potential to forge solidarity across the globe between women of different positioning and interests. In the seminal book *Feminism without Borders: Decolonizing Theory, Practicing Solidarity*, Chandra Talpade Mohanty (2003) argues that that for transnational feminisms to be possible, the politics of solidarity has to be based on "mutuality, accountability, and the recognition of common interests as the basis for relationships among diverse communities" (7).

Sociologist Jyotsna Agnihotri Gupta applies this notion of epistemic honesty to new reproductive technologies to ask, "Can the need of infertile women for donor eggs or surrogacy services and the financial need of women that drives them to offer the same, thus creating a relationship of mutual dependency, be a basis for mutual solidarity?" (2011, 31). Although these mutual dependencies between the gestational and intended mothers may lead to the forging of unexpected and sometimes-reluctant ties of sisterhood, the task of envisioning a politics of solidarity cannot be left to the two sets of women involved in surrogacy. In my previous discussions of surrogacy as a new kind of reproductive labor, I have discussed the salience of placing surrogacy within the continuum of reproductive labor, along with sex work, care work, and other intimate forms of labor (Pande 2014). This may well be the first step toward imagining a broader community of women with common interests. This framing of surrogacy as labor, however, needs to be much more than theoretical maneuvering.

Transnational commercial surrogacy provides a novel opportunity to rethink the meanings and possibilities in transnational feminist dialogue and praxis: to highlight the intersectionality of oppressions and "critique the hegemony of a monolithic notion of Third World Women" (Swarr and Nagar 2010, 5). A meaningful transnational feminist engagement around issues like surrogacy needs to be attentive to the politics of differential locations, as already mentioned, but also to the implicit hierarchies of knowledge production. Gestational mothers cannot remain mere objects of academic theorization and ethnographic knowledge production. The critical second step in addressing the complicated logics of transnational commercial surrogacy and effectively asserting a broader vision of social justice is to recognize the economic and political voice of the gestational mothers themselves. In the spirit of collaborative knowledge production and transnational feminist praxis, there is a dire need to view the women as active participants in a global fertility market, not as vessels or guinea pigs, so that they are the ones participating in these dialogues, not just being written about or saved by concerned third parties.

ACKNOWLEDGMENTS

My gratitude to the women in surrogacy hostels in India who have continued to make me a part of their lives. Thank you to Millie Thayer and Ashwini Tambe for bringing us together and for starting this vital conversation. A part of this research was supported by a National Research Foundation of South Africa grant (number 118573).

NOTES

1 Judaism and Islam allow most techniques of assisted reproduction when the egg and sperm originate from the wife and husband respectively. In Sunni Islam, third-party donation of any kind (including surrogacy) is not allowed. There is no consensus about the same in Shia Islam, although ethnographic work done by anthropologist Marcia Inhorn (2011) indicates that gamete donation happens routinely, albeit secretly, in countries like Lebanon. Most scholars indicate that Islam does not permit surrogacy because of the sacredness of the womb. The attitude toward reproductive practices varies among Christian groups (Schenker 2005). According to traditional Christian views, beginning at conception, the embryo has moral status as a human being, and thus most assisted reproductive technologies are forbidden. For a detailed discussion, see Schenker (2005) and Inhorn (2011).
2 This is partly because these "foreign couples" are ready to spend the extra money for the luxury rooms. The doctor does not, however, offer the luxury rooms to Indian couples even when they are unoccupied and instead reserves the rooms for unexpected visits by white clients.
3 See, for instance, the Stop Surrogacy Now campaign, 2015.

NATIONALISMS AND PLURI-NATIONALISMS

Part V

11

Sporting Transnational Feminisms

Gender, Nation, and Women's Athletic Migrations between Brazil and the United States

CARA K. SNYDER

THIS CHAPTER uses Brazilian and US women's soccer to explore how nationalism functions within the ambit of transnational migration circuits. Through the lens of soccer, I examine and critique how the United States is constructed in the Brazilian imagination and how and why soccer players travel between countries to play for teams other than their national ones. Key moments in Brazilian women's soccer—its introduction and development from the late 1800s to the late 1970s, changes following the first Olympic appearance of the national women's team's (*seleção feminina*) in 1996, and the migrations of women athletes to the United States through the 2000s—suggest that, for Brazilian players trying to negotiate a better life, the United States represents an ideal not only in terms of structural conditions but also in terms of what is imagined to be the relative freedom of gender performance. Analysis of media coverage as well as interviews with women athletes from the 2015 Seleção Permanente Brasileira (Permanent Brazilian Women's Soccer Team), about their experiences of migrating between the United States and Brazil indicates that athletes play a central role in creating and circulating a nationalist discourse about soccer. In particular, the statements by and the activism of Sissi do Amor, who is one of the top women players in the world and who has been outspoken about the problems within Brazilian women's soccer, suggest both economic and identity-based motives for migration. Taking a transnational approach, I argue that the meanings of the United States change depending on one's geographic vantage point.

Professional athletes are transnational actors who cross geographic, political, and cultural borders and who subsequently form multisited relationships. Because sports are used by nation-states to develop cultural and political projects "as they vie for hegemony in relation with other nation-states, with their citizens and 'aliens'" (Kearney 2004, 218), the movement of athletes can uncover nationalist agendas. At the same time, players' transnational migration undermines nationalist goals. The routes taken by professional athletes are linked to flows of global capital, but their multiple migrations back and forth between countries also reveal the ways capitalism, and more specifically supranational industries, rely on the nation-state. Transnational feminist approaches to sport migration can uncover the workings of power and gender within the production of global sport.

A transnational framework questions the fixedness of nations, while also exposing power asymmetries between them. The migration of athletes and their status as transmigrants—people who live between various nations—who both work and come to represent various locales (local, regional, and national teams) serve as an interesting site to study how ideas of the nation operate at distinct scales and to explore how the national and the transnational both constitute and undermine one another. Brazil and the United States serve as particularly fertile sites to examine women athletes' migrations. First, Brazil is known as *o país do futebol*, the country of soccer, and the United States is known as the top country for women's soccer. These facts mark both locations as sites to explore relationships between gender and nation. In the case of sports migration, I look at Brazil because it is one of the top exporters of players and at the United States because it is the top receiver of foreign players (Rial 2014). While such statistics seem to adhere to familiar narratives of Latin America as an exporter of raw materials and of the United States as a consumer of these, the reality is more complex. Player migrations are multisited: several play in as many as three different nations in one year.

I situate these migrations within the context of the long and developed genealogies of racial formation in Brazil and the United States. Transnational scholarship has documented the ways racial configurations in both countries were shaped in comparison to each other. In particular, Brazil's racialized processes of nation building have been carried out, in part, in comparison to the United States. Just as supposedly national forms of racial identity have been constructed using comparative frameworks, so, too, have ideas of gender and nation, as evinced in the transnational migrations of Brazilian women athletes.

BRAZILIAN *FUTEBOL FEMININO*, 1800s–1970s

The history of Brazil's national sport, *futebol*, is a history of how national identity is articulated along masculine lines. Soccer as we might recognize it today arrived in Latin America from the United Kingdom in the late nineteenth century, a period when political and intellectual leaders began looking to Europe for models of modernity (Nadel 2014, 219).[1] Throughout the Americas and Europe, sport and physical education became a way to develop national identity as well as the bodies and minds of citizens. In Brazil advocates encouraged women to practice sports like swimming that reinforced feminine attributes such as delicacy and harmony (Nadel 2014, 216). But policy makers coded soccer as aggressive and physical; futebol was tagged *coisa de macho*, for men only. The athleticism of the sport thereby became bound to notions of national manhood (Mosse 1996, 7).

Although the masculine coding of soccer happened alongside its weaving into Brazil's national fabric, Brazil was also the first Latin American country to introduce an official women's soccer team (Rial 2012).[2] Women's soccer tournaments, which took place in São Paulo and Rio de Janeiro as early as 1931, received accolades in local papers like *O Imparcial* and *Jornal dos Sports*. But even as many supported *futebol feminino* (women's soccer), some government officials sought to exclude women from the national sport, fearing that their desire to compete on the soccer field would threaten their reproductive potential and the traditional gender order (Nadel 2014, 216). National policies drew on "medical justifications" that sports like soccer put female reproduction at risk and discouraged girls from playing soccer. They finally banned it altogether in 1940 (Rial 2012). This ban, which lasted forty years, was directed at middle- and upper-class women—the populations that nationalist, eugenic policies required for reproduction of "desirable" genres of Brazilianness. Thus, the medical industry, the sports industry, and government officials colluded to dampen the potential of women's soccer for decades.

Even after the state overturned the ban in the late 1970s, social barriers remained (Nadel 2014, 234). The most significant barrier included the stigmatization of female masculinity and lesbian baiting (Fisher and Dennehy 2015). Attempts to counter these stereotypes, including a series of tournaments in São Paulo in the early 2000s (Snyder 2018), involved feminizing female athletes by promoting a heteronormative physical appearance. In effect, these attempts trivialized rather than valorized women's sports. In the following section, I explore one effect of this trivialization—the forced migration of Sissi do Amor, one of Brazil's and the world's greatest players of all time.

SISSI DO AMOR AND WOMEN'S SOCCER'S DEBUT
AT THE 1996 OLYMPIC GAMES

The 1996 Olympics were the first games to include women's soccer. The visibility of this international competition—where athletes came to represent the nations they played for—appears to have motivated the formation of local and national women's soccer leagues in Brazil. In an international arena like the Olympics, it became clearer that women's soccer in Brazil and the United States represented national aspirations. On an international stage, women's participation and performance in futebol came to represent a nation's progress with regard to gender rights: the more developed the sport, the more progressive the nation (Franzini 2005, 316; Rubio 2014). The Brazilian team captain's experiences in Brazil, and later in the United States, begin to tell the story of what US women's soccer means for Brazilian players and how they use the idea of US women's soccer to advocate for rights within their home country.

Sissileide do Amor, known as Sissi, was in her thirties when she served as captain of the Brazilian women's national soccer team that placed fourth in the 1996 Olympic Games. It was the first time women's soccer was played at the games, and the seleção feminina returned home to a country shocked by their Olympic success. There were two reasons for such shock: first, despite Brazil's status as the first Latin American nation where women's soccer had been played, few Brazilians could imagine *women* and *soccer* in the same sentence; and, second, the team had little financial support. Notably, Sissi was ranked the second-best player in the world (after Mia Hamm). Shortly after her return home from the Olympics, Sissi received and accepted an offer from the San Jose Cyber Rays. (Three of her closest teammates also received and accepted offers to play on the US West Coast.)

For soccer aficionados, Sissi's move to the United States does not appear surprising because most women's soccer fans and players imagine the country as a mecca. Importantly, it is not just the money and infrastructure that draw the best women players. A specific inflection in the portrayal of the United States as an attractive destination is its purported tolerance of gender and sexual nonnormativity among women soccer players. *Homonationalism*, a term Jasbir Puar uses to describe a favorable association between a nationalist ideology and LGBTQIA people or their rights, is a distinct feature of representations of US women's soccer (2007). In the case of women's soccer, coverage in both the United States and Brazil describes the United States in homonationalist terms. Such homonationalist tones in conversations about women's soccer migration become clear as we look more closely at the Brazilian media's coverage of Sissi's nonnormative gender presentation and of her migration from Brazil to the United States.

Eight out of twenty-five articles about women's soccer within five years of the Olympic Games made reference to Sissi's move, citing financial, professional, and personal reasons. These articles have been collected as an archive of Brazilian news media representations of women's soccer by artist, activist, scholar, and athlete Caitlin Fisher, the cofounder of the Guerreiras Project.[3] For example, an article from the *Estado de São Paulo* was titled "Sissi Shines on the Fields without Prejudice on the Pitch."[4] Below that headline is an image of Sissi; the text beside the image states, "Sissi became a forward and conquered the USA: the player has recognition and working conditions that she never found working in Brazilian women's soccer" (V.Z. n.d.) The unnamed sports journalist goes on to explain that the players earn an average salary of US$25,000 per season (better than they would in Brazil but still not very much by US sporting standards) and benefit from a "professional structure," including scheduled training, gym time, and physical therapists. The journalist also notes that, according to Sissi, "in the United States there's no prejudice that the athlete becomes masculinized" (V.Z. n.d., E6). Fans support women athletes by sporting their jerseys, "which [Sissi] never saw in Brazil." This article and others make reference to Sissi's supposedly masculine-of-center presentation and her use of the language of sanctuary to describe her migration out of Brazil.

Examples abound of media coverage that uses gendered discourses to construct the United States as not only structurally superior but also as a more open place for women to express masculinity.[5] For example, one article states, "Exiled, Experts Become Stars of 'Soccer' in the USA: Without Structure at Home, Brazilian Women Migrate to the WUSA, Which Only Cares about Their Skills When Contracting Players." In the main text, journalist Eduardo Ohata (2001) explains that both structural and social considerations motivate players' migrations: "Besides the structures, they are not harassed about their image, just about soccer." The article goes on to state that the players "seek refuge abroad," presumably from harassment. In this supposedly accepting environment, "Sissi recuperates the pleasure of playing in the American League" (Salgueiro 2001).

The Brazilian media thus frame the United States as a leader in terms of compensation, infrastructure, and gendered politics and as a more progressive and hospitable place for certain women athletes to work. Still, this oasis is always incomplete—shimmering high points are tempered by geographic, cultural, and linguistic discrepancies. The articles also discuss the many things about the United States that players find troubling, including "the distance from their families, the culture and difficulties with the language" (Salgueiro 2001). In addition to playing, they are required to complete hours of community service and to spend time with the media and sponsors. In many ways, the dream of playing in the United States is less attractive on the ground. Players like Kátia, for instance, were "annoyed" and "pissed off" that managers prevented players from going home when the season's championship games finished. The league held them in the United States for a month after the season was over so they could fulfill their duties as "ambassadors of women's soccer" (Ohata 2001). This labor, including visits to schools and hospitals, is contractual but unpaid, and such expectations complicate an easy image of the United States as the best place to play women's soccer.

The way reporters and Sissi frame her national identity during this period also suggests a complex and uneven terrain. Journalists by and large present the US women's soccer league as the top option for *futebolistas* to make a career. But even if Brazilian women play in the United States, they remain *brasileiras*, in both their eyes and the eyes of their compatriots. For instance, one article's headline reads, "Sissi *Dá a Volta por Cima* and Becomes a Champion in the United States" (Beraldo n.d., E6). The phrase *dá a volta por cima* means "to make a comeback" but literally translates as "moves to the top," which references geospatial, and perhaps also power-laden, relations between the United States and Brazil. The phrase comes from Sissi; she is enjoying so much success that the CyberRays' coach, Ian Sawyers, has offered her US citizenship. Yet she ends by reaffirming that she "still hopes to return to the seleção" (Beraldo n.d., E6). Apparently, she shares her status as worthy of US citizenship with the reporter to prove that she is worthy of competing with the *seleção feminina* in the Olympics. In other words, Sissi used the offer of another (much-coveted) citizenship to affirm her place in Brazil, suggesting that even as her home league had failed to give her the

Cara K. Snyder

recognition she deserved, playing with the seleção remained her top priority. Sissi's ambivalence about her nationality tells a more nuanced transnational story that includes multiple affects, trade-offs, and logics of citizenship.

If the United States is imagined as a sanctuary of sorts—a refuge where adequately compensated athletes can dedicate themselves to their trade, supported by a liberal society that cares more about their athletic skills than their feminine presentation—it is the unevenness of the global financial infrastructure that sets the parameters for such a space. One player, Kátia, makes it clear that "if the conditions were the same, I would be in Brazil . . . but that's not how it is" (Ohata 2001). Kátia's statement emphasizes that athletes do have agency, but her assertion also uncovers how US teams take advantage of an uneven playing field to attract the athletic talent that then bolsters their national profile. Writing for the *Folha de São Paulo*, Ohata (2001) quotes Jody Meacham, the director of public relations for the Bay Area CyberRays, as saying, "We want the best athletes. So, for foreigners the best way to the WUSA [women's soccer league] is through their national teams." In an athletic parallel to the academic brain drain, the United States relies on national teams to find the talent so that they can import athletes and exploit their labor for local markets.

What makes the question of nationalism complex is that US soccer is touted as the "greatest power" in the sport for women (Bittencourt and Chaluppe 2001, 33), even as many of the players in women's leagues in the United States are actually from other countries. For instance, in the same breath (in this case, on the same webpage), media outlets like *O Campeão da Rede* can show such contradictory headlines as "The [US] League Promotes Foreign Invasion . . . Besides the Four Brazilians, 23 Other Foreign Players Are Part of the WUSA League: Five Chinese, Five Norwegians, Three Germans, Four Canadians, Two Swiss, One Japanese, One British, One Australian and One Nigerian" and "American Women Are the Best in the World . . . The United States [Is] Considered THE Country of Women's Soccer" (Alonso 2001). In other words, they at once treat "Americans" as a powerhouse *and* present the players of multiple nationalities as the source of this power.

Furthermore, the migration of athletes is accompanied by an exchange of skills and styles that begin to blur and mix as international soccer stars play with and against one another. One article, for instance, brags that four Brazilian players (Sissi, Kátia Cilene, Roseli, and Pretinha), who formed almost half of the starting lineup for the Bay Area CyberRays in 2001, are wowing fans in the United States. Writing about the Brazilian women's performance in the season opener, the journalist observes, "Accustomed to football force, with lots of running and competition, the gringos' jaws literally dropped in response to the brasileiras' touches and assists" (Salgueiro 2001, 8). As the US league and its fans pay and cheer, Brazilian players bring style, skill, and excitement. Through playing in the United States, Brazilian athletes build strength, and the non-Brazilians they play with are in turn influenced by the flair of *futebol brasileiro*. Even while it may be framed as "US" women's soccer, it is in fact transnational—it does not fit neatly within the mapped borders of the nation-state.

Media depictions of gender expression among women soccer players also have interesting implications. Brazilian media coverage of Sissi paints the United States as a haven for gender-queer and more masculine-presenting women. They simultaneously describe a Brazil that is so hostile to "masculinized" athletes that they must either accept this prejudice or leave. It is not my purpose here to deny Sissi's experiences of gender bias in Brazil and the relatively different treatment she experiences in California. I do, however, want to scale out and connect media portrayals of her experience to global distributions of power. This imagining of the United States as a gender sanctuary is crucial to reproducing US hegemony, if one analyzes it using the framework that Jasbir Puar offers. It is a prime example of "sexual exceptionalism" in action—a discourse that both marks the United States as exceptional and allows the United States to act exceptionally, thereby justifying often-violent and unilateral state actions. This form of exceptionalism constructs the United States as "saviors and rescuers of the 'oppressed women'" (2007, 5). Painting the United States as a queer sanctuary, however, masks the ways the US state functions, in many cases, as an oppressor. According to Puar, US homonationalism—its supposed openness to queer people (and Puar makes it very clear that these people are imagined as wealthy and white)—obscures its problematic interventions in other parts of the world. In the case of Latin America, US involvement is deep: its long Cold War history of supporting conservative and authoritarian military rulers has been extended in the Trump era to specifically supporting explicitly homophobic leaders such as Jair Bolsonaro. Furthermore, the US liberal stance is then used in the service of racist, xenophobic, and Islamophobic policy aimed at criminalizing immigration, for instance. Marking the United States as an oasis for queer folk, as journalists in Brazil are doing, also hides the discrimination that many LGBTQIA people, especially those of color, face in the United States.

If, on the one hand, the Brazilian media's framing of Sissi's migration may feed into US sexual exceptionalism, it is possible, on the other hand, that the media and Sissi use such comparisons to fight for improved conditions within Brazilian women's soccer. Their critique, in other words, could be motivated by patriotism for their own nation rather than by support for the United States. While Sissi was perhaps the first high-profile Brazil woman soccer player to migrate semipermanently to the United States, and maybe the only Brazilian player who has been explicitly vocal about how gender norms influenced this migration, many futebolistas have lived and played in the United States after her migration in the late 1990s. The following section tracks some of these athletes' migrations and the discourses around women's soccer in Brazil and in the United States, which evince the ways national identities are transnationally constructed through comparison, movement, sport, and gender.

SOCCER'S TRANSMIGRANTS: BRAZILIAN
FUTEBOLISTAS FROM 2000 TO 2015

On June 1, 2015, a team from the research center at the Football Museum in the city of São Paulo was invited to visit the Brazilian women's national soccer team at a training center in Itu, in the state of São Paulo, Brazil. The researchers' visit preceded the team's participation in the Fédération Internacionale de Football Association (FIFA) Women's World Cup in Canada (June 5–July 6, 2015). The principal investigator on this research team, journalist Aira Bonfim, video-recorded interviews with twelve players from the Brazilian seleção feminina. The archive of these interviews offers a fascinating counterpoint to my narrative thus far because these were primarily conversations between Brazilians and meant for a Brazilian audience. I analyze them (with permission from the Centro de Referência do Futebol Brasileiro) in the following, focusing on exchanges about the interviewees' time abroad and how it compares to their experiences with Brazilian soccer.[6]

The interviewees were players from the Seleção Permanente, an experimental group of the best players in Brazilian women's soccer, picked to train for six months before the Women's World Cup in Canada.[7] As could be expected from athletes of this caliber, they had long athletic histories. Those interviewed had much in common: they began playing between the ages of four and seven, they left home to play at fourteen, and they had played abroad (outside of Brazil) at some point in their careers. Playing abroad is typical for professional Brazilian futebolistas, according to Carmen Rial (2014). Many played with boys and were the only girls to play in their family, neighborhood, or league, until they joined established women's teams in São

Paulo or Rio. Ten of the twelve had played in the United States, and three of these came to the United States on a university scholarship.

When asked to compare their experiences in Brazil and the United States, all interviewees spoke of a difference in how the game is played, and they described distinctions in playing style in similar ways. North Americans play with "strength," "force," and "focus," and Brazilians play with "skill," "creativity," and "fun." Several players contrasted the unique, individual talent Brazilian players possessed with the unity and teamwork of the North Americans. Francielle, for example, affirmed differences, while arguing against a simplistic ranking:

> It's not about imitating, it's not that they are better than us, but I think the organization, the structure, yes, these are better than us. . . . We see girls there, four or five years old, already starting. And here we start really late.[8] So I think they [the United States] are a great power; it's not by accident that they win. But we can get there. In terms of individual talent, without a doubt Brazil is way in front. But we lose in the *colectivo*. They know they are not so good individually, but as a collective they are strong. Obedience, discipline, this makes a difference. In these ways we sometimes lose a bit.[9]

The way to tap into the potential of Brazilian women's soccer, according to Francielle, is to combine this individual talent with collective organizational strength.

Another player, Rafaela, speaks to the ways the US women's leagues seek and encourage these differences and then use them, potentially for profit:

> We can't be the *Americanas* [the North American soccer players], because they already have the profile of the *Americanas* there. He [the coach of the Boston Breakers] said he doesn't want us to be the same as them. He wants us to go and play Brazilian soccer, because that is what is needed, the cadence of Brazilian players, the technique, ability, creativity. Because they don't have that, they are very mechanized. What they are told to do, they will do 100 percent correct. But to go outside of what they are asked, they aren't able to quickly think of another possibility, of another play. Brazilians no, Brazilians are very improvisational. And the structure, too, yeah? The American league is one of the strongest in the world. You see the power they have there. You go to a stadium, there are so many more people than here, many kids. You spend thirty minutes giving autographs after the game ends. Like three hundred kids who come to tell you how cool the game was. They

have your shirts for sale, kids buy your shirt. The [Boston] Breakers just made a cool shirt that says "Breaker Brasileiras" on the front, and then the back of the shirt has the names of Brazilian players. So when people go to the stadium, they know they have the Brazilian women playing, and they want the Brazilian women's shirt. I get chills just thinking about it, because it's really cool. Imagine if Brazil was like this.[10]

Rafaela articulates clearly the essentialized notions of Brazilian versus US futebol that the majority of the interviewees describe. Whether or not these accounts are true, they certainly reflect national stereotypes about *ginga*, or the swing of Brazilians compared to the rigidity of Americans. These characteristics, of course, depend on a comparison to define each style. Rafaela's quote points out the mutual influence between Brazil and the United States, as Brazilian players discuss how they are benefiting from cultural interaction. Yet it is largely a one-sided exchange in terms of the flow of players: ultimately, the United States is receiving and profiting from the most skilled players.

The Breakers shirt is also an interesting example of transnational exchange. On the one hand, it is an homage to the team's Brazilian players and a recognition of where they come from. On the other hand, it can be read as one US women's league team asserting its dominance by advertising its acquisitions—Brazilian teams, after all, do not acquire US players in the same way. Furthermore, leagues display their international base only when marketers recognize the possibility for profit. In moments of competition like the Olympics or the Women's World Cup, when nations are performing on an international stage in competition with one another, this internal contradiction—of Brazilian players who train and play with US teams except during these international events—is downplayed. Interviewees from the Seleção Permanente in 2015 suggest that women's athletics reveals how sports can both strengthen and undermine the nation and how soccer is linked to global capital even as its flows must work through the nation-state.

The role of Brazilian metropolitan centers such as Rio de Janeiro and São Paulo in these circuits of women's soccer and capital is complex. On the one hand, they are bypassed in the Brazilian popular imagination. For example, for Aline, who was born in Macapá, Amapá, in the Amazon region, women's soccer was imagined as a reality only in the United States. When asked during her interview with Bonfim, for instance, whether she grew up watching regional soccer or knew of Brazilian women's teams, she replied, "I don't remember seeing anything from here in Brazil. For me, women's soccer didn't exist in Brazil, if I wanted to play, I would have to go to the United

States, because in our country we had nothing."[11] On the other hand, the two Brazilian cities are crucial nodes. Only when Aline's family moved to Rio de Janeiro was she recruited to play professionally in a women's league in São Paulo. Similarly, Marta, from Dois Riachos, Alagoas, in the Northeast, also did not have the opportunity for a soccer career until moving to Rio at the age of fourteen.[12] The differences in resources and opportunities between these regions are evident in multiple ways, including access to women's soccer leagues. Players talk about the different regions of Brazil as if they are separate countries. In other words, São Paulo and Rio represent a "First World" within their own country. These stark differences between the metropolitan centers and other regions work to undermine the notion of a cohesive nation-state.

CONCLUSIONS

Brazil's status as the país do futebol and the simultaneously contentious history of its futebol feminino marks it as a field ripe for studying the relationship among gender, sport, and nation. And since the soccer nation is a top exporter of players, both women and men, the migrations of its athletes uncover complicated transnational power dynamics, informed by global capital and filtered through the nation-state.

If sports propagate nationalism, studying athletes who migrate exposes the many illusions of nationalism. Several transnational analytic insights can be gleaned from looking at the process of athlete migration during key transitions in Brazilian women's soccer—its internationalization following the 1996 Olympics and subsequent mainstreaming during the 2000s. First, international sporting events that promote hegemonic forms of competition elide national origins and interchanges. At events such as the World Cup, for instance, athletes often represent the country where they have become naturalized citizens, rather than their country of birth. Their origin stories are seldom analyzed in countries such as the United States, which claim the multinational athletes as their own.[13]

Second, the United States plays a leading role in shaping women's soccer in ways both real and imagined, structural and social. And yet the United States (and its women's soccer league) that is imagined is not self-contained. As the leading importer of athletes, it comprises players from all over the world. Even as the league propagates the myth that US women are the best soccer players in the world, what is ostensibly US soccer actually represents women from all over the world.

Cara K. Snyder

This leads to the third point my analysis highlights: women athletes are drawn to the homonationalist and sexual-exceptionalist narratives that serve to benefit US women's soccer. The US league can claim moral high ground, even as its primary motivator is the acquisition of top players for financial profit. Taken together, Sissi and the Seleção Permanente members who were interviewed suggest that players both generate and reinforce gendered and hegemonic discourses about Brazil and the United States.

ACKNOWLEDGMENTS

Muita obrigada to Sissi do Amor, Caitlin Fisher, Raphael H. Martins, Lu Castro, Aira Bonfim, Brenda Elsey, and all the *futebolistas* in the struggle for more equitable *futebóis* (plural). *Gratidão* to Ashwini Tambe and Millie Thayer for their organizational work in bringing us together in Florianópolis, Brazil, and for their editorial work on this volume. Thank you to my colleagues at the University of Louisville and to The Harriet Tubman Department of Women, Gender, and Sexuality Studies as well as the Latin American Studies Center at the University of Maryland for their financial support of this research.

NOTES

1 Historian Alex Bellos (2014) notes that Pareci Indians (he does not note their gender) played a game similar to soccer long before the British established regimented soccer. Parecis made rubber balls from the sap of *mangaba* trees and bounced the ball using only their heads. During a journey through the Amazon in 1913, Theodore Roosevelt witnessed a game and called the sport "headball."

2 There is some debate about the exact date, but historian Fábio Franzini notes that there were over forty official teams in Rio de Janeiro by 1940 (2005, 317). Many historians consider a match between Tremembe and Cantareira in São Paulo in 1921 to be the first match in Brazil (Nadel 2014, 216).

3 Fisher played soccer in São Paulo in the late 1990s and early 2000s. Because of her physical location but also because of the concentration of print media in São Paulo (Brazil's financial capital), nearly all of the sources in Fisher's archive of newspaper and magazine clippings are from the city and state of São Paulo. Because of the dates I am examining (the 1990s were a transition period between print and online media that has made locating sources difficult), the scarcity of coverage about women's sports (TV and radio coverage are nonexistent), and my location in the United States, Fisher's archive is my primary source. I certainly do not assume this source is complete, although it

is thorough; she has done an impressive job collecting and recording materials. For more information about the Guerreiras Project—which, according to its website, is "a collective of athletes, academics, activists, and artists, [who are] using futebol through various channels to raise questions around the regulation of bodies, the significance of empowerment, possibilities for resistance, and social justice within and beyond the game"—visit https://guerreirasproject.wordpress.com.

4 All translations are my own.

5 Sexuality is not explicitly referenced, although scholars have noted that female masculinity and lesbianism are often conflated (Fisher and Dennehy 2015).

6 Bonfim's interviews comprised a series of questions, with some deviations, depending on the responsiveness of the interviewee: name, age, position, soccer origin story, incidents of prejudice or machismo, experiences playing on national teams, experiences playing abroad, predictions about outcomes in the Brazilian Confederation of Football (Confederação Brasileira de Futebol) if they won the 2015 FIFA Women's World Cup, their knowledge of the forty-year ban on women's soccer in Brazil, and a request to provide a quick blurb to advertise the museum's upcoming exhibition on women's soccer.

7 The group was referred to as "experimental" by researchers, players, and coaches alike, since it was the Brazilian Confederation's first attempt to gather a team to train leading up to the Women's World Cup.

8 By "start late," Francielle means that many Brazilian women athletes begin playing when they are older, often in their early teens.

9 "Seleção Permanente Brasileira: Francielle," interview by Aira Bonfim, accessed January 8, 2017. All interviews were conducted on June 1, 2015. They may be accessed at the Football Museum, housed in the Pacaembu Stadium in the city of São Paulo, Brazil.

10 "Seleção Permanente Brasileira: Rafaela," interview by Aira Bonfim, accessed January 8, 2017. All interviews were conducted on June 1, 2015. They may be accessed at the Football Museum, housed in the Pacaembu Stadium in the city of São Paulo, Brazil.

11 "Seleção Permanente Brasileira: Aline," interview by Aira Bonfim, accessed January 8, 2017. All interviews were conducted on June 1, 2015. They may be accessed at the Football Museum, housed in the Pacaembu Stadium in the city of São Paulo, Brazil.

12 "Seleção Permanente Brasileira: Marta," interview by Aira Bonfim, accessed January 8, 2017. All interviews were conducted on June 1, 2015. They may be accessed at the Football Museum, housed in the Pacaembu Stadium in the city of São Paulo, Brazil.

13 To give an idea of the scale of this practice, during the 2018 FIFA World Cup for men, ninety-seven foreign-born players competed for the thirty-two qualifying-country teams (Champine 2018).

12

Mozambican Feminisms

Between the Local and the Global

ISABEL MARIA CORTESÃO CASIMIRO &
CATARINA CASIMIRO TRINDADE

IN RECENT YEARS Mozambique has been the site of an intense culture war that has targeted feminists. One powerful aspect of state repression of feminist activism has been the framing of feminism as a foreign intrusion. An incident that took place in March 2016 highlights this dynamic. Five feminist activists were imprisoned in the capital, Maputo, after a failed attempt to present a street theater performance against the policy of the Ministry of Education and Human Development requiring female primary and secondary school students to wear full-length maxiskirts as part of their school uniform. Several schools had recently introduced new regulations to this effect, claiming that covering up girls would protect them from rampant sexual harassment and rape. As education minister Jorge Ferrão put it, "School is not a place for fashion shows" (AFPQC 2016). Feminist organizations denounced this as a measure that stigmatized young girls and aimed to control their bodies (AFPQC 2016). The feminist who most directly bore the brunt of government force, however, was a foreigner: two weeks after the incident, the Mozambican authorities announced the expulsion from the country of Eva Anadón Moreno, a Spanish feminist militant who had been living in Mozambique for four years. According to the order of expulsion signed by the minister of the interior, Jaime Basilio Monteiro, "By participating in an illegal demonstration, by leading a group of children dressed in school uniforms and by using/chanting slogans against the good customs of the Republic of Mozambique, Citizen Eva Anadón Moreno violated the law in a clear and open way" (AFPQC 2016). The police claimed the gathering was an illegal demonstration on a public street. However, according to Graça Samo, the Mozambican coordinator of the International Secretariat of the World March of Women (WMW), "This supposed protest was not a demonstration, it was just a play [performance], like those we often do." Eva was not "leading a group of children"; she was one of the participants as a militant of the WMW. What Eva and the other four detainees *were* doing was challenging one of the patriarchal practices of the state, as well as questioning the violence of the police and their use of force, with dogs and military tanks, against unarmed protestors (AFPQC 2016).[1]

During the past decade, women's and feminist organizations have been concerned with the growing and worrying efforts to control Mozambican women's bodies and their form of dress. On repeated occasions, like the one just described, Fórum Mulher ([FM] Women's Forum), a network of organizations working on women's issues, has taken positions and issued statements expressing their discontent with these efforts. The state has, perhaps rightly, identified alliances among local, regional, and international women's and feminist organizations as a problem for the maintenance of order: these alliances are indeed strengthening the organizations' capacities to challenge dominant gendered structures in Mozambique. In this chapter, using the case just described as a lens, we reflect on the nature of Mozambican patriarchy and the involvement of the state in controlling women's and girls' bodies, as well as on the resilience and transnational connections of the country's feminist movements.

HUMAN AND WOMEN'S RIGHTS IN MOZAMBIQUE

Economic growth has been a priority in Mozambique over the past decades. Poverty reduction and higher gender equality are high on the political agenda. However,

> standard indicators such as the UN Development Programme (UNDP) Human Development Index (with a ranking of 178 out of 187 countries) and the Gender-Related Development Index (also with a ranking of 178 out of 187 countries) reveal that Mozambicans remain poor overall as well as in gender equality terms. A total of 36.6 per cent of all households are

female-headed, which are poorer than their male-headed counterparts, with the proportion showing an increasing trend. During the past eight years, former reductions in the poverty rate have also come to an abrupt halt: poverty stood at 54.7 per cent in 2008/09 compared with 54.1 per cent in 2002/03 and 69.4 per cent in 1996/97. (Tvedten et al. 2015, 6)

Substantial progress has been made regarding the participation of women in decision-making spaces in Mozambique. This is due to a combination of factors, from the ad hoc quota system for women holding seats in the legislature, their increased access to education and literacy, and a greater awareness of their importance at all levels of Mozambican society. However, concrete improvements in the status of women and girls related to the exercise of their rights and the explicit inclusion of women's strategic priorities in various approved policies and programs are not yet equally visible (Lubrino, Buque, and Lipapa 2016). There are more women in positions of power at the national level than at the local and district levels, but their representation is not reflected in greater opportunities for decision-making, as women are trapped by the policies of their political parties. In other words, women are *in* power, but they do not *have* power.

According to the Constitution of the Republic of Mozambique (República de Moçambique 2004), women and men have the same rights and duties. However, their daily life experiences are quite different. It is considered a woman's destiny to marry, have children, take care of her husband and his family, and also attend to community issues. Women suffer violence at all ages: babies can be raped or sold; girls are forced to marry as soon as they menstruate in order to pay family debts or bring needed income to a poor family; and older or widowed women in rural areas are sometimes accused of being witches and killed.

Cultural and social practices lead to gender-based violence, especially sexual violence against girls and women, in public and private spaces, such as schools, health centers, hospitals, markets, police stations, prisons, bus stops, public and private transport, abandoned ruins, and alleys and streets with low or absent public lighting (ASCHA 2018). According to ASCHA (Associação Sócio-Cultural Horizonte Azul, or Blue Horizon Sociocultural Association), citing data compiled by the emergency and gynecological services of the National Health System, in 2017 Mozambique was the scene of 4,907 rapes. The number reveals frightening violence: thirteen women are reported to be raped in the country every day, and more than half are children under fourteen. The victims of rape include children younger than eleven months old. The figures also show that 199 baby girls between one and four years of age were victims of such violence in 2017. Maputo city and Maputo and Nampula provinces have the highest numbers of rapes and/or assassinations and are the regions where the most cases were reported, with 554, 356, and 335, respectively. In sum, it is dangerous to be born a woman in Mozambique.

CRIMINALIZATION OF FEMINIST MILITANTS
AND SOCIAL MOVEMENTS IN MOZAMBIQUE

Over the past two decades, Mozambique has developed a lively and active feminist and women's movement that includes multiple organizations and a variety of practices. Women's rights organizations have played and continue to play a pioneering role in the democratization process through local, regional, and global articulations. This role is crucial in a changing environment where feminist activists are often perceived as a threat by the patriarchal state. Generations of feminist activists from various organizations—such as Fórum Mulher, a network of associations, unions, and institutions; Women and Law in Southern Africa Research and Education Trust (WLSA Moçambique), a regional organization; Marcha Mundial das Mulheres (World March of Women); Movimento das Jovens Feministas de Moçambique (Mozambican Young Feminists' Movement [MOVFEMME]); and ASCHA—are challenging the increasingly conservative nature of Mozambique's governmental institutions, which limit women's spaces and voices.

Girls and young women, human rights activists, and various organizations joined together in 2016 with the aim of creating a permanent space for discussion and building an agenda of advocacy for girls and young women in the municipalities, a collective construction involving everybody from the conception of the idea to the completion of municipal and district forums.[2] Programa Diálogo (Dialogue Program), FM, ASCHA, WMW, WLSA Moçambique, and Associação KUTENGA (KUTENGA Association) conceived and carried out the first Municipal Forum on Gender, Culture, Urban Safety and Public Policies for girls and young women in Maputo city during that year. In 2017 other organizations such as United Nations agencies (UN Women) and the embassy of Canada joined this agenda, organizing the first district forum and the second municipal forum, both in Maputo city.[3]

Women's and girls' growing activism and visibility at various levels in urban and rural areas, and in alliance with local, regional, and international women's and feminist organizations, have been strengthening their capacities and creating better conditions for challenging patriarchal structures in Mozambique. At the same time, the militancy and visibility of young girls and women in feminist organizations have given rise to various forms of control and/or repression by the government and the Frelimo Party in power. Efforts at control have occurred in different ways: through the actions of party militants in women's organizations, through threats or the creation of parallel associations designed to undermine feminist institutions, through the offer of more funds to pursue externally designed agendas, and also through direct repression and the prohibition of activities, such as marches, street theater performances, and so on.

Graça Samo, then executive director of Fórum Mulher, was one of the first feminist militants to speak openly about persecution. In October 2013 she posted on Facebook that she had been threatened, saying, "I got a phone call from someone close to me who was assigned the task of calling my attention to the fact that I'm talking too much. 'Call Graça Samo's attention because she is talking too much. She may criticize but she must have limits. The Women's Forum is not a non-party organization as she thinks, because inside there are party members. Why don't they speak and why is she the only one?' More things have been said that interfere in my private sphere" (pers. post, May 27, 2013). She finished her post by declaring that she would not accept the threat or be silenced and that she would continue to "denounce, protest and create solidarity among all, for otherwise oppression will win." These threats are part of a larger pattern in the relations between the state and its critics. In 2013 there was a mass demonstration against war, violence, and kidnappings.[4] Afterward, Mozambican citizen Carlos Nuno Castel-Branco was accused by the Attorney General's Office of insulting and disrespecting the then president of the Republic of Mozambique, Armando Emílio Guebuza (2005–14), through a Facebook post.[5] He and a journalist who published the post in a private newspaper faced the court in August 2015. Though they were released by the judge in Kampfumo District Court, the Attorney General's Office appealed the decision. The City Court of Maputo confirmed the first instance decision and the Prosecution appealed again before the Supreme Court. The case remains open and undecided.

In May 2016 Jaime Macuane, a teacher and political scientist from Eduardo Mondlane University who also served as a commentator on a private TV station (STV) program, was kidnapped and shot four times in his knees after hearing his captors say that they had not been ordered to kill him, just to warn him. The previous day, Macuane had participated in the usual TV program, drawing attention to the situation in Mozambique: corruption, bad governance, and the possibility of falling into the networks of organized crime.

In the past fifteen years, especially under the former president Guebuza, the Frelimo Party and state institutions have practiced a policy of criminalizing those who criticize or oppose the policies and positions of the party, calling them "apostles of doom" and accusing them of being aligned with international donors who seek to undermine national sovereignty by imposing their own agendas.[6] A lawyer, a judge, and a prosecutor were shot dead in 2015 and 2016. Journalists, economists, law professionals, and about fifteen other people have been killed or threatened for various reasons. Some of them were handling specific judicial cases of corruption involving state bodies; others were calling attention to or criticizing government decisions on political and economic issues.

TURNING POINT: REPRESSION OF A WOMEN'S DAY EVENT

The imprisonment of five feminists and the deportation of Eva Anadón Moreno from the International Secretariat of the World March of Women in Mozambique represents a turning point in the behavior of the government apparatus toward dissenting voices that challenge its policies and practices. It was the first time the Frelimo Party and the government attacked women's organizations this aggressively, using the arrest as intimidation to say "enough is enough" to those who are not aligned with them. These actions have profoundly affected women's organizations, undermining their actions and leading them to rethink the way activism is done.

The presence of feminists who were Spanish and Brazilian citizens was exploited to raise the specter of intervention by foreigners as compromising national sovereignty. Of course, this accusation referred only to *feminist* foreigners, because the many other foreigners who have taken control of the country's economy suffer no consequences. In any case, the apparently well-prepared media coverage drove the point home, bombarding people to convince them of the dangers of foreign influence on Mozambican culture.

Eva's deportation and ensuing ban on reentering the country for a period of ten years were based on an order issued by the minister of the interior on March 28, 2016, the same day she was deported.[7] This order was never presented to the person concerned (Eva), which led to the intervention of a woman magistrate from the Public Prosecutor's Office in the International Airport of Mavalane, where Eva had been taken after being summoned to appear at Migration Services (WLSA Moçambique 2016; Trindade 2016).[8]

Isabel Casimiro & Catarina Trindade

The failure to notify the person affected by an order is a serious breach of an essential procedural requirement, since it would have enabled Eva to exercise her right to bring an action before the expulsion order had been executed, even if that order had no suspensive effect (WLSA Moçambique 2016; Trindade 2016). Why did this happen, and what reasons may lie behind this strong reaction and weighty decision from the government of Mozambique?

Twelve days before the deportation, on March 16, as part of the International Women's Day activities in Mozambique, a group of civil society organizations coordinated by the Fórum Mulher network had scheduled a street intervention.[9] It consisted of the public reading of a press release (Fórum Mulher 2016a) referring to several examples of violations of women's and girls' rights in education, as well as the presentation of a play performed by a group of girls, activists, actresses, and secondary school students. The play was about violence against girls in school and was conceived by a group of girls who wanted to talk about the problems they face every day related to sexual harassment, rape, and unwanted pregnancies (Fórum Mulher 2016b; WLSA Moçambique 2016; Trindade 2016). Street theater is part of a larger campaign to draw attention and awareness to violence against women and girls, a global problem affecting one in three women, destroying lives and breaking families and communities apart. It takes various forms and knows no geographic or cultural boundaries.

As part of the 2017 International Women's Day actions, the street theater was not communicated ahead of time to the civil and police authorities of the area in which it would occur, because the promoters considered that it was a "small-scale activity, located on a sidewalk, without interrupting the normal movement of people and vehicles" (WLSA Moçambique 2016; Trindade 2016). A similar action with a play had previously taken place in other cities of Mozambique, presented by more members of a Brazilian theater group, with no problems (WLSA Moçambique 2016; Trindade 2016).

The planned program was not even carried out because at 11:00 a.m., when it was scheduled to start, the place chosen—in the vicinity of Francisco Manyanga Secondary School—was taken over by uniformed and plain-clothed agents of the police of the Republic of Mozambique with dogs and a military car. The police confiscated the prepared posters before they were even displayed. The statement was not read, nor the play presented (WLSA Moçambique 2016; Trindade 2016).

At a certain point, a number of activists and militants—some of them very young members of ASCHA—decided to move away from the place where the gathering was to be held and start dancing, singing a song that

FIGURE 12.1 Poster produced by the organizing associations on March 18, 2017. It reads, "Women say 'enough!' on the control of their bodies"; "Against the compulsion of the maxiskirts, let's defend our rights!!"; and "Because my safety does not depend on my skirt!!!" Source: Fórum Mulher.

said, "When women unite, patriarchy will fall / When girls unite, machismo will fall / When women unite, violence will fall / It will fall, will fall, will fall . . ." This song triggered the ire of the police officers, who, wielding weapons and dogs, chased the group of participants with the intent of preventing them from continuing their action. Some of the activists questioned the agents about their behavior while trying to photograph and film the police. In response, the police arrested, handcuffed, and took five of them to the Seventh Police Station, where they remained for five hours, until the end of the afternoon. The detainees were three Mozambicans from different civil society associations, Eva Anadón Moreno, and a Brazilian member of the theater group. Up to this point, no official report had been drawn up, nor had any procedural formalities been carried out. The police officers in the police station did not allow the intervention of a lawyer and a prosecutor

Isabel Casimiro & Catarina Trindade

who went there right away to find out about the situation and defend the detainees. They were released around 5:30 p.m., after the intervention of the president of the Human Rights League, Alice Mabota; diplomats from Brazil, Spain, and France; and a representative of UN Women (WLSA Moçambique 2016; Trindade 2016). From this day on until her deportation from Mozambique, Eva continued to receive anonymous phone calls threatening her. Fortunately, the Brazilian activist and theater group member detained with Eva was able to return to her country on the morning of the following day, March 19. The five detainees stayed in the Seventh Police Station together until they were released.

The day before Eva was ultimately deported from Mozambique, she received an order to go to the city Migration Services office, where she stayed all day long without knowing what was happening and without being allowed to leave or to eat. In the afternoon she was told she was being taken to the national Migration Services office, but in fact she was taken to the airport to be deported. Her colleagues, who had remained vigilant, realized that Eva was being driven to the airport and immediately informed a lawyer and called the clients' line of the city attorney's office. Both the prosecutor and the lawyer were prevented from demanding due process for Eva (WLSA Moçambique 2016; Trindade 2016). These actions—the behavior of the government agents, the illegalities that led to Eva's deportation, and the fear that was instilled among activists in the aftermath—are the reason the events of March 16 and 28, 2016, are viewed as a milestone in the struggle for women's and girls' human rights in the region.

A COUNTRY "FOREVER AGAINST WOMEN AND GIRLS"

The use of moralistic policies to control women's bodies is not new in the history of Mozambique.[10] Shortly after independence, on June 25, 1975, a series of extremist measures that reflected religious and political influences were taken against women and girls, without analyzing how they would impact public health and human rights (Arthur and Cabral 2004). Among other measures, women thought to be prostitutes were sent to reeducation camps, and women married to foreigners lost their Mozambican nationality and were stateless for some time. A number of policies today are based on Protestant Christian ethics and morality, combined with the vigilante morality of the *guerrilha* (guerrilla) of the Mozambican Liberation Front (FRELIMO). These policies refer to dignity (only) in marriage, the (nuclear) family, the father as the head of the household, and the mother as a stay-at-home wife and reject vagrancy, alcoholism, prostitution, and marginalization (Arnfred 1990).[11] It is, effectively, a "Marxist ideology grafted in Christian morality" owing to the influence of these values on some of the leaders of Frelimo and the party through their education in the Catholic and Protestant missions (Casimiro 1999, 2003, 2014).

One example of how this ideology surfaces in governmental action is the policy of expelling girls from elementary or secondary school if they become pregnant, as if they alone were responsible for their pregnancies. In most cases, the father of the baby (normally a peer or teacher) suffers no consequences. This subject has been discussed several times since independence in 1975 within the Mozambican Women's Organization (Organização da Mulher Moçambicana), which has been unable to dissuade the Frelimo Party and the government from continuing to impose these unjust measures that further penalize girls who are often victims.[12]

In 2003, Order 39/GM/2003, issued by the minister of education, forced pregnant students to be transferred to the evening school.[13] This effectively penalized them twice: first because they are blamed for their pregnancies and then because they are forced to endure the dangers of travel to evening schools when there is a lack of street lighting and security. Evening schools are also usually farther from home, have a predominance of adult students, higher dropout rates, and so on. Although the order refers to disciplinary measures directed at the male student responsible for the pregnancy (who should also be transferred to the evening school), this does not normally occur. Punishment of teachers, who are often responsible for pregnancies or sexually harass their students (a crime punishable by law), is rare.[14]

Beginning in 2015, the Education for All Movement (Movimento Educação Para Todos) resumed negotiations with the Ministry of Education and Human Development for the repeal of this old order that forces pregnant girls to be transferred to the evening school. For this purpose, it has produced a document laying out the legal foundation for revoking the order. In the course of these negotiations, the minister of education and human development not only did not repeal the order but also imposed the wearing of long skirts in primary and secondary schools as a way of "solving" the problem of harassment and teenage pregnancy in schools.

The conservative effort to exert explicit control over women's clothing began slowly and imperceptibly over the past ten years and has now become explicit with written orders about how women in certain kinds of workplaces—mainly banks and public institutions—should dress; it prevents women from entering public buildings when wearing clothing without sleeves.[15] Pregnant women who are not properly dressed are prevented from entering health centers, for example, and university professors are not permitted to teach in sleeveless attire, no matter how hot the weather. In contrast, in contexts such as advertising and dance shows, it is expected that women cover only the bare minimum.[16] Both extremes reflect a male desire to control women's bodies. Women and feminist organizations raised this issue with the previous minister of women and social action and with women members of the parliament, with no results.[17]

Society's attitudes also influence the way in which women's bodies are controlled. On February 22, 2006, FM and WLSA Moçambique drafted a press release titled "It Is Not by Controlling Women's Clothing That One Can Stop the AIDS Epidemic" (Fórum Mulher 2006) In this press release, they denounced the attitude of a few journalists who misrepresented the content of a meeting that the president of the republic, Armando Emílio Guebuza, held on February 16 with women's organizations involved in the fight against AIDS. Instead of accounting for all the richness of the debate, the majority of the media "chose to divulge a monolithic and reductive vision of the event," claiming that the women's organizations had defended the idea of controlling young women's clothing as a way to avoid "provok[ing]" men, when in fact their position was the opposite (Fórum Mulher 2006). The feminists had argued that neither the girls nor their clothing was to blame but rather that the existing heteropatriarchal culture of harassment and rape had to be tackled.

In 2006 the Community Development Foundation (Fundação para o Desenvolvimento da Comunidade) launched a campaign for HIV/AIDS awareness with the message that adults were buying pants imported from Brazil (called *tchuna babes*) for adolescent and younger girls in order to gain sexual favors. Tchuna babes are tight jeans that can reveal the shape of women's bodies. The campaign contained sentences such as "Quem te dá uma 'tchuna babes' também te dá o HIV" (The person who gives you "tchuna babes" also gives you HIV) and "Com 'tchuna babes' você também pode ser portadora do HIV" (With "tchuna babes" you can also be infected with HIV). Because of this campaign and the disinformation in it, women and girls were attacked in the streets for wearing jeans and also became associated with the disease. Once again, women's and girls' bodies were blamed for sexual violence.

FIGURE 12.2 "It's wrong to not let Manuela attend our class just because she's pregnant. She's a girl like us. We are used to helping our sisters and our mothers when they get pregnant." This cartoon represents an example of the images distributed in the campaign. For further information about this struggle, see WLSA Moçambique (2016a). *Artist: Zacharias Chemane.*

"WHEN WOMEN AND GIRLS UNITE, PATRIARCHY, MACHISMO, AND VIOLENCE WILL FALL"

The arrest of five feminist activists and the deportation of Spanish citizen Eva Anadón Moreno in 2016 thus came on the heels of growing feminist protest. Rape, sexual harassment, pregnancies among adolescents, and forced unions led Mozambican associations to organize the street theater performance in March 2016, during the activities commemorating International Women's Day. The idea was to reflect on and respond to the control of girls' and women's bodies by powerful social and political institutions. Their actions were in line with feminist activism in other African countries, where women have participated in movements and collective actions around a variety of subjects, inspired by international feminisms and matrilineal traditions, and with support from external partners and donors. African women

Isabel Casimiro & Catarina Trindade

activists have critically contributed to analyzing, conceptualizing, and forging their own agendas, actions, and ways of creating movements (Badri and Tripp 2017).

Reflecting on the trajectory of the women's movement in Mozambique, which has been stitched together through the relationships among academia, women's organizations and associations, labor unions, female leagues within political parties, public institutions and international organizations, and regional and international networks, we can affirm, without a doubt, that the movement has won many battles. Its most striking successes include the Land Law (1997), the Family Law (2004), and the Law of Domestic Violence against Women (2009); gender-related focal points in the ministries; and women's associations and organizations on all levels. In December 2018, Order 39 was overturned in response to pressure from various civil society organizations. These are all important achievements.

However, the movement is deeply challenged by the violation of both the Constitution and international legal instruments ratified by the Mozambican government (Convention on the Elimination of All Forms of Discrimination against Women [CEDAW]) and the Southern Africa Development Community [SADC] Gender Protocol, for example). It is hampered by the lack of enforcement of laws at various levels. We struggle with, and are challenged to change, heteropatriarchal mentalities in a society deeply influenced by Christian and Muslim religious ideas mixed with an authoritarian Marxist ideology that emerged during the armed struggle for independence. As long as a woman continues to be an object, seen only as a mother, wife, and breeder of future laborers, unremunerated and invisible in her multiple and simultaneous activities and with a body that is subject to regulation and containment by patriarchal power, the struggle will remain urgent.

ACKNOWLEDGMENTS

We would like to give a big *khanimambo* (thank you) to all the Mozambican feminists who struggle daily for a more just and egalitarian Mozambique where women's rights are respected.

NOTES

This chapter is a longer version of an article published in *Spotlight Magazine* titled "Criminalization of Feminist Activists and Social Movements in Mozambique" (Casimiro 2016).

1 Eva had been working in Mozambique since 2014, when the International Secretariat of the World March of Women moved from Brazil to Mozambique.

2 Mozambique is organized territorially into provinces, districts, administrative posts, localities, and settlements. The district, as the second territorial level after the province, covers the administrative, locality, and settlement levels. In addition, Maputo city is divided into seven municipal districts, formerly known as urban districts.

3 Other organizations that participated in the Municipal Forum were Fórum da Sociedade Civil para os Direitos da Criança (Civil Society Forum for Children's Rights), Centro de Aprendizagem e Capacitação da Sociedade Civil (Civil Society Learning and Training Center), and muva (a women's economic empowerment program).

4 The poster about the event, which took place in Maputo city, was titled "movimento da sociedade civil mocambicana indignada pela tensão político militar e com os raptos. marcha pacífica pela paz e contra os raptos—31 de outubro 2013. Um grito de socorroooo!!!" (Mozambican Civil Society Movement outraged by the political-military tension and kidnappings. Peaceful march for peace and against kidnappings—October 31, 2013. A cry for help!!!) (Fórum Mulher 2013).

5 Castel-Branco is a Mozambican economist who was the founder and first director of the Institute for Social and Economic Studies.

6 *Apóstolos da desgraça* is an expression used to label people with different opinions and positions.

7 An interesting metaphor: Eve is expelled again from paradise! The order was no. 01/EA/GMI/2016.

8 Eva was taken to the airport after being in the Maputo city Migration Services office for almost twelve hours. She was not aware of her impending deportation.

9 The organizations included PathFinder International, wlsa Moçambique, the World March of Women (wmw), ascha, the Mozambican Young Feminists' Movement, Lambdamozi (lgbt Mozambique), Rede de Defesa dos Direitos Sexuais e Reprodutivos (Network for the Defense of Sexual and Reproductive Rights), Fórum das Rádios Comunitárias (Community Radio Forum), muleide (Associação Mulher, Lei e Desenvolvimento, Woman, Law and Development Association), and Associação Levanta-te Mulher e Siga o Seu Caminho, Chimoio (Stand Up, Woman, and Go Your Own Way). Also participating in this group were two Brazilian feminists, members of a theater group.

10 The quotation in the heading is taken from the article "Um ministério eternamente contra a rapariga" (A ministry forever against girls), by journalist Rui Lamarques (2016).

11 It is expected that a woman will marry and have children, combining endogenous cultural aspects and, more recently, the Christian and Islamic religions.

12 The Mozambican Women's Organization was created by FRELIMO in 1973 during the armed struggle (1962–74) against Portuguese colonialism.

13 Order 39 from the Government of Mozambique (GM).

14 Many organizations are involved in a campaign against Order 39, considered to violate girls' human rights and the Mozambican Constitution. Mozambique is one of the countries in southern Africa with the highest percentage of girls who drop out of school owing to early pregnancy: 39 percent in secondary education and 9 percent in primary education (Lubrino, Buque, and Lipapa 2016).

15 For example, an announcement from the Directorate for Community Affairs (Direcção dos Assuntos Comunitários) of Zambeze University (a public institution) reads, "[The Directorate for Community Affairs] [h]ereby notifies all staff, faculty and students of this institution that it is prohibited to have access to the university campus with inappropriate clothing. For women, inappropriate clothing is considered to be: clothes that stick to the body, clothing above the knee, sleeveless clothing, low necklines, transparent or shiny fabrics, clothing that shows the bra, torn jeans, and shorts. For men, inappropriate clothing is considered to be: shorts, torn jeans, undershirts, low waist pants, hats inside the buildings, slippers, braids, dreadlocks, punk, earrings, and long hair. The announcement will be in effect from April 3, 2017" (Zambeze University, 2017).

16 Fórum Mulher campaigned against the racist, *machista* (sexist), and misogynist outdoor publicity for a Mozambican beer. The advertising showed a bottle of black (root) beer in the shape of a woman's body, with the words "Esta preta está muito boa" (This black one is very good). After the protest, the advertising was removed.

17 The Ministry of Gender, the Child and Social Action was previously known as the Ministry of Women and Social Action.

13

Plural Sovereignty and la Familia Diversa in Ecuador's 2008 Constitution

CHRISTINE "CRICKET" KEATING & AMY LIND

IN SEPTEMBER 2008 the Ecuadorian people voted to approve a new constitution, the twentieth in the country's history. Along with innovations such as codifying the rights of nature, guaranteeing the right to food, and affirming the right to nondiscrimination on the basis of gender identity, a key component of the 2008 Constitution is that it redefines Ecuador as a plurination, one that recognizes and enables the sovereignty of the Indigenous and Afro-Ecuadorian groups within it. Another important innovation of the Constitution is that it introduces the concept of *la familia diversa* (the family in its diverse forms) as a means of expanding what it means to be a family as well as who might constitute one. This chapter analyzes the linked resignifications of the nation and the family in contemporary Ecuadorian politics. We suggest that these redefinitions share a similar logic of multiplicity and open-endedness that works to challenge monolithic and hegemonic social and political forms that had been imposed on Ecuador in the colonial context and then preserved in the postcolonial period. In doing so, we pay particularly close attention to the development of these concepts in contemporary Ecuadorian politics, as well as to the ways in which their implementation has been limited, compromised, and forestalled. We argue that, far from being a change only on paper, the opening up of the definitions of the nation and the family in the Ecuadorian Constitution is an important aspect of linguistic and institutional resistance to the coloniality of power in Ecuador.

Feminist and queer scholars, among others, have focused closely on ways that heterosexualism and the heteropatriarchal family have been key to the articulation and consolidation of hegemonic configurations of the racialized state across multiple contexts (Alexander 2006; Lugones 2007; Canaday 2009). This chapter explores the possibilities that emerge when, in the words of Ecuador's Indigenous activists, the "uninational" and "monocultural" state is challenged and when both sovereignty and the family are affirmed as plural. How might these pluralized formations of both state and family echo and reinforce each other across and within different levels of social organization? What are the possibilities and challenges involved in engaging with the state in doing this work? Finally, what are the implications of these linked resignifications for transnational feminist practice?

PLURINATIONALIST REFOUNDINGS

The concept of plurinationalism articulated by Indigenous groups in Ecuador is grounded in a demand for the recognition of Indigenous and Afro-Ecuadorian groups as distinct nations within the state, with rights to territorial, cultural, economic, and political self-determination. The struggle for recognition of Ecuador as a plurinational state is rooted in a deep critique of the ways that Indigenous groups have been oppressed, marginalized, and excluded by and from the state. Until the late 1970s, for example, people who could not read or write in Spanish were barred from voting in Ecuador—effectively disenfranchising Indigenous communities. These franchise restrictions were finally removed in Ecuador's 1979 Constitution. Since then the Indigenous movement in Ecuador has become one of the most politically effective movements in the world, organizing massive uprisings throughout the 1990s and successfully forcing the resignation of President Abdalá Bucaram in 1996 and President Jamil Mahuad in 2000, leading mass uprisings in October 2019 that halted President Lenín Moreno's austerity measures and supporting Ecuador's first Indigenous Pachakutik Party presidential candidate, Yaku Pérez, in 2020–21 (Yashar 2005; Zamosc 2007; Becker 2008; Novo 2014).

Of particular importance to the organizational strengthening of the Indigenous movement in Ecuador was the formation of the Confederation of Indigenous Nationalities of Ecuador (CONAIE) in 1986, a group that would become Ecuador's largest Indigenous organization (Prieto et al. 2006). The organization serves as an umbrella, linking together the fourteen different

Indigenous nations of Ecuador. According to Leon Zamosc, the effectiveness of Indigenous mobilization in Ecuador in recent decades lies in part in its strong network of communities. He explains:

> Ecuador has about 2,100 Indian communities, functioning as self-regulated entities based on the authority of their *asambleas* (in which everybody participates) and *cabildos* (executive committees of five members). All important issues are discussed in the *asambleas*, where agreement is usually reached by consensus rather than by voting. The decisions are binding for all members. . . . Thus, joining in a mobilization is always the result of a decision of the community, which exerts its influence to make sure that the members join in the roadblocks and rallies. The secret of CONAIE's power, then, lies in its ability to harness the resources for collective action that exist in the Indian communities. (Zamosc 2007, 16)

In 1988 CONAIE first presented their demand for the constitutional refounding of Ecuador as a plurinationalist state, calling for a recognition of "Indigenous territoriality, organization, education, culture, medicine, and judicial systems" (Becker 2008, 172). In CONAIE's framing, plurinationalism is closely related to the concept of interculturalism, which denotes the process by which different autonomous groups can interact and coexist with respect and equality. According to CONAIE, the state has the function of simultaneously strengthening groups' autonomy (plurinationalism) and working toward their unity (interculturalism) on a national level (Walsh 2009, 78). Such a unity is to be built through dialogue between groups, not imposed from above or assumed. Interculturalism, in other words, is to be state enabled, not state centered.

In an indication of its centrality in the Indigenous struggle in Ecuador, the demand for the constitutional recognition of Ecuador as a plurination was the first among *los 16 puntos* (the sixteen points) that CONAIE presented to the government in the 1990 *levantamiento*, a massive weeklong uprising in which thousands of people blockaded roads leading into Ecuador's major cities in protest over the continued social, economic, and political marginalization of Indigenous groups.[1] This demand remained central to the powerful Indigenous uprisings and protests that followed throughout the 1990s. In 1998 the movement partially achieved its goal when the Constituent Assembly agreed to declare Ecuador a "pluricultural and multi-ethnic" state and to include a statement asserting that "Indigenous peoples, who self-define as nationalities of ancestral races, and Negro and Afro-Ecuadorian peoples, form part of a united and indivisible Ecuadorian state" (República del Ecuador 1998, quoted in Becker 2011, 58).

The inclusion of such language in the 1998 Constitution was a break-through. Unfortunately, however, such language did not translate into con-crete policy, and it became evident that the changes were part of a regional shift toward neoliberal multiculturalism in which Indigenous groups gained recognition but little else. Soon the Indigenous movement called for another constitution that would enact deeper transformations. In her explanation of why a shift from a neoliberal multiculturalist toward a plurinationalist approach was necessary, CONAIE leader and Constituent Assembly member Mónica Chuji (2008) notes that "the multiculturalism recognized by the Ecuadorian State had no legal power to change the unjust power relations to which indigenous people have been subject."[2] As a result, there was what Chuji calls an "implementation gap" between the state's commitment to In-digenous peoples, implied in the affirmation of the state as pluricultural and multiethnic, and its actions. She argues that plurinationalism is a strategy to challenge that implementation gap, in that it "returns to indigenous peoples their capacities for territorial, institutional, and political management." Such a concept functions, she argues, as a challenge to the domination and exclu-sion of Indigenous groups and other marginalized peoples that is endemic to a uninational or monocultural political framework.

In the 2006 Ecuadorian presidential elections, Rafael Correa made the demand for a new constitution, one that would reject neoliberalism as a social, economic, and political model and would construct a new path for Ecuador, a central part of his campaign platform. Some saw his embrace of this goal as responsive to the demands of the Indigenous movement, while others saw it as Correa's attempt to co-opt the movement. Correa and his political party, Alianza PAIS, won the election with 56 percent of the popular vote and, soon after taking office, called for a referendum to decide whether to convene a Constituent Assembly.[3] The referendum passed by a huge mar-gin, with 82 percent voting in favor of a new constitution. Elections for the Constituent Assembly were held, and in 2007 the body convened to begin the work of drafting a new constitution, meeting in Montecristi, a small hillside village near the coast, famous for being the birthplace of Ecuador's revolutionary leader Eloy Alfaro.

Although constituent assemblies are privileged spaces, recent efforts toward making constitution building more open, inclusive, and dialogic have trans-formed many of them into much more participatory forums for reimagining the political. Indeed, the Ecuadorian Constituent Assembly opened with a pledge that it "would be more inclusive than any previous government and would incorporate the concerns of indigenous peoples, Afro-Ecuadorians, and others who lacked representation" (Becker 2011, 48). Because of a gender quota imposed on the parties during the assembly elections, half of the assembly members were women. Out of the 130 members, eight were Indigenous (6.2 percent of the total), and seven were Afro-Ecuadorian (5.4 percent), up from three Indigenous members and one Afro-Ecuadorian representative in the 1998 Constituent Assembly (Castro and Ocles 2012, 8, 10). In addition to these elected members, CONAIE opened an office in Montecristi and regularly organized marches and delegations to the assembly. Further, an organized group of five hundred Afro-Ecuadorians regularly attended the proceedings as witnesses (10).

The members of the assembly elected Alberto Acosta, an economist who had worked closely with CONAIE, as its president, and all the members were divided into ten working groups, each of which concentrated on a particular topic. The assembly practiced gender equity in establishing the leadership of these committees, with ten women and ten men designated as leaders of the groups. Two of these working groups were led by Indigenous leaders: Mónica Chuji, who chaired the roundtable that focused on natural resources and biodiversity, and Pedro de la Cruz, who chaired the roundtable that focused on development. The working groups began their deliberations by holding town meetings across Ecuador to hear concerns and obtain proposals from a wide variety of civil society groups.

The assembly also experimented with technology in order to open up the proceedings to as many people as possible, with the slogan "Everybody can participate in the Assembly by Internet" (Albornoz and Albornoz 2010, 55). Diego López, whose company set up and maintained the assembly's website, explained that the assembly's goals were to provide access to information about the assembly, to foster participation, to enable transparency, and to document the proceedings (Albornoz and Albornoz 2010, 62). Toward these ends, minute-by-minute reports from the assembly's proceedings were put up on the assembly's website, and each roundtable had a blog in which they shared their work and invited feedback and proposals. In addition, many of the assembly members had their own blogs in which they would also solicit input. Given these multiple avenues for engagement and dialogue, Catherine Walsh, who served as an adviser to Acosta, notes that the Constituent Assembly was "an incredibly open space, a rare space" for the political exploration and deliberation of ideas.[4]

In anticipation of the Constituent Assembly's proceedings, CONAIE prepared a draft constitution that they presented to the assembly upon its convening. The draft constitution articulated a deep critique of the state and its role in the institutionalization and legitimization of processes of colonial and neocolonial discrimination, oppression, and exploitation (CONAIE 2007a, 1). Proclaiming that "the construction of a plurinational state . . . will end forever the colonial and monocultural shadows that have marked Ecuador over the past 200 years" and will serve as a "model of political organization for the decolonization of our nationalities and peoples" (CONAIE 2007b, 7, 9), the draft constitution included measures that would strengthen institutions of Indigenous community governance, provide for judicial autonomy, increase legislative representation for Indigenous and Afro-Ecuadorian groups, and foster the deepening of democracy and a multiplication of its forms across several areas.

The concept of the plurinational state articulated in CONAIE's draft constitution not only challenges the exclusion of Indigenous peoples and Afro-Ecuadorians from Ecuadorian politics but also works against the hegemonic imposition of liberal democracy as a political form. As CONAIE explains, "The colonial State made a single type of democracy possible, liberal democracy . . . even though Ecuador is a multicultural society in which different peoples and nationalities have developed different ways of understanding and exercising democracy" (2007b, 9). In particular, CONAIE notes that "Indigenous peoples have a long tradition in the exercise of forms of democracy" that the Ecuadorian state not only has refused to recognize but has "even tried for centuries to exterminate" (14).

In his work, decolonial scholar Boaventura de Sousa Santos argues that one of the ways that processes of colonialism, neocolonialism, and neoliberalism have operated (and continue to operate) is by negating modes of being, of relating, of producing, and of understanding the world that could serve as the bases for alternative ways of living. In his words, such modes of being are "actively produced as nonexistent" or as "non-credible alternatives" (2014, 181, 173). To challenge this politics of negation, CONAIE replaced a term (the *nation*) that emphasizes cultural and political singularity with one that signifies multiplicity (the *plurination*). This resignification opens up, in CONAIE's words, "enormous possibilities for the enrichment of the Ecuadorian democratic system, so that Ecuadorians can have a real democracy," one that takes up the many "different ways of exercising democracy" and is both "participatory and deeply rooted in our history and our cultural roots" (2007b, 14). According to Chuji, plurinationalism activates "a new form of a social contract that respects and harmonizes the rights of indigenous peoples and nationalities with the judicial structure and political force to recognize their status as political subjects" (quoted in Becker 2011, 55).

When the Constituent Assembly convened to draft the new constitution, the first article they produced took up the question of the identity of the Ecuadorian state. Meeting CONAIE's demand, Article 1 of the assembly's draft declared Ecuador "a social, democratic, sovereign, independent, unitary, intercultural, plurinational, and secular state" (República del Ecuador 2008). After twenty years of struggle, the resignification of Ecuador as a plurinational and intercultural state in the first article of the 2008 Constitution was a truly momentous victory; many analysts and participants saw this move as a crucial step toward decolonizing formal democracy and refounding the state in inclusive terms. In the words of Acosta, "the construction of the plurinational state opens the door to a path of continuous democracy" (2009, 18).

Even though the recognition of Ecuador as a plurination in the 2008 Constitution was a critical turning point, the principle of plurinationalism was compromised or left ambiguous in several ways. First, as Carmen Martínez Novo asserts, "the question of indigenous territories and control of nonrenewable natural resources remains a problematic and ambiguous arena in the constitutional text" (2014, 114). For example, even though the Constitution states that Indigenous groups should be consulted before any decision that affects them, there is ambiguity in the clause, an ambiguity that the government has leveraged so as to ignore this directive, particularly in relation to the extraction of oil and minerals. Second, instead of naming Kichwa as Ecuador's second official language, as CONAIE sought, after much debate and tension, the assembly gave it the ambiguous category of an official language of "intercultural relation" (113). Third, although CONAIE's draft constitution included institutional designs for new modes of plurinational representation, such as a plurinational legislature and a Supreme Court in which Indigenous groups and Afro-Ecuadorians would be ensured seats, these measures were not included in the 2008 Constitution (113).

Furthermore, in contemporary Ecuadorian politics, the principle of plurinationalism has been violated in several ways by the Ecuadorian government. For example, in blatant disregard of the plurinationalist mandate, the Ecuadorian government has sought to undercut community water management organizations and has intensified rather than eased up on resource extraction on Indigenous lands. These moves have been met with vigorous protest. For example, in 2009 thousands of members of water-user associations marched to Quito against a proposed law that would have centralized water governance (Armijos 2013, 86). These protesters invoked the 2008 Constitution and argued that such a move violated their rights as autonomous communities of Ecuador. Their protest was successful, and in 2010 the National Assembly suspended its negotiations over the proposed law (99). Not all of these protests have been as successful, particularly in relation to the question of oil and mineral extraction.

Additionally, while continuing to use rhetoric affirming the importance of plurinationalism, during his time in office, Correa aggressively moved to dismantle and centralize locally controlled initiatives in matters such as health and education (Lang 2019, 181). In the face of these policies, some local municipalities drew upon the language of plurinationalism to resist the centralizing pull from the national government and introduced, in the words of Miriam Lang, "different logics of doing government . . . into existing governmental structures" (176). For example, the municipalities of Nabón and Cayambe "not only gave recognition to the logics of Indigenous communitarian democracy where it existed in their territories, but placed those logics at the core of political transformation" (181). Lang explains that such examples represent ways that "plurinationality as a strategy" can be used to transform local government institutions despite state policies to the contrary (176).

Building a plurinational state along the lines of what Chuji and others envisioned during the Constituent Assembly discussions is no doubt an incomplete project. Despite setbacks and lingering questions, however, the resignification of Ecuador from nation to plurination is a significant victory in the struggle for economic, social, and political justice, one that points to new possibilities for struggles for autonomy and self-determination. According to Chuji, the new constitution "is the product of a collective force. It is one step forward in this process. Maybe that's an end for Alianza país but for me and for the Ecuadorian people, it is just a step forward" (quoted in Denvir 2008). Echoing this assertion, Acosta writes, "The constitutional declaration of the plurinational state opened a road, without a doubt, a very long one, towards the eventual achievement of plurinationalism itself. The constitutional declaration of the plurinational state is an important step, but not enough, now we must build it" (2009, 20).

REDEFINING THE FAMILY: LA FAMILIA DIVERSA

If redefining the state was a central Indigenous demand, redefining the family was a central focus for feminist and LGBTQI groups working with the Constituent Assembly. These groups worked to shift from the hegemonic conception of the nuclear family to an open-ended notion of the diverse family. The work of the legal division of the Quito-based Proyecto Transgénero (Transgender Project), a group that is at the forefront of the movement for transgender and intersex rights in Ecuador, was particularly pivotal to efforts to introduce the language of the diverse family into the Constitution. One of the keys to their success was that Elizabeth Vásquez, a Proyecto Transgénero activist and lawyer, served as an adviser to Constituent Assembly member Tania Hermida and was able to work within the assembly itself to draft and lobby for several important measures relating to gender and sexual diversity. In addition to measures that prohibit discrimination on the basis of gender and cultural identity, they were successful in passing Article 67 of the Constitution, which affirms that "the family in its diverse forms" is recognized and protected by the Ecuadorian state (República del Ecuador 2008).

In advocating for an affirmation of the diverse family in the Constitution, Vásquez drew on a transfeminist approach that, in her words, seeks to "profoundly question male privilege from an alliance that aimed to challenge social and legal institutions such as the family" (quoted in Lind and Pazmiño 2009, 100). For transfeminists working across movements to challenge multiple normativities based on gender, race, ethnicity, sexuality, class, and geopolitical location, decentering patriarchy, gender normativity, and heteronormativity is key to social change. Vásquez distinguishes such a transfeminist approach from a "corporatist" approach. In her framing, corporatist groups, which tend to be led by urban middle-class gay men, many of whom work for relatively well-funded HIV/AIDS nongovernmental organizations, tend to focus on the more traditional struggle for inclusion. In contrast, transfeminist groups tend to focus on diversifying the family to make possible forms of families that do not privilege patriarchy, heteronormativity, and other social norms sustained through scripts of respectability (2008, 101). For example, the notion of the diverse family is also compatible with the work the Indigenous movement had long done toward expanding the institution of marriage and state practices toward the recognition of communal rights.

A strength of a transfeminist approach to sexual justice that is grounded in an affirmation of multiple modes of familial relationality, Vásquez notes, is that "the legalization of the notion of family diversity does not conflict with the struggle for same-sex marriage but includes it as one more manifestation of diversity. In contrast, struggling only for same-sex marriages excludes struggles for a more broad conception of a diversity of families" (101). In many ways, this intersectional approach to redefining the family reflects the grounded process of social movement organizing in Ecuador, distinguishing it from countries in the region that have focused more exclusively on same-sex marriage and other normative legal advances regarding same-sex partner recognition (De la Dehesa 2010, 2014).

Linking the movement for migrant rights with the movement for sexual diversity was particularly key to the measure's success. Ana Almeida (2010), an activist with Proyecto Transgénero, explains that these struggles came together in the Constituent Assembly in its questioning of what is considered the "fundamental unit of society—the family." She writes, "At first glance, the organized movements for the rights of sexually diverse people and for the rights of migrants do not seem to share a broad common agenda beyond both being movements for human rights. But there are deep underlying symmetries in the two experiences, not only because migrants themselves are sexually diverse and because there is sexual diversity in migration patterns." What links the two experiences, she explains, is that transnational families and sexually diverse families are both instances where people craft their own lives in ways that push against traditional, hegemonic modes of being a family. In making choices that go outside of these culturally and geographically prescribed ways of being, people in these families "face the punishment of being deprived, to varying degrees, of full citizenship." Almeida writes that "the confluence of the movement for sexual diversity and the movement for human mobility in the Constituent Assembly should be just the beginning of a shared political project" of an intercultural struggle for full citizenship that can foster "other ways of being, other solidarities, other life projects and other relationships" beyond the norm that holds that a person "can only live in one place . . . with only one way of understanding gender and family."

In her influential essay "Toward a Decolonial Feminism," María Lugones emphasizes the need for a decolonial feminist politics that takes up the hierarchical and dichotomous gender system as a colonial imposition that persists in what she calls "the colonial/modern gender system" (2007, 187). For Lugones, "the imposition of dichotomous hierarchies became woven into the historicity of relations, including intimate relations" (by which she means not only sexual relations but intimacy in the sense of sharing an "interwoven social life") (2010, 743). These intimate relations, however, are also important spaces for the perseverance of people's resistant meanings and meaning-making practices. She writes that such perseverance "shows the power of communities of the oppressed in constituting resistant meaning . . . against the constitution of meaning and social organization by power. In our colonized, racially gendered, oppressed existences we are also other than what the hegemon makes us be" (746). Lugones proposes as a central task of decolonial feminism the work of "learning about each other as resistors to the coloniality of gender," a task that requires, in her words, "a furthering of the logic of difference and multiplicity and of coalition" (755). Lugones's emphasis on everyday forms of intimate relationality as important sites of decolonial resistance and meaning making highlights the importance of the *transfeministas'* work in resignifying the family in Ecuador. By opening up the definition of the family, the transfeministas' work not only promotes the flourishing of a multiplicity of modes of intimate relationality but also can help to make these modes of relationality visible in a way that enables us to learn about the resistant meanings and practices potentially embedded in them.

Such a multiplicitous resignification of the family—one that makes room for a variety of relational forms—echoes the emphasis on multiplicity in the concept of plurinationalism. Indeed, if the constitutional embrace of Ecuador as plurinational challenges the hegemony of the monocultural, uninational model of the state, the inclusion of the notion of the diverse family in the 2008 Constitution challenges the hegemony of the heteronormative nuclear family. Further, even though the struggles to resignify the nation as plurinational and to resignify the family as diverse were rooted primarily in particular movements, activists within these movements worked to open up the terms to link with other groups more broadly. For example, Chuji (2008) argued that the concept of plurinationalism could have broad implications for thinking about multiple differences: "In Ecuador, the concept of plurinationalism has been proposed by the indigenous movement to challenge the racism, exclusion, and violence that has characterized the relationship of the modern nation-state with indigenous peoples, but plurinationalism can also generate conditions of possibility for the state recognition for gender diversity, for example. . . . Plurinationalism is not only a concept having to do with ethnicity, it is a concept that opens the social contract to multiple differences, be they differences of ethnicity, or of gender, or of culture, or of age, etc." Similarly, the transfeministas worked to open up the term *family* in a way that would enable many groups to claim it and would open up spaces for multiple modes of relationality. In the words of Vásquez (2008), such an approach takes up the "overwhelming diversity of families that exist," families that are distinct because they are grounded in "different understandings of solidarity, different circumstances, different arrangements for survival, love, and even chances that often have nothing to do with sex." These, she

Christine "Cricket" Keating & Amy Lind

explains, "are the 'other families' that are demanding basic protections in the constitutional process."

Chuji's and Vásquez's formulations of the notions of plurinationalism and the diverse family are both deeply open ended. While the multiplicity at the heart of the concepts of plurinationalism and the diverse family takes up and links already-existing identities and communities, Chuji's and Vásquez's insistence on keeping the concepts open leaves room for yet-unknown and yet-unnamed possibilities for solidarity.

CONTROVERSY, COMPROMISE, AND CHALLENGE

This redefinition of the family was deeply controversial in the assembly. Protests from conservative assembly members from within the Alianza PAís, in particular Rosana Queirolo and Diana Acosta, threatened to undercut support for passage of the new constitution. On the assembly floor, for example, Queirolo argued, "For thousands of years, the family has been always a natural institution, whose meaning should not be changed. . . . We cannot change the meaning of family in this new Constitution, I don't know any constitution in the world that might be committing this barbarity" (quoted in Hoffman 2008). In response to this opposition within his party, Correa acquiesced to a compromise that would enable same-sex couples as well as others to form free unions that would be recognized by the state, while barring gay couples from marrying or adopting children. In a statement published shortly after a meeting with Queirolo and other conservative members, Alianza PAís published a statement explaining its position that "the state will strengthen the family as a nuclear unit of society. Marriage will continue to be the union of a man and a woman, recognizing free unions" (quoted in *El Comercio* 2008). Given these positions, Articles 67 and 68 were amended to read as follows:

> Article 67. The family in its diverse forms is recognized. The State shall protect it as the fundamental core of society and shall guarantee conditions that integrally favor the achievement of its goals. They shall be comprised of legal or common-law ties and shall be based on the equality of rights and the opportunities of their members.
>
> Marriage is the union of man and woman and shall be based on the free consent of the persons entering into this bond and on the equality of rights, obligations and legal capacity.

Article 68. The stable and monogamous union between two persons without any other marriage ties who have a common-law home, for the lapse of time and under the conditions and circumstances provided for by law, shall enjoy the same rights and obligations of those families bound by formal marriage ties.

Adoption shall only be permitted for different-gender couples. (República del Ecuador 2008)

This juxtaposition of the constitutional embrace of the family in its diverse forms and the subsequent restrictions on same-sex marriage and adoption in these articles is, of course, deeply contradictory.

Despite these limits and contradictions, activists in Ecuador have worked to make sure that the constitutional commitments to the protection of the family in its diverse forms translate into concrete policy changes and advances. As legal activist Verónica Potes (2012) explains, "The 2008 Constitution made important advances in the recognition of diversity.... Since then there have been efforts by stakeholders and activists (individuals and groups) who work so that these laws, rights, freedoms and guarantees do not remain simple statements on paper." Potes notes that although advances have been difficult, there have been notable successes in pushing forward the notion of diverse families. For example, activists have pressed the state to grant same-sex couples the same benefits received by heterosexual married couples. One important achievement in this realm was that in 2011, for the first time in Ecuador, a lesbian widow, Janneth Peña, was able to gain full pension and social security benefits upon the death of her partner, Thalía Álvarez Carvallo. Carvallo had been a feminist and LGBTQI activist and had worked with the Constituent Assembly in 2007 and 2008 on issues of gender and sexual rights. Peña noted that the ruling was in part a legacy of Carvallo's hard work in the assembly: "She fought to include Article 68 in the Constitution, which says that the stable and monogamous union between two people without matrimonial ties constitutes a family that generates the same rights and obligations as those of families joined through marriage. Now our ideal is realized" (quoted in *El Comercio* 2011).

In another milestone in the struggle for legal recognition for diverse families in Ecuador, in July 2018 the Constitutional Court overturned a 2012 ruling that barred two lesbians from registering as joint mothers of their daughter, Satya Amani. In explaining the significance of the case for Ecuadorian family law, Constitutional Court justice Tatiana Ordeñana (2018) explained that the ruling was an important step toward, in her words, "the recognition of the diversity of families within Ecuador" and noted that the ruling established an opening not only for same-sex couples but also "for the general recognition of all models of the family."

In June 2019, after years of struggle by LGBTQI activists and petitions by same-sex couples to have their unions recognized as marriages, the Constitutional Court issued a ruling that legalized same-sex marriage in Ecuador. In their ruling, the court declared the restrictions on same-sex marriage in both the Civil Code and the Organic Law of Identity and Civil Data Management to be unconstitutional. Noting that the Constitution must be interpreted in the sense that favors rights for all, they urged the "National Assembly to fully review the rest of the legal provisions on civil marriage, in order for it to provide spouses of the same sex with the same treatment that is granted to couples of different sex" (Corte Constitucional 2019). Legalizing same-sex marriage was an important step in resolving the deep contradiction between the 2008 Constitution's affirmation of diverse forms of the family and its incongruous restrictions on marriage.

Among the ongoing struggles toward the fruition of the concept of the diverse family in Ecuadorian life is Proyecto Transgénero's work to gain legal recognition for a family of several trans sex workers who live as "street sisters," sharing "housing and economic solidarity without being related by blood, by marriage, or by any relationship of spousal or equivalent type" (Proyecto Transgénero n.d.). Besides being groundbreaking in terms of challenging the legal system to extend protection and recognition to an unconventional family, it is also innovative in its political and legal process, as the litigants engaged in a process of photographing their everyday lives in order to demonstrate their lives together as a family. Although it is on hold for the moment, the case represents an important intervention toward making visible the diverse ways in which, in the words of Vásquez (2008), "human beings make—and live—family."

CONCLUSION

The concepts of plurinationalism and la familia diversa/the diverse family— have important implications for thinking about transnational feminist praxis. From a transnational feminist perspective, the plurinationalist critique of uninationalism can be useful in adding to transnational feminist critiques of the state and can provide another lens through which to critically interrogate who is being included and who is being left out in understandings of the "national," even in feminist analyses; it also underscores the multiplicity of feminisms within different contexts. These concepts also form the groundwork of an alternative structuring of the state, one rooted in a commitment to the autonomy and self-determination of nations and communities and to the self-definition of families within it—even if, as in Ecuador, the struggle for a gender-just plurinational and intercultural state is far from complete. Indeed, given the contradictions within the Constitution itself, with its juxtaposition of the language of the diverse family with restrictions on same-sex marriage and adoption, as well as the varied ways that the implementation of the concept of plurinationalism has been limited and forestalled, it might be tempting to understand the resignification of the nation and the family as merely changes on paper, ones that do not fundamentally shift or challenge the hegemony of racialized heteronormative understandings of political and social life in Ecuador. While certainly acknowledging these limitations, we do not want to lose sight of the resignifications as tremendously momentous achievements. As Vásquez suggests, "Institutions, especially legal ones, operate by naming—or sometimes more significantly—by leaving things unnamed. I think that to contest this mode of institutionalization with our own definitions is one of the most powerful forms of subversion, above all for people who historically have been defined by others who have been made invisible" (quoted in Lind and Pazmiño 2009, 100).

In Ecuador we have an important example of the constitutional codification of alternatives to the hegemony of the monocultural state and the heteronormative family. What remains to be seen, of course, is how these changes will manifest in people's lives and how the limits and contradictions embedded in the Constitution will be pushed both on the democratic collective level and in an everyday sense. In doing this work in Ecuador, Indigenous groups, LGBTQI groups, feminist groups, groups fighting for environmental justice, and others face the difficult political challenge of not only a hostile right-wing opposition but also a left-wing government that helped to facilitate the decolonial resignifications in the 2008 Constitution but subsequently became obstructionist as groups worked to use these constitutional gains in struggles for justice. Indeed, activists across a number of sectors were deeply critical of Correa owing to the government's aggressive pursuit of mining and oil exploration on Indigenous lands and its violent crackdown on social movements and activists. Protesters argued that with actions such as these, the government betrayed both the spirit and the fundamental principles of the political project that brought the Alianza PAÍS to power in 2006 and that soon thereafter were codified in the 2008 Constitution.

Observers had hoped that Lenín Moreno, Correa's successor as Ecuador's president, might work toward a more conciliatory relationship with its social movements. These hopes were dashed, however, when, shortly after his election in 2017, he shifted sharply to the right and infuriated Indigenous groups, feminists, environmentalists, workers' rights activists, and students, among others, for his stance on questions of public spending, trade liberalization, oil drilling, and abortion, as well as over his deals with the United States military and the International Monetary Fund. Tensions came to a head in October 2019, when Moreno signed an austerity package that would cut public salaries and fuel subsidies in order to comply with IMF credit conditions. In response, CONAIE led a massive, two-week demonstration in Quito in protest. The protests were successful and Moreno was forced to withdraw the package. This victory, however, came at a terrible cost, with seven protesters killed, scores more injured, and more than 2000 arrested (Higgins 2019). Despite these ongoing challenges, Vásquez urges people to be bold and creative in putting the innovative principles of Ecuador's 2008 Constitution into practice. In her words, "the transformative potential of these legal innovations is developed only through their use. If they are not used, they will not develop. If they are used only timidly or conventionally, they develop less than if they were used ambitiously or creatively" (quoted in Lind and Pazmiño 2009).

In this chapter we have highlighted resignifications of the nation and of the family as important decolonial political interventions in Ecuador, ones that can be potentially instructive in struggles for social change more generally. A central task of transnational feminist pedagogy is to challenge the way that states—especially the US state—act to suppress learning about political innovations in other contexts. The stakes of such suppression are tremendously high, given the ways in which epistemic suppression enables geopolitical violence, both within states and between them. The transnational feminist flip side of that equation is that epistemic openness can enable geopolitical solidarity. Indeed, learning about each other's political innovations can help generate transnational feminist coalitions in which we can back up each other's political interventions and cutting-edge ideas as well as foster the expansion of our political imaginations in ways that enable the building of transformative alternatives. One of the most notable features of the struggle for just significations in Ecuador is the coalitional open-endedness of the resignifications themselves: the ways, for example, that the concept of the plurinational and intercultural state can be used to animate LGBTQI movements for justice or that the notion of la familia diversa can be conceptualized to include all kinds of nonnormative families. Struggles in Ecuador and beyond can draw on this model to generate coalitional approaches that weave together not only alternative imaginaries but also the movements themselves.

ACKNOWLEDGMENTS

We are deeply grateful to both Ashwini Tambe and Millie Thayer for their wonderful work in conceptualizing this volume and for all their efforts in making it a reality. We also would like to give our heartfelt thanks to Ana Almeida, Maylei Blackwell, Diego López, María Lugones, Elizabeth Vásquez, Virginia Villamediana, and Maria Amelia Viteri for thinking closely with us about the ideas in the chapter.

NOTES

Portions of this chapter were previously published as "Plural Sovereignty and the Diverse Family in Ecuador's 2008 Constitution," *Feminist Studies* 43, no. 2 (2017): 291–313.

1 The sixteen points are listed online in a website project by Marc Becker that seeks to make archival material from the Indigenous movement in Ecuador more accessible. See CONAIE (1990).

2 Unless otherwise noted, all translations from the original Spanish are the authors' own.

3 Alianza PAIS was founded as a political party in 2006. The acronym PAIS is derived from *Patria Altiva y Soberana* (Proud and Sovereign Homeland). Of course, PAIS is also a homonym for *país*, which means "is also" in Spanish. For these reasons, Alianza PAIS is also commonly referred to as Alianza País.

4 Catherine Walsh, interview with author, Quito, Ecuador, January 30, 2015.

Abeysekera, Sunila. 2013. "Transnational Feminisms." In *Gender: The Key Concepts*, edited by Mary Evans and Caroline Williams, 208–15. New York: Routledge.

Abram, Ruth. 1978. Introduction to *Perspectives on Non-sexist Early Childhood Education*, edited by Barbara Sprung, 1–19. New York: Teachers College Press.

Abramovitz, Mimi. 2017. *Regulating the Lives of Women: Social Welfare Policy from Colonial Times to the Present*. 3rd ed. New York: Routledge.

Abu-Lughod, Lila. 2015. *Do Muslim Women Need Saving?* Cambridge, MA: Harvard University Press.

Ackland, Richard. 2014. "Surrogacy Is Still Available to Paedophiles. This Must Change—But How?" *Guardian,* August 15, 2014. https://www.theguardian.com/commentisfree/2014/aug/15/surrogacy-is-still-available-to-paedophiles-this-must-change-but-how.

Acosta, Alberto. 2009. "El estado plurinacional, puerta para una sociedad democrática." In *Plurinacionalidad: Democracia en la diversidad,* edited by Alberto Acosta and Esperanza Martínez. Santiago, Chile: Editorial Universidad Bolivariana.

Adey, Peter, David Bissell, Kevin Hannam, Peter Merriman, and Mimi Sheller, eds. 2017. *The Routledge Handbook of Mobilities*. London: Routledge.

AFPQC. 2016. "Mozambique: Une Espagnole expulsée pour manifestation 'illégale' liée au port de mini-jupes." *Huffington Post*, March 30, 2016. https://quebec.huffingtonpost.ca/2016/03/30/mozambique-une-espagnole-expulsee-pour-manifestation-illegale-liee-au-port-de-mini-jupes_n_9575336.html.

Albornoz, Consuelo, and María Belén Albornoz. 2010. *La esfera pública en la blogosfera política ecuatoriana*. Quito: Facultad Latinoamericana de Ciencias Sociales Sede Ecuador.

Alexander, M. Jacqui. 1991. "Redrafting Morality: The Postcolonial State and the Sexual Offenses Bill of Trinidad and Tobago." In *Third World Women and the Politics of Feminism*, edited by Chandra Mohanty, Ann Russo, and Lourdes Torres, 113–52. Bloomington: Indiana University Press.

Alexander, M. Jacqui. 2006. *Pedagogies of Crossing: Meditations on Feminism, Sexual Politics, Memory, and the Sacred*. Durham, NC: Duke University Press.

Alexander, M. Jacqui, and Chandra Talpade Mohanty, eds. 1997. *Feminist Genealogies, Colonial Legacies, Democratic Futures*. New York: Routledge.

Ali, Nosheen, Mona Bhan, Sahana Ghosh, Hafsa Kanjwal, Zunaira Komal, Deepti Misri, Shruti Mukherjee, Nishant Upadhyay, Saiba Varma, and Ather Zia. 2019. "Geographies of Occupation in South Asia." *Feminist Studies* 45 (2–3): 574–80.

Allen, Anita L. 1991. "The Black Surrogate Mother." *Harvard BlackLetter Law Journal*, no. 8, 17–31.

Almeida, Ana. 2010. "'Las hermanas Lafayette.'" *Género, Justicia y Derechos Humanos* (blog), October 19, 2010. http://paralegalidades.blogspot.com/2010/10/las-hermanas-lafayette.html.

Alonso, Márcio. 2001. "Fenômeno de saias no futebol." *O Campeão da Rede*, April 14, 2001.

Alvarez, Sonia E. 1990. *Engendering Democracy in Brazil: Women's Movements in Transition Politics*. Princeton, NJ: Princeton University Press.

Alvarez, Sonia E. 1999. "Advocating Feminism: The Latin American Feminist NGO 'Boom.'" *International Feminist Journal of Politics* 1 (2): 181–209.

Alvarez, Sonia E. 2009. "Beyond NGO-ization? Reflections from Latin America." *Development*, no. 52, 175–84.

Alvarez, Sonia E. 2014. "Para além da sociedade civil: Reflexões sobre o campo feminista," *Cadernos Pagú*, no. 43: 13–56, https://doi.org/10.1590/0104-8333201400430013.

Alvarez, Sonia E., Claudia de Lima Costa, Verónica Feliu, Rebecca J. Hester, Norma Klahn, and Millie Thayer, eds. 2014. *Translocalities/Translocalidades: Feminist Politics of Translation in the Latin/a Américas*. Durham, NC: Duke University Press.

Alvarez, Sonia E., Elisabeth Jay Friedman, Ericka Beckman, Maylei Blackwell, Norma Stoltz Chinchilla, Nathalie Lebon, Marysa Navarro, and Marcela Ríos Tobar. 2002. "Encountering Latin American and Caribbean Feminisms." *Signs: Journal of Women in Culture and Society* 28 (2): 537–79.

Alves, José Eustáquio Diniz, and Sônia Corrêa. 2003. "Demografia e ideologia: Trajetos históricos e os desafios do Cairo + 10." *Revista Brasileira de Estudos de População* 20 (2): 129–56.

Amar, Paul. 2013. *The Security Archipelago: Human-Security States, Sexuality Politics, and the End of Neoliberalism*. Durham, NC: Duke University Press.

Amos, Valerie, and Pratibha Parmar. 1984. "Challenging Imperial Feminism." *Feminist Review*, no. 17, 3–19.

Anzaldúa, Gloria. 2012. *Borderlands/La Frontera: The New Mestiza*. 4th ed. San Francisco: Aunt Lute Books.

Appadurai, Arjun. 1996. *Modernity at Large: Cultural Dimensions of Globalization*. Minneapolis: University of Minnesota Press.

Armijos, Maria Teresa. 2013. "'They Cannot Come and Impose on Us': Indigenous Autonomy and Resource Control through Collective Water Management in Highland Ecuador." *Radical History Review*, no. 116, 86–103.

Arnfred, Signe. 1990. "Notes on Gender and Modernisation—Examples from Mozambique." In *The Language of Development Studies*, edited by Signe Arnfred and Agnete Weis, 71–101. Copenhagen, Denmark: New Social Science Monographs.

Arthur, Maria José, and Zaida Cabral. 2004. "Essas gravidezes que embaraçam as escolas: Violação dos direitos humanos das jovens adolescentes." *Outras Vozes 7*. http://www.wlsa.org.mz/artigo/essas-gravidezes-que-embaracam-as-escolas-violacao-dos-direitos-humanos-das-jovens-adolescentes.

ASCHA (Associação Sócio-Cultural Horizonte Azul). 2018. "Relatório do Fórum Distrital de Género, Cultura, Segurança e Políticas Públicas para a Rapariga e Mulher Jovem." Distrito Municipal KaMaxakeni, December 12–13, Maputo, Mozambique.

Australian Broadcasting Network. 2011. "Surrogacy." Episode of *Overnights with Trevor Chappell*, January 21, 2011. https://www.abc.net.au/radio/programs/overnights/surrogacy/7737398.

Bacchetta, Paola, and Margaret Power, eds. 2013. *Right Wing Women: From Conservatives to Extremists around the World*. New York: Routledge.

Bacon, David. 2004. *The Children of NAFTA: Labor Wars on the U.S./Mexico Border*. Berkeley: University of California Press.

Badri, Balghis, and Aili Mari Tripp, eds. 2017. *Women's Activism in Africa*. London: Zed Books.

Bailey, Alison. 2011. "Reconceiving Surrogacy: Toward a Reproductive Justice Account of Indian Surrogacy." In "Feminist Ethics and Social Theory," edited by Diane T. Meyers. Special issue, *Hypatia* 26 (4): 715–41.

Banerjee, Amrita. 2013. "Race and a Transnational Reproductive Caste System: Indian Transnational Surrogacy." *Hypatia* 29 (1): 113–28.

Banet-Weiser, Sarah. 2018. *Empowered: Popular Feminism and Popular Misogyny*. Durham, NC: Duke University Press.

Barbosa, Mariana Granato. 2013. "Todo brinquedo é unissex?" Accessed July 23, 2017, http://maesamigas.com.br/todo-brinquedo-e-unissex/.

Barbosa, Fábia Cristina Mendes, and Helisangela Andrade. 2017. "Gênero na prática: Uma educaçao não-sexista nas escolas." Seminário Internacional Fazendo Gênero, 11th and 13th Women's Worlds Congress, Anais Eletrônicos (Electronic annals), July 30–August 4, 2017, Florianópolis, Brazil.

Barnett, Evelyn Brooks. 1978. "Nannie Burroughs and the Education of Black Women." In *The Afro-American Woman: Struggles and Images*, edited by Sharon Harley and Rosalyn Terborg-Penn, 97–108. Port Washington, NY: Kennikat.

Basu, Amrita, ed. 2010. *Women's Movements in the Global Era: The Power of Local Feminisms*. San Francisco: Westview.

Baxi, Pratiksha. 2013. "We Must Resist the Cunning of Judicial Reform." *Critical Legal Thinking* (blog), January 9, 2013. https://criticallegalthinking.com/2013/01/09/we-must-resist-the-cunning-of-judicial-reform.

Baxi, Pratiksha. 2015. "Law, Visuality and Sexual Violence: Leslee Udwin's *India's Daughter*." Mukta Salve Lecture Series, Krantijyoti Savitribai Phule Women's Studies Centre, Savitribai Phule Pune University, March 14, 2015.

BBC News. 2018. "How WhatsApp Helped Turn an Indian Village into a Lynch Mob." July 18, 2018. https://www.bbc.co.uk/news/world-asia-india-44856910.

Bear, Laura, Karen Ho, Anna Lowenhaupt Tsing, and Sylvia Yanagisako. 2015. "Gens: A Feminist Manifesto for the Study of Capitalism." Society for Cultural Anthropology, March 30, 2015. https://culanth.org/fieldsights/652-gens-a-feminist-manifesto-for-the-study-of-capitalism.

Becker, Marc. 2008. *Indians and Leftists in the Making of Ecuador's Modern Indigenous Movements*. Durham, NC: Duke University Press.

Becker, Marc. 2011. *¡Pachakutik! Indigenous Movements and Electoral Politics in Ecuador*. Lanham, MD: Rowman and Littlefield.

Belkhir, Jean Ait. 2009. "The 'Johnny's Story': Founder of the Race, Gender, and Class Journal." In *The Intersectional Approach: Transforming the Academy through Race, Class, and Gender*, edited by Michelle Tracy Berger and Kathleen Guidroz, 303–38. Chapel Hill: University of North Carolina Press.

Bellos, Alex. 2014. *Futebol: The Brazilian Way of Life*. New York: Bloomsbury.

Beraldo, Marcon. [n.d.] "Sissi dá a volta por cima e é campeã nos Estados Unidos." *O Estado de São Paulo*.

Bergeron, Suzanne, and Stephen Healy. 2015. "Beyond the 'Business Case': A Community Economies Approach to Gender, Development and Social Economy." In *Social and Solidarity Economy beyond the Fringe*, edited by Peter Utting, 72–85. London: Zed Books.

Berlant, Lauren, ed. 2000. *Intimacy*. Chicago: University of Chicago Press.

Bernstein, Elizabeth. 2007. *Temporarily Yours: Intimacy, Authenticity, and the Commerce of Sex*. Chicago: University of Chicago Press.

Bernstein, Mary, and Nancy A. Naples. 2010. "Sexual Citizenship and the Pursuit of Relationship Recognition Policies in Australia and the U.S." *Women's Studies Quarterly* 38 (1–2): 132–56.

Bernstein, Mary, and Nancy A. Naples. 2015. "Altared States: Legal Structuring and Relationship Recognition in the United States, Canada, and Australia." *American Sociological Review* 80 (6): 1226–49.

Bernstein, Mary, and Verta Taylor. 2013. "The Debate Over Marriage in the Lesbian and Gay Movement." In *The Marrying Kind: Debating Same-Sex Marriage Within the Lesbian and Gay Movement*, edited by Mary Bernstein and Verta Taylor, 1–35. Minneapolis: University of Minnesota Press.

Bharadwaj, Aditya. 2006. "Sacred Modernity: Religion, Infertility, and Techno-scientific Conception around the Globe." In "Sacred Conceptions: Religion and the Global Practice of IVF." Special issue, *Culture, Medicine, and Psychiatry* 30 (4): 423–25.

Biella, Andrea Alexandra do Amaral Silva, Nádia Conceição Vernes Almeida, and Roseli Kubo Gonzalez. 2010. "Consumption of Toys: A Gender Deviation." *Olhar de Professor* 13 (2): 255–66.

Bignall, Simone, and Paul Patton. 2010. *Deleuze and the Postcolonial*. Edinburgh: Edinburgh University Press.

Bittencourt, Carla, and Michele Chaluppe. 2001. "Futebol pra homem? Eles e elas debatem o mais masculino dos esportes." *Lance!*

Bliss, James. 2016. "Black Feminism Out of Place." *Signs: Journal of Women in Culture and Society* 41 (4): 727–49.

Briggs, Laura. 2003a. "Mother, Child, Race, and Nation: The Visual Iconography of Rescue and the Politics of Transnational and Transracial Adoption." *Gender and History* 15 (2): 179–200.

Briggs, Laura. 2003b. *Reproducing Empire: Race, Sex, Science and U.S. Imperialism in Puerto Rico*. Berkeley: University of California Press.

Briggs, Laura, Gladys McCormick, and J. T. Way. 2008. "Transnationalism: A Category of Analysis." *American Quarterly* 60 (3): 625–48.

Burton, Antoinette. 1994. *Burdens of History: British Feminists, Indian Women, and Imperial Culture, 1865–1915*. Chapel Hill: University of North Carolina Press.

Burton, Antoinette. 1998. "Some Trajectories of 'Feminism' and 'Imperialism.'" *Gender and History* 10 (3): 558–68.

Caetano, André Junqueira. 2014. "Esterilização cirúrgica feminine no Brasil, 2000–2006: Aderência à lei de planejamento familiar e demanda frustrada." *Revista Brasileira de Estudos de População* 31 (2): 309–31.

Caetano, André Junqueira, and Joseph E. Potter. 2004. "Politics and Female Sterilization in Northeast Brazil." *Population and Development Review* 30 (1): 79–108.

Caldwell, Kia. 2007. *Negras in Brazil: Re-envisioning Black Women, Citizenship, and the Politics of Identity*. New Brunswick, NJ: Rutgers University Press.

Canaday, Margot. 2009. *The Straight State: Sexuality and Citizenship in Twentieth-Century America*. Princeton, NJ: Princeton University Press.

Carastathis, Anna. 2016. *Intersectionality: Origins, Contestations, Horizons*. Lincoln: University of Nebraska Press.

Carby, Hazel V. 1999. *Cultures in Babylon: Black Britain and African America*. London: Verso.

Carby, Hazel V. 2000. "White Woman Listen! Black Feminism and the Boundaries of Sisterhood." In *Black British Culture and Society*, edited by Kwesi Owusu, 82–88. Abingdon, UK: Routledge.

Cartwright, Lisa. 2005. "Images of 'Waiting Children': Spectatorship and Pity in the Representation of the Global Social Orphan in the 1990s." In *Cultures of Transnational Adoption*, edited by Toby Alice Volkman, 185–212. Durham, NC: Duke University Press.

Casimiro, Isabel Maria. 1999. "Paz na terra, guerra em casa: Feminismo e organizações de mulheres em Moçambique." Master's thesis, Universidade de Coimbra, Portugal.

Casimiro, Isabel Maria. 2003. "Feminism and Women's Human Rights." In *Outras Vozes* (Suplemento do Boletim no. 3, WLSA Moçambique): 26–27.

Casimiro, Isabel Maria. 2014. *Paz na terra, guerra em casa: Feminismo e organizações de mulheres em Moçambique*. Maputo, Mozambique: Edição PROMÉDIA.

Casimiro, Isabel Maria. 2016. "Criminalization of Feminist Activists and Social Movements in Mozambique." *Spotlight Magazine*, no. 39. http://archiv.vidc .org/news/spotlight-392016/criminalization-of-feminist-activists-and -social-movements-in-mozambique/index.html.

Castilho, Inês. 1985. "O Plano do Ministério mudando mentalidades." *Mulherio* 5 (21): 10.

Castro, Luis Alberto Tuaza, and Maria Alexandra Ocles. 2012. *Political Representation and Social Inclusion: Ecuador Case Study*. New York: The Americas Society and Council of the Americas. https://www.as-coa.org/sites/default /files/EcuadorFINAL.pdf.

Ceregatti, Alessandra, with Brigitte Verdière, Célia Alldridge, Miriam Nobre, and Nathalia Capellini. 2008. *Marcha Mundial de las Mujeres: Una década de lucha internacional feminista*. São Paulo, Brazil: SOF–Sempreviva Organização Feminista. http://www.inmujer.gob.es/publicacioneselectronicas /documentacion/Documentos/DE1196.pdf.

Chakrabarty, Dipesh. 2007. *Provincializing Europe: Postcolonial Thought and Historical Difference*. Princeton, NJ: Princeton University Press.

Champine, Riley D. 2018. "See Which World Cup Teams Have the Most Foreign-Born Players." *National Geographic*, July 2018. https://www.national geographic.com/magazine/2018/07/world-cup-fifa-soccer-players-national -teams-foreign-born.

Chang, Robert S., and Jerome McCristal Culp Jr. 2002. "After Intersectionality." *University of Missouri Kansas City Law Review* 71 (2): 485–91.

Chant, Sylvia. 2006. "Re-thinking the 'Feminization of Poverty' in Relation to Aggregate Gender Indices." *Journal of Human Development* 7 (2): 201–20.

Chernilo, Daniel. 2006. "Social Theory's Methodological Nationalism: Myth and Reality." *European Journal of Social Theory* 9 (1): 5–22.

Chow, Rey. 1993. *Writing Diaspora: Tactics of Intervention in Contemporary Cultural Studies*. Bloomington: Indiana University Press.

Chowdhury, Elora Halim. 2011. *Transnationalism Reversed: Women Organizing against Gendered Violence in Bangladesh*. Albany: State University of New York Press.

Chowdhury, Elora Halim, and Liz Philipose. 2016. *Dissident Friendships: Feminism, Imperialism, and Transnational Solidarity*. Urbana: University of Illinois Press.

Chubb, Laura. 2016. "Gay Dads in Australia Call for Government to Legalize Commercial Surrogacy." *Gay Star News*, May 28, 2016. https://www .gaystarnews.com/article/gay-dads-australia-legalize-commercial-surrogacy.

Chuji, Mónica. 2008. "Diez conceptos básicos sobre plurinacionalidad e interculturalidad." *Agencia Latinoamericana de Información*, April 8, 2008. https://www.alainet.org/es/active/23366.

Clifford, James. 1997. *Routes: Travel and Translation in the Late Twentieth Century*. Cambridge, MA: Harvard University Press.

Colen, Shellee. 1995. "Like a Mother to Them: Stratified Reproduction and West Indian Childcare Workers and Employers in New York." In *Conceiving the New World Order: The Global Politics of Reproduction*, edited by Faye D. Ginsberg and Rayna Rapp, 78–102. Berkeley: University of California Press.

Collins, Patricia Hill, and Sirma Bilge. 2016. *Intersectionality: Key Concepts*. Cambridge, UK: Polity.

Comaroff, Jean, and John L. Comaroff, eds. 2001. *Millennial Capitalism and the Culture of Neoliberalism*. Durham, NC: Duke University Press.

Comaroff, Jean, and John L. Comaroff. 2012. *Theory from the South: Or, How Euro-America Is Evolving toward Africa*. Boulder, CO: Paradigm.

El Comercio. 2008. "Asamblea aprueba cinco primeros artículos de nueva Constitución." April 1, 2008. http://www.elcomercio.com/noticias/Asamblea -aprueba-primeros-articulos-Constitucion_0_164984838.html.

El Comercio. 2011. "Una lesbiana recibió pensión de montepío por su pareja fallecida." December 14, 2011. http://www.elcomercio.com/sintesis -noticiosa/Redaccion_Sociedad_0_608939332.html.

Comissão Parlamentar Mista de Inquérito. 1993. *Relatório final*. Brasilia: Congresso Nacional.

CLADEM (Committee for Latin America and the Caribbean for the Defense of Women's Rights). n.d. "Educación no sexista y antidiscriminatoria." Accessed July 20, 2019. https://cladem.org/campanha-educacion-no-sexista/.

CONAIE (Confederation of Indigenous Nationalities of Ecuador). 1990. "Los 16 puntos." E-Archivo Ecuatoriano, website of Mark Becker. http://www .yachana.org/earchivo/conaie/hoy_en.php.

CONAIE (Confederation of Indigenous Nationalities of Ecuador). 2007a. *Constitución del estado plurinacional de la república del Ecuador: Propuesta de la Confederación de Nacionalidades Indígenas del Ecuador*. Quito: CONAIE. https://www.yachana.org/earchivo/conaie/propuesta_constitucion_conaie.pdf.

CONAIE (Confederation of Indigenous Nationalities of Ecuador). 2007b. "Propuesta de la CONAIE frente a la Asamblea Constituyente: Principios y lineamientos para la nueva constitución del Ecuador." Quito: CONAIE. https://www.yachana.org/earchivo/conaie/ConaiePropuestaAsamblea.pdf.

Connelly, Matthew. 2006. "Seeing beyond the State: The Population Control Movement and the Problem of Sovereignty." *Past and Present*, no. 193, 197–233.

Connelly, Matthew. 2008. *Fatal Misconceptions: The Struggle to Control World Population*. Cambridge, MA: Harvard University Press.

Conway, Janet M. 2008. "Geographies of Transnational Feminisms: The Politics of Place and Scale in the World March of Women." *Social Politics: International Studies in Gender, State and Society* 15 (2): 207–31.

Conway, Janet M. 2017. "Troubling Transnational Feminism(s): Theorizing Activist Praxis." *Feminist Theory* 18 (2): 205–27.

Corrêa, Sonia Onufer. 1982. "Projeto: Causas e condições da esterilização feminina voluntária na região metropolitana do Recife, ou, Por que as mulheres da periferia ligam as trompas? O que aconteceu depois? O que significa isso do ponto de vista da estratégia política da reprodução humana?" Unpublished report. Recife, Brazil: SOS Corpo.

Corrêa, Sonia Onufer. 1989. "Uma recusa da maternidade?" In *Os direitos reprodutivos e a condição feminina: Textos*, 26–38. Recife, Brazil: SOS Corpo.

Corrêa, Sonia, with Rebecca Reichmann. 1994. *Population and Reproductive Rights: Feminist Perspectives from the South*. Boston: Zed Books.

Corte Constitucional de Ecuador. 2019. Caso 10–18-CN. http://portal
.corteconstitucional.gob.ec:8494/BuscadorRelatoria.aspx.

Cowan, Benjamin Arthur. 2017. "How Machismo Got Its Spurs—in English: Social Science, Cold War Imperialism, and the Ethnicization of Hypermasculinity." *Latin American Research Review* 52 (4): 606–22.

Crenshaw, Kimberlé. 1989. "Demarginalizing the Intersection of Race and Sex: A Black Feminist Critique of Antidiscrimination Doctrine, Feminist Theory and Antiracist Politics." *University of Chicago Legal Forum* 1989 (1): 138–67.

Crenshaw, Kimberlé. 1991. "Mapping the Margins: Intersectionality, Identity Politics, and Violence against Women of Color." *Stanford Law Review* 43 (6): 1241–99.

Cresswell, Tim, and Peter Merriman, eds. 2013. *Geographies of Mobilities: Practices, Spaces, Subjects*. Farnham, UK: Ashgate.

Cross, Gary. 1997. *Kids' Stuff: Toys and the Changing World of American Childhood*. Cambridge, MA: Harvard University Press.

Cushman, John H., Jr. 1998. "Nike Pledges to End Child Labor and Apply U.S. Rules Abroad." International Business, *New York Times*, May 13, 1998. https://www.nytimes.com/1998/05/13/business/international-business
-nike-pledges-to-end-child-labor-and-apply-us-rules-abroad.html.

Cuthbert, Denise, and Patricia Fronek. 2014. "Perfecting Adoption? Reflections on the Rise of Commercial Offshore Surrogacy and Family Formation in Australia." In *Families, Policy and the Law*, edited by Alan Hayes and Daryl Higgins, 55–66. Melbourne: Australian Institute of Family Studies.

Da Costa, Dia. 2018. "Academically-Transmitted Caste Innocence." *Raiot* (blog), August 23, 2018. http://raiot.in/academically-transmitted-caste
-innocence.

Damasco, Mariana Santos. 2009. "Feminismo negro: Raça, identidade e saúde reprodutiva no Brasil (1975–1996)." Master's thesis, Fiocruz, Rio de Janeiro.

Dasgupta, Sayantani, and Shamita Das Dasgupta. 2010. "Motherhood Jeopardized: Reproductive Technologies in Indian Communities." In *The Globalization of Motherhood: Deconstructions and Reconstructions of Biology and Care*, edited by Wendy Chavkin and JaneMaree Maher, 131–53. New York: Routledge.

Davis, Angela Y. 1983. *Women, Race and Class*. New York: Vintage.

De Aza Mejía, Carmen C. n.d. "Article de Carmen C. De Aza Mejía." Accessed July 20, 2019. http://www.educando.edu.do/files/5313/4030/8627/Dia _Internacional_Educacion_No_Sexista.pdf.

Deeb-Sossa, Natalia. 2007. "Helping the 'Neediest of the Needy': An Intersectional Analysis of Moral-Identity Construction at a Community Health Clinic." *Gender and Society* 21 (5): 749–72.

De la Dehesa, Rafael. 2010. *Queering the Public Sphere in Mexico and Brazil: Sexual Rights Movements in Emerging Democracies.* Durham, NC: Duke University Press.

De la Dehesa, Rafael. 2014. "In Brazil, AIDS Activism Led to Political Connections." Room for Debate, "Why Is Latin America So Progressive on Gay Rights?" *New York Times*, January 29, 2014. https://www.nytimes.com /roomfordebate/2014/01/29/why-is-latin-america-so-progressive-on-gay -rights/in-brazil-aids-activism-led-to-political-connections.

De la Dehesa, Rafael. 2019. "Social Medicine, Feminism and the Politics of Population: From Transnational Knowledge Networks to National Social Movements in Brazil and Mexico." *Global Public Health* 14 (6–7): 803–16.

Deleuze, Gilles, and Félix Guattari. 1987. *A Thousand Plateaus: Capitalism and Schizophrenia.* Translated by Brian Massumi. London: Continuum.

della Porta, Donatella, and Sidney Tarrow. 2012. "Interactive Diffusion: The Co-evolution of Police and Protest Behavior with Application to Transnational Contention." *Comparative Politics Studies* 45 (1): 119–52.

Dempsey, Deborah. 2013. "Surrogacy, Gay Male Couples and the Significance of Biogenetic Paternity." *New Genetics and Society* 32 (1): 37–53.

Denvir, Daniel. 2008. "Whither Ecuador? An Interview with Indigenous Activist and Politician Monica Chuji." *Upside Down World*, November 6, 2008. http:// upsidedownworld.org/main/ecuador-archives-49/1563-whither-ecuador -aninterview-with-indigenous-activist-and-politician-monica-chuji.

Deo, Nandini. 2018. "#MeToo Sparks Debate on Gender and Caste in Indian Feminism." *Fletcher Forum of World Affairs*, January 31, 2018. http://www .fletcherforum.org/home/2018/1/31/from-metoo-to-himtoo-gender-and -caste-in-indian-feminism.

Deomampo, Daisy. 2013. "Transnational Surrogacy in India: Interrogating Power and Women's Agency." *Frontiers: A Journal of Women's Studies* 34 (3): 167–88.

Deomampo, Daisy. 2016. *Transnational Reproduction: Race, Kinship, and Commercial Surrogacy in India.* New York: New York University Press.

Desai, Jigna, Danielle Bouchard, and Diane Detournay. 2010. "Disavowed Legacies and Honorable Thievery: The Work of the 'Transnational' in Feminist and LGBTQ Studies." In *Critical Transnational Feminist Praxis*, edited by Amanda Swarr and Richa Nagar, 46–62. Albany: State University of New York Press.

Donchin, Anne. 2010. "Reproductive Tourism and the Quest for Global Gender Justice." *Bioethics* 24 (7): 323–32.

Dufour, Pascale, and Isabelle Giraud. 2007. "Globalization and Political Change in the Women's Movement: The Politics of Scale and Political

Empowerment in the World March of Women." *Social Science Quarterly* 88 (5): 1152–73.

Duggan, Lisa. 2003. *The Twilight of Equality? Neoliberalism, Cultural Politics, and the Attack on Democracy.* Boston: Beacon.

Dutta, Debolina, and Oishik Sircar. 2013. "India's Winter of Discontent: Some Feminist Dilemmas in the Wake of a Rape." *Feminist Studies* 39 (1): 293–306.

Ehrick, Christine. 1998. "*Madrinas* and Missionaries: Uruguay and the Pan-American Women's Movement." *Gender and History* 10 (3): 406–24.

Elliott, Josh K. 2018. "India WhatsApp Killings: Why Mobs Are Lynching Outsiders over Fake Videos." *Global News*, July 16, 2018.

Eng, David L. 2010. *The Feeling of Kinship: Queer Liberalism and the Racialization of Kinship.* Durham, NC: Duke University Press.

Enloe, Cynthia. 1990. *Bananas, Beaches and Bases: Making Feminist Sense of International Politics.* Berkeley: University of California Press.

Escobar, Arturo. 2001. "Culture Sits in Places: Reflections on Globalism and Subaltern Strategies of Localization." *Political Geography*, no. 20, 139–74.

Evans, Richard J. 1977. *The Feminists: Women's Emancipation Movements in Europe, America and Australasia, 1840–1920.* New York: Routledge.

Ewig, Christina. 2006. "Hijacking Global Feminism: Feminists, the Catholic Church, and the Family Planning Debacle in Peru." *Feminist Studies* 32 (3): 632–59.

Falcón, Sylvanna M. 2016. *Power Interrupted: Antiracist and Feminist Activism inside the United Nations.* Seattle: University of Washington Press.

Falcón, Sylvanna M., and Jennifer C. Nash. 2015. "Shifting Analytics and Linking Theories: A Conversation about the 'Meaning-Making' of Intersectionality and Transnational Feminism." *Women's Studies International Forum*, no. 50, 1–10.

Family Court of Australia. 2016. "What Is a De Facto Relationship?" May 3, 2016. http://www.familycourt.gov.au/wps/wcm/connect/fcoaweb/family-law -matters/separation-and-divorce/defacto-relationships.

Farrow, Ronan. 2017. "Harvey Weinstein's Army of Spies." *New Yorker*, November 6, 2017. https://www.newyorker.com/news/news-desk/harvey -weinsteins-army-of-spies.

Farrow, Ronan. 2019. *Catch and Kill: Lies, Spies, and a Conspiracy to Protect Predators.* New York: Little, Brown.

Fass, Paula S. 2007. *Children of a New World: Society, Culture, and Globalization.* New York: New York University Press.

Felix, Beatriz. 2009. PINKSTINKS. "Our Campaigns." Accessed September 12, 2018, http://www.pinkstinks.co.uk/our-campaigns.html.

FeministsIndia. 2020. "Statement by Indian Feminists on the Police Violence That Killed George Floyd." *Mainstream Weekly*, June 6, 2020. http://www .mainstreamweekly.net/article9453.html.

Fernandes, Leela. 2013. *Transnational Feminism in the United States: Knowledge, Ethics, Power.* New York: New York University Press.

Finlayson, Lorna. 2019. "Travelling in the Wrong Direction." *London Review of Books*, July 4, 2019.

FirstPost staff. "Niharika Singh Shares Her #MeToo Account: Neo-liberal, Savarna Feminism Isn't Going to Liberate Anyone." FirstPost, November 10, 2018. https://www.firstpost.com/entertainment/niharika-singh-shares-her-metoo-account-neo-liberal-savarna-feminism-isnt-going-to-liberate-anyone-5528681.html.

Fisher, Caitlin Davis, and Jane Dennehy. 2015. "Body Projects: Making, Remaking, and Inhabiting the Woman's Futebol Body in Brazil." Sport in Society 18 (8): 995–1008.

Fixmer-Oraiz, Natalie. 2013. "Speaking of Solidarity: Transnational Gestational Surrogacy and the Rhetorics of Reproductive (In)Justice." Frontiers: A Journal of Women's Studies 34 (3): 126–63.

Fórum Mulher. 2006. "Comunicado: Não é controlando o vestuário das mulheres que se pode travar a epidemia do SIDA." Boletim Outras Vozes, no. 14.

Fórum Mulher. 2013. "Movimento da sociedade civil Moçambicana indignada pela tensão político-militar e com os raptos." WLSA, October 31, 2013. http://www.wlsa.org.mz/wp-content/uploads/2013/11/Manifesto.pdf.

Fórum Mulher. 2016a. "Mulheres e raparigas dão um Basta a violação dos seus direitos nas escolas." Press release. WLSA, March 17, 2016. http://www.wlsa.org.mz/contra-a-violaca-dos-direitos-das-raparigas-nas-escolas.

Fórum Mulher. 2016b. "Nós todas somos Eva." WLSA, March 31, 2016. http://www.wlsa.org.mz/comunicado-do-forum-mulher.

Franzini, Fábio. 2005. "Futebol é 'coisa para macho'? Pequeno esboço para uma história das mulheres no país do futebol." Revista Brasileira de História 25 (50): 315–28.

Friedman, Susan Stanford. 1998. "(Inter)disciplinarity and the Question of the Women's Studies Ph.D." Feminist Studies 24 (2): 301–25.

The George Washington University. n.d. "GW Women's, Gender, & Sexuality Studies Program." The Gender Equality Initiative in International Affairs. https://geia.elliott.gwu.edu/gw-womens-gender-and-sexuality-studies-program.

Gibson-Graham, J. K. 2006. The End of Capitalism (as We Knew It): A Feminist Critique of Political Economy. Minneapolis: University of Minnesota Press.

Gilligan, Carol, and Naomi Snider. 2018. Why Does Patriarchy Persist? Cambridge, UK: Polity.

Gilroy, Paul. 1990. "Nationalism, History and Ethnic Absolutism." History Workshop, no. 30, 114–20.

Gilroy, Paul. 1995. The Black Atlantic: Modernity and Double-Consciousness. New York: Verso.

Go, Julian. 2013. "For a Postcolonial Sociology." Theory and Society 42 (1): 25–55.

Godin, Mélissa, and Chahrazade Douah. 2020. "A Young Man Died in France in Police Custody. Now Thousands Are Protesting in His Name." Time, June 4, 2020. https://time.com/5847396/france-protests-anti-racism.

Golden, Tim. 1992. "New Ball Game for Mexican Toys." New York Times, August 28, 1992.

Gordon, Avery. 1994. Ghostly Matters: Haunting and the Sociological Imagination. Minneapolis: University of Minnesota Press.

Greenberg, Janet. 1990. "Toward a History of Women's Periodicals in Latin America: Introduction." In *Women, Culture and Politics in Latin America: Seminar on Feminism and Culture in Latin America*, 173–81. Berkeley: University of California Press.

Gregory, Andy. 2020. "Black Lives Matter: Aerial Images Show Protests around the World after George Floyd's Death." *Independent*, June 7, 2020. https://www.independent.co.uk/news/world/black-lives-matter-protests-global-george-floyd-death-us-police-racism-a9553356.html.

Grewal, Inderpal. 1996. *Home and Harem: Nation, Gender, Empire, and the Cultures of Travel*. Durham, NC: Duke University Press.

Grewal, Inderpal. 2005. *Transnational America: Feminisms, Diaspora, Neoliberalism*. Durham, NC: Duke University Press.

Grewal, Inderpal. 2013. "Outsourcing Patriarchy: Feminist Encounters, Transnational Mediations and the Crime of 'Honour Killings.'" *International Feminist Journal of Politics* 15 (1): 1–19.

Grewal, Inderpal. 2017. *Saving the Security State: Exceptional Citizens in Twenty-First-Century America*. Durham, NC: Duke University Press.

Grewal, Inderpal, and Caren Kaplan. 1994. "Introduction: Transnational Feminist Practices and Questions of Postmodernity." In *Scattered Hegemonies: Postmodernity and Transnational Feminist Practices*, edited by Inderpal Grewal and Caren Kaplan, 1–33. Minneapolis: University of Minnesota Press.

Grewal, Inderpal, and Caren Kaplan. 2001. "Global Identities: Theorizing Transnational Studies of Sexuality." GLQ: *A Journal of Lesbian and Gay Studies* 7 (4): 663–97.

Grewal, Inderpal, and Srila Roy. 2017. "The Positive Side of Co-optation? Intersectionality: A Conversation between Inderpal Grewal and Srila Roy." *International Feminist Journal of Politics* 19 (2): 254–62.

Gupta, Jyotsna Agnihotri. 2011. "Towards Transnational Feminisms: Some Reflections and Concerns in Relation to the Globalization of Reproductive Technologies." *European Journal of Women's Studies* 13 (1): 23–38.

Gupta, Jyotsna Agnihotri. 2012. "Reproductive Biocrossings: Indian Egg Donors and Surrogates in the Globalized Fertility Market." *International Journal of Feminist Approaches to Bioethics* 5 (1): 25–51.

Guy, Donna J. 1995. *Sex and Danger in Buenos Aires: Prostitution, Family, and Nation in Argentina*. Lincoln: University of Nebraska Press.

Hall, Stuart. 1996. "Race, Articulation, and Societies Structured in Dominance." In *Black British Cultural Studies: A Reader*, edited by Houston A. Baker Jr., Manthia Diawara, and Ruth H. Lindeborg, 16–47. Chicago: University of Chicago Press.

Halley, Janet. 2006. *Split Decisions: How and Why to Take a Break from Feminism*. Princeton, NJ: Princeton University Press.

Hancock, Ange-Marie. 2007. "When Multiplication Doesn't Equal Quick Addition: Examining Intersectionality as a Research Paradigm." *Perspectives on Politics* 5 (1): 63–79.

Harcourt, Wendy. 2013. *Gender and Environment*. London: Zed Books.

Harrison, Laura. 2016. *Brown Bodies, White Babies: The Politics of Cross-Racial Surrogacy*. New York: New York University Press.

Hartmann, Betsy. 1995. *Reproductive Rights and Wrongs: The Global Politics of Population Control*. Boston: South End Press.

Harvey, David. 1990. *The Condition of Postmodernity: An Enquiry into the Origins of Cultural Change*. Malden, MA: Blackwell.

Hemmings, Clare. 2011. *Why Stories Matter: The Political Grammar of Feminist Theory*. Durham, NC: Duke University Press.

Higgins, Eoin. 2019. "In Victory for People's Movement, Ecuador Protests End with Government Capitulation on Fuel Subsidies." *Common Dreams*, October 14, 2019. https://www.commondreams.org/news/2019/10/14/victory -peoples-movement-ecuador-protests-end-government-capitulation-fuel -subsidies.

Hoffman, Matthew Cullinan. 2008. "New Ecuadorian Constitution Endangered by Pro-abortion, Anti-family Language." *LifeSiteNews*, December 23, 2008. http://www.lifesitenews.com/news/archive//ldn/2008/jul/08071606.

Holloway, Karla F. C. 2006. "'Cruel Enough to Stop the Blood': Global Feminisms and the U.S. Body Politic, or: 'They Done Taken My Blues and Gone.'" *Meridians* 7 (1): 1–18.

hooks, bell. 2014. *Feminist Theory: From Margin to Center*. 3rd ed. New York: Routledge.

Horton, Sarah. 2008. "Consuming Childhood: 'Lost' and 'Ideal' Childhoods as a Motivation for Migration." *Anthropological Quarterly* 81 (4): 925–43.

Human Rights and Equal Opportunity Commission of Australia. 2007. *Same-Sex: Same Entitlements*. Sydney: Human Rights and Equal Opportunity Commission of Australia. https://humanrights.gov.au/sites/default/files /content/human_rights/samesex/report/pdf/SSSE_Report.pdf.

Ikemoto, Lisa C. 2009. "Reproductive Tourism: Equality Concerns in the Global Market for Fertility Services." Minnesota Journal of *Law and Inequality* 27 (2): 277–310.

INE (Instituto Nacional de Estatística). 2011. *Moçambique: Inquérito demográfico e de saúde*. Maputo, Mozambique: INE. https://dhsprogram.com/pubs/pdf /FR266/FR266.pdf.

Inhorn, Marcia C. 2011. "Globalization and Gametes: Reproductive 'Tourism,' Islamic Bioethics, and Middle Eastern Modernity." *Anthropology and Medicine* 18 (1): 87–103.

Inhorn, Marcia C. 2015. *Cosmopolitan Conceptions: IVF Sojourns in Global Dubai*. Durham, NC: Duke University Press.

Jackson, Cecile. 1996. "Rescuing Gender from the Poverty Trap." *World Development* 24 (3): 489–504.

Jayawardena, Kumari. 1986. *Feminism and Nationalism in the Third World*. London: Zed.

Jha, Sonora, and Alka Kurian, eds. 2018. *New Feminisms in South Asia: Disrupting the Discourse through Social Media, Film, and Literature*. New York: Routledge.

John, Mary E. 1999. "Feminisms and Internationalisms: A Response from India." In *Feminisms and Internationalism*, edited by Miralini Sinha, Donna Guy, and Angela Woollacott, 195–204. Oxford: Blackwell.

John, Mary E. 2014. "Feminist Trajectories in Time and Space: Perspectives from India." *Economic and Political Weekly* 49 (22): 121–31.

Jolly, Jallicia. 2016. "On Forbidden Wombs and Transnational Reproductive Justice." *Meridians* 15 (1): 166–88.

Jornal da Rede. 1992. "Aborto: A grande hipocrisia nacional." *Jornal da Rede* 1 (2): 4.

Kabeer, Naila. 2003. *Gender Mainstreaming in Poverty Eradication and the Millennium Development Goals: A Handbook for Policy-Makers and Other Stakeholders*. London: Commonwealth Secretariat.

Kandiyoti, Deniz. 1995. *Gendering the Middle East: Emerging Prospects*. London: I. B. Tauris.

Kappal, Bhanuj. 2017. "Breaking the 'Savarna Feminism' Rules—How Raya Sarkar's List of Alleged Harassers Divided Opinion in India." *New Statesman*, November 30, 2017. https://www.newstatesman.com/politics /feminism/2017/11/breaking-savarna-feminism-rules-how-raya-sarkar-s -list-alleged-harassers.

Kapur, Ratna. 2013. "Gender, Sovereignty and the Rise of a Sexual Security Regime in International Law and Postcolonial India." *Melbourne Journal of International Law* 14 (2): 317–45.

Karthick, R. M. 2015. "India's Patriotic Feminist Daughters." *Round Table India*, March 6, 2015. http://roundtableindia.co.in/index.php?option=com _content&view=article&id=8095:india-s-patriotic-feminist-daughters&catid =119:feature&Itemid=132.

Kearney, Michael. 2004. *Changing Fields of Anthropology: From Local to Global*. Lanham, MD: Rowman & Littlefield.

King, Tiffany Lethabo. 2015. "Post-identitarian and Post-intersectional Anxiety in the Neoliberal Corporate University." *Feminist Formations* 27 (3): 114–38.

Kirkpatrick, David D., and Eric Lipton. "Behind Trump's Dealing with Turkey: Sons-in-Law Married to Power." *New York Times*, November 12, 2019. https://www.nytimes.com/2019/11/12/us/politics/trump-erdogan-family -turkey.html.

Knudsen, Britta Timm, and Carsten Stage. 2014. *Global Media, Biopolitics and Affect: Politicizing Bodily Vulnerability*. New York: Routledge.

Krishnan, Prabha. 1990. "In the Idiom of Loss: Ideology of Motherhood in Television Serials." *Economic and Political Weekly* 25 (42–43): 103–15.

Kroløkke, Charlotte Halmø, and Saumya Pant. 2012. "'I Only Need Her Uterus': Neo-liberal Discourses on Transnational Surrogacy." *NORA: Nordic Journal of Feminist and Gender Research* 20 (4): 233–48.

Kropeniscki, Fernanda Battagli, and Fátima Cristina Vieira Perurena. 2017. "Gender Relations in Toys Catalogs: (Contra)indications to Play." *Educação e Sociedade* 38 (141): 965–81.

Kumar, Radha. 1993. *History of Doing: An Illustrated Account of Movements for Women's Rights and Feminism in India, 1800–1990*. New Delhi: Kali for Women.

Kwan, Peter. 1997. "Jeffrey Dahmer and the Cosynthesis of Categories." *Hastings Law Journal* 48: 1257–92.

Lamarques, Rui. 2016. "Um ministério eternamente contra a rapariga." Facebook, April 19, 2016. https://www.facebook.com/rui.lamarques/posts /1334458989903757?fref=nf.

Lang, Miriam. 2019. "Plurinationality as a Strategy: Transforming Local State Institutions toward *Buen Vivir*." In *Postdevelopment in Practice: Alternatives, Economies, Ontologies*, edited by Elise Klein and Carlos Eduardo Morreo, 176–89. New York: Routledge.

Lebon, Nathalie. 2013. "Taming or Unleashing the Monster of Coalition Work: Professionalization and the Consolidation of Popular Feminism in Brazil." *Feminist Studies* 39 (3): 759–89.

Leite, Rosalina de Santa Cruz. 2003. "Brasil mulher e nós mulheres: Origens da imprensa feminista brasileira." *Revista de estudos feministas* 11 (1): 234–41.

Lemos, Nina. 2016. "Nem rosa, nem azul: Por um natal com briquedos gender free." *UOL*, July 12, 2016. http://revistatrip.uol.com.br/tpm/nina-lemos-natal -brinquedos-sem-estereotipo-de-genero.

Leon, Ethel. 1984. "Contracepção: O drama nosso de cada dia." *Mulherio* 4 (17): 6.

Lewis, Sophie. 2017. "Defending Intimacy against What? Limits of Antisurrogacy Feminisms." *Signs: A Journal of Women in Culture and Society* 43 (1): 97–125.

Lewis, Sophie. 2018. "International Solidarity in Reproductive Justice: Surrogacy and Gender-Inclusive Polymaternalism." *Gender, Place and Culture: A Journal of Feminist Geography* 25 (2): 207–27.

Libardoni, Marlene. 1996. "A arte de dialogar com o legislativo." *Jornal da Rede* 4 (11): 4–5.

Lind, Amy, and Sofía Argüello Pazmiño. 2009. "Activismo LGBTIQ y ciudadanías sexuales en el Ecuador: Un diálogo con Elizabeth Vásquez." *Íconos: Revista de ciencias sociales* 35: 97–101.

"Lisa Ling Investigates: Wombs for Rent." 2007. *Oprah Winfrey Show*, October 9, 2007. http://www.oprah.com/world/Wombs-for-Rent.

Locke, Richard M. 2002. "The Promise and Perils of Globalization: The Case of Nike." Working paper, Industrial Performance Center, Massachusetts Institute of Technology, Cambridge, Massachusetts. https://ipc.mit.edu/sites /default/files/2019–01/02–007.pdf.

Lopez, Iris. 1993. "Agency and Constraint: Sterilization and Reproductive Freedom among Puerto Rican Women in New York City." *Urban Anthropology and Studies of Cultural Systems and World Economic Development* 22 (3–4): 299–323.

Lorde, Audre. *Sister Outsider: Essays and Speeches*. Trumansburg, NY: Crossing Press, [1984] 2007.

Lowe, Lisa. 2015. *The Intimacies of Four Continents*. Durham, NC: Duke University Press.

Lubrino, Angelina, Sansão Buque, and Ernesto Lipapa. 2016. *Perfil de género de Moçambique*. Maputo, Mozambique: Ministério de Género, Criança e Acção Social. http://www.mgcas.gov.mz/st/FileControl/Site/Doc/4021perfil _de_genero_de_mocambique.pdf.

Lugones, María. 2007. "Heterosexualism and the Colonial/Modern Gender System." *Hypatia* 22 (1): 186–209.

Lugones, María. 2010. "Toward a Decolonial Feminism." *Hypatia* 25 (4): 742–59.

Luna, Zakiya, and Kristin Luker. 2013. "Reproductive Justice." *Annual Review of Law and Social Science*, no. 9, 327–52.

Maddison, Sarah. 2007. *Black Politics: Inside the Complexity of Aboriginal Political Culture*. Crows Nest, NSW, Australia: Allen and Unwin.

Mann, Joseph A., Jr. 2015. "Hasbro's Toys and Games Post Strong Growth in Latin America." *Miami Herald*, March 20, 2015. https://www.miamiherald .com/news/business/biz-monday/article15519500.html.

Marino, Katherine M. 2019. *Feminism for the Americas: The Making of an International Human Rights Movement*. Chapel Hill: University of North Carolina Press.

Markens, Susan. 2007. *Surrogate Motherhood and the Politics of Reproduction*. Berkeley: University of California Press.

Massey, Doreen. 1994. "A Global Sense of Place." In *Space, Place, and Gender*, 146–54. Minneapolis: University of Minnesota Press.

Masson, Dominique. 2010. "Transnationalizing Feminist and Women's Movements: Towards a Scalar Approach." In *Solidarities beyond Borders: Transnationalizing Women's Movements*, edited by Pascale Dufour, Dominique Masson, and Dominique Caouette, 35–55. Vancouver: University of British Columbia Press.

Mbembe, Achille. 2001. *On the Postcolony*. Berkeley: University of California Press.

McCall, Leslie. 2005. "The Complexity of Intersectionality." *Signs: Journal of Women in Culture and Society* 30 (3): 1771–800.

McClintock, Anne. 1995. *Imperial Leather: Race, Gender, and Sexuality in the Colonial Contest*. New York: Routledge.

McDonnell, Patrick J., and Kate Linthicum. 2020. "U.S. Protests Prompt Reflections on Class, Race and Police Violence in Mexico." *Los Angeles Times*, June 6, 2020. https://www.latimes.com/world-nation/story/2020–06–06/us -protests-prompt-reflections-on-class-race-and-police-violence-in-mexico.

McLaren, Margaret A., ed. 2017. *Decolonizing Feminism: Transnational Feminism and Globalization*. London: Rowman and Littlefield.

Mehta, Purvi. 2017. "Dalit Feminism at Home and in the World: The Conceptual Work of 'Difference' and 'Similarity' in National and Transnational Activism." In *Women's Activism and "Second Wave" Feminism: Transnational Histories*, edited by Barbara Molony and Jennifer Nelson, 231–48. London: Bloomsbury.

Menon, Nivedita, ed. 2007. *Sexualities*. New Delhi: Women Unlimited.

Merino, Roger. 2011. "What Is 'Post' in Post-neoliberal Economic Policy? Extractive Industry Dependence and Indigenous Land Rights in Bolivia and Ecuador." SSRN, October 4, 2011.

Mignolo, Walter D., and Catherine E. Walsh. 2018. *On Decoloniality: Concepts, Analytics, Praxis*. Durham, NC: Duke University Press.

Millán, Cecilia. n.d. "Education to Not Discriminate." Network of Popular Education among Women [REPEM]. Accessed September 15, 2018, http://agendadelasmujeres.com.ar/notadesplegada.php?id=1256.

Millbank, Jenni. 2011. "The New Surrogacy Parental Laws in Australia: Cautious Regulation or '25 Brick Walls'?" *Melbourne University Law Review*, no. 35, 201–3.

Mintz, Steven. 2004. *Huck's Raft: A History of American Childhood*. Cambridge, MA: Belknap Press of Harvard University Press.

Misra, Joya, and Mary Bernstein. 2019. "Sexuality, Gender, and Social Policy." In *The New Handbook of Political Sociology*, edited by Thomas Janoski, Cedric de Leon, Joya Misra, and Isaac William Martin, 1375–444. Cambridge: Cambridge University Press.

Modern Girl around the World Research Group. 2008. *The Modern Girl around the World: Consumption, Modernity, and Globalization*. Durham, NC: Duke University Press.

Moeller, Kathryn. 2018. *The Gender Effect: Capitalism, Feminism, and the Corporate Politics of Development*. Oakland: University of California Press.

Mohanty, Chandra Talpade. 2003. *Feminism without Borders: Decolonizing Theory, Practicing Solidarity*. Durham, NC: Duke University Press.

Mohanty, Chandra Talpade. 1984. "Under Western Eyes: Feminist Scholarship and Colonial Discourses." *Boundary* 2 12 (3): 333–58.

Mohanty, Chandra Talpade, Ann Russo, and Lourdes Torres, eds. 1991. *Third World Women and the Politics of Feminism*. Bloomington: Indiana University Press.

Montague, Clara, and Ashwini Tambe. 2020. "Women's Studies." In *Companion to Women's and Gender Studies*, edited by Nancy A. Naples, 25–39. London: Wiley Blackwell.

Mooney, Jadwiga E. Pieper. 2012. "Forging Feminisms under Dictatorship: Women's International Ties and National Feminist Empowerment in Chile, 1973–1990." *Women's History Review* 19 (4): 613–30.

Morgan, Lynn M., and Elizabeth F. S. Roberts. 2012. "Reproductive Governance in Latin America." *Anthropology and Medicine* 19 (2): 241–54.

Morgan, Robin, ed. 1996. *Sisterhood Is Global: The International Women's Movement Anthology*. New York: Feminist Press at the City University of New York.

Mosse, George L. 1996. *The Image of Man: The Creation of Modern Masculinity*. New York: Oxford University Press.

Mudimbe, V. Y. 1988. *The Invention of Africa: Gnosis, Philosophy, and the Order of Knowledge*. Bloomington: Indiana University Press.

Murphy, Michelle. 2012–13. "The Girl: Mergers of Feminism and Finance in Neoliberal Times." *Scholar and Feminist Online* 11 (1–2). http://sfonline.barnard

.edu/gender-justice-and-neoliberal-transformations/the-girl-mergers-of
-feminism-and-finance-in-neoliberal-times.

Nadel, Joshua H. 2014. *Fútbol! Why Soccer Matters in Latin America.* Gainesville:
University Press of Florida.

Nahman, Michal Rachel. 2013. *Extractions: An Ethnography of Reproductive
Tourism.* New York: Palgrave Macmillan.

Najar, Nida. 2015. "India Wants to Ban Birth Surrogacy for Foreigners." *New York
Times,* October 28, 2015. https://www.nytimes.com/2015/10/29/world/asia
/india-wants-to-ban-birth-surrogacy-for-foreigners.html.

Naples, Nancy A. 2003. *Feminism and Method: Ethnography, Discourse Analysis,
and Activist Research.* New York: Routledge.

Naples, Nancy A. 2013. "Sexual Citizenship and Reproductive Rights: Creating
Dialogue between Feminist and Queer Approaches." Paper presented at
the 8th International Meetings Against Homophobia, Koas-GL, Ankara,
Turkey, May 18, 2013.

Naples, Nancy A. 2016. "Transnational Activism, Feminist Praxis, and Cultures
of Resistance." In *Globalizing Cultures: Theories, Paradigms, Actions,* edited
by Vincenzo Mele and Marina Vujovic, 143–73. Leiden, Netherlands: Brill.

Naples, Nancy A. 2017. "Intersectional Transnational Organizing and Shifting
Border Politics." Paper presented in the workshop on "Whither Transna-
tional Feminism?" at the Women's World Conference, Florianópolis, Brazil,
August 30, 2017.

Naples, Nancy A. 2018. "What's in a Word? Austerity, Precarity, and Neoliberal-
ism." In *Feminists Rethink the Neoliberal State: Inequality, Exclusion, and
Change,* edited by Leela Fernandes, 32–70. New York: New York University
Press.

Narayan, Uma. 1997. *Dislocating Cultures: Identities, Traditions, and Third World
Feminism.* New York: Routledge.

Narrain, Arvind, and Gautam Bhan, eds. 2005. *Because I Have a Voice: Queer
Politics in India.* New Delhi: Yoda.

Nash, Jennifer C. 2017. "Intersectionality and Its Discontents." *American Quarterly* 69 (1): 117–29.

Nash, Jennifer C. 2019. *Black Feminism Reimagined: After Intersectionality.* Durham, NC: Duke University Press.

Neill, Rosemary. 2003. *White Out: How Politics Is Killing Black Australia.* Crows
Nest, NSW, Australia: Allen and Unwin.

Neverdon-Morton, Cynthia. 1989. *Afro-American Women of the South and the Advancement of the Race, 1895–1925.* Knoxville: University of Tennessee Press.

Nicholls, Walter, Byron Miller, and Justin Beaumont. 2013. "Introduction: Conceptualizing the Spatialities of Social Movements." In *Spaces of Contention:
Spatialities and Social Movements,* edited by Walter Nicholls, Byron Miller,
and Jason Beaumont, 1–23. Farnham, UK: Ashgate.

Nike, Inc. 2006. "Workers in Contract Factories." In *Innovate for a Better World:
Nike FY 05–06 Corporate Responsibility Report,* 15–50. https://purpose-cms

-production01.s3.amazonaws.com/wp-content/uploads/2018/05/14214955
/Nike_FY05_06_CR_Report_C_original.pdf.

Nike, Inc. 2012. "Nike Foundation Launches New Girleffect.org." https://news
.nike.com/news/nike-foundation-launches-new-girleffectorg.

Nike Foundation. 2005. "Investor News Details: Nike Foundation Steps on to
New Field." *Nike News*, March 8, 2005. http://investors.nike.com/investors
/news-events-and-reports/investor-news/investor-news-details/2005/Nike
-Foundation-Steps-on-to-New-Field/default.aspx.

Nike Foundation. 2007. "Request for Proposals: She's an Economic Powerhouse:
Economic Empowerment Models for Girls." Accessed October 2007,
www.nikefoundation.com.

Nobre, Miriam, and Sarah de Roure. 2012. "La construcción de la Marcha
Mundial de las Mujeres: Formas organizativas y sostenimiento de nuestro
movimiento." In *Movimientos sociales y cooperación: Ideas para el debate*,
edited by Janaina Stronzake, Judite Stronzake, Daniel Von Freyberg, Lorena
Cabnal, and Jesus González, 53–68. Leioa, Spain: Universidad del Pais
Vasco.

Novo, Carmen Martínez. 2014. "Managing Diversity in Postneoliberal Ecuador."
Journal of Latin American and Caribbean Anthropology 19 (1): 103–25.

Núñez, Roselia. n.d. "21 de Junio: Día Nacional para una Educación No Sexista."
Accessed July 20, 2019, http://genero.ues.edu.sv/index.php/sexismo/57–21
-de-junio-dia-nacional-para-una-educacion-no-sexista.

Ohata, Eduardo. 2001. "Exiladas, craques são estrelas do 'socer' nos EUA." *Folha
de São Paulo*, December 16, 2001.

The Ohio State University. 2020. "Vision and Mission." Department of Women's,
Gender, and Sexuality Studies. https://wgss.osu.edu/about/vision-mission.

O'Leary, Cathy. 2018. "WA Same-Sex Couples Could Have Children Using
Surrogates under Planned Law Changes." *West Australian*, January 12,
2018. https://thewest.com.au/news/wa/wa-same-sex-couples-could-have
-children-using-surrogates-under-planned-law-changes-ng-b88711588z.

Oliver, Pamela E., and Daniel J. Myers. 2003. "The Coevolution of Social Movements." *Mobilization: An International Journal* 8 (1): 1–25.

Omi, Michael, and Howard Winant. 1994. *Racial Formation in the United States:
From the 1960s to the 1990s*. 2nd ed. New York: Routledge.

Ordeñana, Tatiana. 2018. "Tatiana Ordeñana: 'El fallo de Satya reconoce que hay
más tipos de familia.'" Interview by Mariela Rosero. *El Comercio*, July 17,
2018. https://www.elcomercio.com/actualidad/tatianaordenana-fallo
-corteconstitucional-satya-familias.html.

Orellana, Marjorie Faulstich, Barrie Thorne, Anna Chee, and Wan Shun Eva
Lam. 2001. "Transnational Childhoods: The Participation of Children in
Processes of Family Migration." *Social Problems* 48 (4): 572–91.

Oyěwùmí, Oyèrónké. 2003. *African Women and Feminism: Reflecting on the
Politics of Sisterhood*. Trenton, NJ: Africa World Press.

Pande, Amrita. 2010a. "'At Least I Am Not Sleeping with Anyone': Resisting the Stigma of Commercial Surrogacy in India." In "Re-inventing Mothers." Special issue, *Feminist Studies* 36 (2): 292–312.

Pande, Amrita. 2010b. "Commercial Surrogacy in India: Manufacturing a Perfect Mother-Worker." *Signs: Journal of Women in Culture and Society* 35 (4): 969–92.

Pande, Amrita. 2014. *Wombs in Labor: Transnational Commercial Surrogacy in India*. New York: Columbia University Press.

Pande, Amrita. 2017. "Gestational Transnational Commercial Surrogacy in India: To Ban or Not to Ban." In *Babies for Sale: Transnational Surrogacy, Human Rights and the Politics of Reproduction*, edited by Miranda Davies, 328–43. London: Zed Books.

Pande, Amrita. 2020. "Revisiting Surrogacy in India: Domino Effects of the Ban." *Journal of Gender Studies*.

Pande, Amrita. 2021. "Mix or Match? Transnational Fertility Industry and White Desirability." *Medical Anthropology*. https://www.tandfonline.com/eprint /WMSBWJPJIZRZBZGX7EZM/full?target=10.1080/01459740.2021.1877289.

Pande, Amrita. Forthcoming. "Desiring Whiteness and Global Fertility Markets." In *Routledge Handbook of Critical Whiteness Studies*, edited by Shona Hunter and Christi Van der Westhuizen. New York: Routledge.

Panitch, Vida. 2013a. "Global Surrogacy: Exploitation to Empowerment." *Journal of Global Ethics* 9 (3): 329–43.

Panitch, Vida. 2013b. "Surrogate Tourism and Reproductive Rights." *Hypatia* 28 (2): 274–89.

Paris, Leslie. 2011. "Happily Ever After: *Free to Be . . . You and Me*, Second-Wave Feminism, and 1970s American Children's Culture." In *The Oxford Handbook of Children's Literature*, edited by Julia Mickenberg and Lynne Vallone, 519–39. New York: Oxford University Press.

Patil, Anushka. 2020. "How a March for Black Trans Lives Became a Huge Event." *New York Times*, June 15, 2020. https://www.nytimes.com/2020/06 /15/nyregion/brooklyn-black-trans-parade.html.

Pereira, Amilcar Araujo, Julio Cesar Correia de Oliveira, and Thayara Cristine Silva de Lima, eds. 2015. *Memories of Baobá: From Roots to Seeds*. Translated by Janny Llanos. Rio de Janeiro: Kitabu Editora.

Perrett, Molly. 2011. "Surrogacy." Australian Broadcasting Company [ABC] News Local, January 28, 2011.

Perrigo, Billy. 2020. "Crowds Protest in New Zealand against George Floyd's Death and Police Brutality against Indigenous Communities." *Time*, June 1, 2020. https://time.com/5845981/new-zealand-george-floyd.

Pessoa, Francisco Lagge, ed. 1967. *Brasil: Control de la natalidad, Agosto 1966–67: Algunos documentos clave*. Cuernavaca, Brazil: Centro Intercultural de Documentacion.

Petchesky, Rosalind Pollack. 1979. "Reproduction, Ethics and Public Policy: The Federal Sterilization Regulations." *Hastings Center Report* 9 (5): 29–41.

Petchesky, Rosalind Pollack. 2003. *Global Prescriptions: Gendering Health and Human Rights*. New York: Zed Books.

Piketty, Thomas. 2014. *Capital in the Twenty-First Century*. Cambridge, MA: Belknap Press of Harvard University Press.

PINKSTINKS. 2010. "Wow—What a Month!" Accessed September 12, 2018, https://pinkstinks.wordpress.com/2010/01/05/wow-what-a-month/.

PINKSTINKS. 2018. "Our Campaigns." Accessed September 12, 2018, http://www.pinkstinks.co.uk/our-campaigns.html.

Pogrebin, Letty Cottin. 1974. "Toys for Free Children." *Ms.*, 48–53, 82–85.

Ponce, Karina, Andrés Vásquez, Pablo Vivanco, and Ronaldo Munck. 2020. "The October 2019 Indigenous and Citizens' Uprising in Ecuador," *Latin American Perspectives* 47 (5): 9–19.

Potes, Verónica. 2012. "Carta abierta al candidato Lasso (y llamado de atención al resto de candidatos)." Post reproduced on Diane Rodriguez's website, October 24, 2012. https://dianerodriguez.net/2012/10/24/candidatos-no-incluyen-temas-lgbti-ni-aborto-en-propuestas-de-gobierno-ecuatoriano-candidates-exclude-lgbti-and-abortion-issues-in-ecuadorian-government-proposals.

Pratt, Geraldine, and Victoria Rosner. 2012. Introduction to *The Global and the Intimate: Feminism in Our Time*, edited by Geraldine Pratt and Victoria Rosner, 1–27. New York: Columbia University Press.

Price, Kimala. 2017. "Queering Reproductive Justice: Toward a Theory and Praxis for Building Intersectional Political Alliances." In *LGBTQ Politics: A Critical Reader*, edited by Marla Brettschneider, Susan Burgess, and Christine Keating, 72–88. New York: New York University Press.

Prieto, Mercedes, Clorinda Cuminao, Alejandro Flores, Gina Maldonado, and Andrea Pequeño. 2006. "Respeto, discriminación y violencia: Mujeres indígenas en Ecuador, 1990–2004." In *De lo privado a lo público: 30 años de lucha ciudadana de las mujeres en América Latina*, edited by Nathalie Lebon and Elizabeth Maier, 158–80. Mexico City: Siglo XXI Editores.

Proyecto Transgénero. n.d. "Entendiendo a la comunidad transgénero." Accessed January 15, 2021, http://www.proyecto-transgenero.org.

Puar, Jasbir. 2007. *Terrorist Assemblages: Homonationalism in Queer Times*. Durham, NC: Duke University Press.

Puri, Jyoti. 2004. *Encountering Nationalism*. Malden, MA: Blackwell.

Ragoné, Helena. 1994. *Surrogate Motherhood: Conception in the Heart*. Boulder, CO: Westview.

Rahman, Maseeh. 2014. "Indian Prime Minister Claims Genetic Science Existed in Ancient Times." *The Guardian*, October 28, 2014. https://www.theguardian.com/world/2014/oct/28/indian-prime-minister-genetic-science-existed-ancient-times.

Ramamurthy, Priti. 2004. "Why Is Buying a 'Madras' Cotton Shirt a Political Act? A Feminist Commodity Chain Analysis." *Feminist Studies* 30 (3): 734–69.

Ramamurthy, Priti, and Ashwini Tambe. 2017. Preface to "Decolonial and Postcolonial Approaches: A Dialogue." Special issue, *Feminist Studies* 43 (3): 503–11.

Ray, Raka. 1998. *Fields of Protest: Women's Movements in India*. Minneapolis: University of Minnesota Press.

Reichmann, Rebecca, ed. 1999. *Race in Contemporary Brazil: From Indifference to Inequality*. University Park: Pennsylvania State University Press.

República del Ecuador. 2008. Constitución de 2008. Political Database of the Americas, Georgetown University. http://pdba.georgetown.edu /Constitutions/Ecuador/ecuador08.html#mozTocId215170.

República de Moçambique. 2004. Constituição da República. Ministério da Agricultura de Desenvolvimento Rural. https://www.masa.gov.mz/wp-content /uploads/2018/01/Constituicao_republica_mocambique.pdf.

Rial, Carmen. 2012. "Women's Soccer in Brazil: Invisible but Under Pressure." *ReVista: Harvard Review of Latin America* 11 (3): 25–28. http://revista.drclas .harvard.edu/book/womens-soccer-brazil.

Rial, Carmen. 2014. "New Frontiers: The Transnational Circulation of Brazil's Women Soccer Players." In *Women, Soccer and Transnational Migration*, edited by Sine Agergaard and Nina Clara Tiesler, 86–112. London: Routledge.

Riggs, Damien W., and Clemence Due. 2010. "Gay Men, Race Privilege and Surrogacy in India." *Outskirts* 22. http://www.outskirts.arts.uwa.edu.au /volumes/volume-22/riggs.

Riggs, Damien W., and Clemence Due. 2013. "Representations of Reproductive Citizenship and Vulnerability in Media Reports of Offshore Surrogacy." *Citizenship Studies* 17 (8): 956–69.

Ringle, Paul B. 2015. *Commercializing Childhood: Children's Magazines, Urban Gentility, and the Ideal of the Child Consumer in the United States, 1823– 1918*. Amherst: University of Massachusetts Press.

Roberts, Dorothy. 2011. *Fatal Invention: How Science, Politics, and Big Business Re-create Race in the Twenty-first Century*. New York: New Press.

Roberts, Elizabeth F. S. 2012. *God's Laboratory: Assisted Reproduction in the Andes*. Berkeley: University of California Press.

Robinson, Nova. 2016. "Arab Internationalism and Gender: Perspectives from the Third Session of the United States Commission on the Status of Women, 1949." *International Journal of Middle East Studies* 48 (3): 578–83.

Rodney, Walter. 1981. *How Europe Underdeveloped Africa*. Washington, DC: Howard University Press.

Rodrigues, Walter. 1984. "Using the Reproductive Risk Concept to Link Community-Based Distribution (CBD) and Voluntary Surgical Contraception (VSC) in Brazil." Presentation at the Meeting of the International Council of the Johns Hopkins Program for International Education in Gynecology and Obstetrics, Izmir, Turkey, March 31–April 4, 1984. Centro de Documentação-BEMFAM.

Rosemberg, Fúlvia. 1969. "La famille et les relations familiales dans les livres pour enfants." PhD diss., University of Paris.

Rosemberg, Fúlvia. 1975. "A escola e as diferenças sexuais." *Cadernos de Pesquisa*, no. 15, 78–85.

Rosemberg, Fúlvia, Neide Cardoso de Moura, and Paulo Vinícius Baptista Silva. 2009. "Fighting Sexism in Textbooks: Agenda Construction and Its Critics." *Cadernos de Pesquisa* 30 (137): 489–519.

Rosemberg, Fúlvia, and Edith Piza. 1995. "As meninas na literatura infanto-juvenil brasileira." *Revista Psicologia: Teoria e Pesquisa* 11 (3): 217–21.

Roshanravan, Shireen. 2012. "Staying Home While Studying Abroad: Anti-imperial Praxis for Globalizing Feminist Visions." *Feminist Visions* 2 (2): 1–23.

Ross, Loretta, Lynn Roberts, Erika Derkas, Whitney Peoples, and Pamela Bridgewater Toure. 2017. *Radical Reproductive Justice: Foundation, Theory, Practice.* New York: The Feminist Press at City University of New York.

Rotabi, Karen Smith, and Nicole F. Bromfield. 2017. *From Intercountry Adoption to Global Surrogacy: A Human Rights History and New Fertility Frontiers.* New York: Routledge.

Rotabi, Karen Smith, Susan Mapp, Kristen Cheney, Rowena Fong, and Ruth McRoy. 2017. "Regulating Commercial Global Surrogacy: The Best Interests of the Child." *Journal of Human Rights and Social Work* 2: 64–73.

Rothman, Barbara Katz. 2005. *Weaving a Family: Untangling Race and Adoption.* Boston: Beacon Press.

Roy, Ananya. 2010a. "Millennial Woman: The Gender Order of Development." In *The International Handbook of Gender and Poverty: Concepts, Research, Policy,* edited by Sylvia Chant, 548–53. Cheltenham, UK: Edward Elgar.

Roy, Ananya. 2010b. *Poverty Capital: Microfinance and the Making of Development.* New York: Routledge.

Roy, Anupama. 2014. "Critical Events, Incremental Memories and Gendered Violence." *Australian Feminist Studies* 29 (81): 238–54.

Roy, Srila, ed. 2012. *New South Asian Feminisms: Paradoxes and Possibilities.* London: Zed Books.

Roy, Srila. 2015. "The Indian Women's Movement: Within and beyond NGOization." *Journal of South Asian Development* 10 (1): 96–117.

Roy, Srila. 2016. "Breaking the Cage." *Dissent Magazine,* Fall 2016. https:// www.dissentmagazine.org/article/breaking-cage-india-feminism-sexual -violence-public-space.

Roy, Srila. 2017. "Whose Feminism Is It Anyway?" *The Wire,* November 1, 2017. https://thewire.in/gender/whose-feminism-anyway.

Roychowdhury, Poulami. 2013. "'The Delhi Gang Rape': The Making of International Causes." *Feminist Studies* 39 (1): 282–92.

Rubio, Katia. 2014. "The Participation of Women in Brazilian Olympic Sport." In *Routledge Handbook of Sport, Gender and Sexuality,* edited by Jennifer Hargreaves and Eric Anderson, 129–38. New York: Routledge.

Rudrappa, Sharmila. 2015. *Discounted Life: The Price of Global Surrogacy.* New York: New York University Press.

Rudrappa, Sharmila. 2016. "Why Is India's Ban on Commercial Surrogacy Bad for Women?" *Huffington Post,* August 27, 2016. https://www.huffpost

.com/entry/why-indias-new-surrogacy-bill-is-bad-for-women_b_57c075 f9e4b0b01630de83ad.

Rudrappa, Sharmila, and Caitlyn Collins. 2015. "Altruistic Agencies and Compassionate Consumers: Moral Framing of Transnational Surrogacy." *Gender and Society* 29 (6): 937–59.

Said, Edward. 1978. *Orientalism*. New York: Pantheon Books.

Salem, Sara. 2014. "Decolonial Intersectionality and a Transnational Feminist Movement." *Feminist Wire*, April 17, 2014. http://www.thefeministwire.com /2014/04/decolonial-intersectionality.

Salgueiro, Fabio. 2001. "Meninas encantam os EUA." *Diário Popular*, May 5, 2001.

Sameh, Catherine. 2016. "Solidarity." In *Gender: Love*, edited by Jennifer C. Nash, 181–96. Macmillan Interdisciplinary Handbooks. Farmington Hills, MI: Macmillan.

Sanchez-Eppler, Karen. 2000. "Playing at Class." ELH (*English Literary History*) 67 (3): 819–42.

Sangtin Writers and Richa Nagar. 2006. *Playing with Fire: Feminist Thought and Activism through Seven Lives in India*. Minneapolis: University of Minnesota Press.

Santos, Boaventura de Sousa. 2009. *Una epistemología del Sur. La reinvención del conocimiento y la emancipación social*. México City: Siglo XXI Editores.

Santos, Boaventura de Sousa. 2014. *Epistemologies of the South: Justice Against Epistemicide*. New York: Routledge.

Sarat, Magda, Miria Izabel Campos, and Edilaine de Mello Macedo. 2016. "Childhood, Gender, Toys and Games for Boys and Girls." *Horizontes: Revista de Educação* 4 (7): 121–34.

Sassen, Saskia. 2000. "Women's Burden: Counter-geographies of Globalization and the Feminization of Survival." *Journal of International Affairs* 53 (2): 503–24.

Saúde em Debate. 1980. "Editorial." *Saúde em Debate*, no. 10, 3–4.

Schenker, Joseph G. 2005. "Assisted Reproduction Practice: Religious Perspectives." *Reproductive BioMedicine Online* 10 (3): 310–19.

Schoen, Johanna. 2005. *Choice and Coercion: Birth Control, Sterilization and Abortion in Public Health and Welfare*. Chapel Hill: North Carolina University Press.

Schor, Juliet B. 2004. *Born to Buy: The Commercialized Child and the New Consumer Culture*. New York: Scribner.

Schwartzman, Simon. 1988. "Brazil: Opportunity and Crisis in Higher Education." *Higher Education* 17 (1): 99–119.

Shandilya, Krupa. 2015. "Nirbhaya's Body: The Politics of Protest in the Aftermath of the 2012 Delhi Gang Rape." *Gender and History* 27 (2): 465–86.

Sharma, Aradhana. 2008. *Logics of Empowerment: Development, Gender, and Governance in Neoliberal India*. Minneapolis: University of Minnesota Press.

Shohat, Ella, and Robert Stam. 1994. *Unthinking Eurocentrism: Multiculturalism and the Media*. New York: Routledge.

Sinha, Mrinalini. 1995. *Colonial Masculinity: The "Manly Englishman" and the "Effeminate Bengali" in the Late Nineteenth Century*. Manchester, UK: Manchester University Press.

Smerdon, Usha Rengachary. 2008. "Crossing Bodies, Crossing Borders: International Surrogacy between the United States and India." *Cumberland Law Review* 39 (1): 15–86.

Smith, Anna Marie. 2007. *Welfare Reform and Sexual Regulation*. New York: Cambridge University Press.

Smith, Dorothy E. 1990. *Conceptual Practices of Power: A Feminist Sociology of Knowledge*. Boston: Northeastern University Press.

Snyder, Cara. 2018. "The Soccer Tournament as Beauty Pageant: Eugenic Logics in Brazilian Women's *Futebol Feminino*." *Women's Studies Quarterly* 46 (1/2): 181–98.

Soares, Vera, Ana Alice Alcantara Costa, Cristina Maria Buarque, Denise Dourado Dora, and Wania Sant'Anna. 1995. "Brazilian Feminism and Women's Movements: A Two-Way Street." In *The Challenge of Local Feminisms: Women's Movements in Global Perspective*, edited by Amrita Basu, 302–23. Boulder, CO: Westview.

Sobrinho, Délcio da Fonseca. 1993. *Estado e população: Uma história do planejamento familiar no Brasil*. Rio de Janeiro: Rosa dos Tempos and United Nations Population Fund.

Sociedade Civil Bem-Estar Familiar no Brasil (BEMFAM). 1987. *Pesquisa nacional sobre saúde materno-infantil e planejamento familiar*. Rio de Janeiro: BEMFAM and IRD.

Sociedade Civil Bem-Estar Familiar no Brasil (BEMFAM). 1997. *Pesquisa nacional de demografia e saúde, 1996*. Macro International, Inc. DHS Program, 26–38. Rio de Janeiro: BEMFAM and Programa de Pesquisas de Demografia e Saúde (DHS).

Sorj, Bila. 2017. "O 'reencantamento' da política institucional: O feminismo na conjuntura conservadora do Brasil." Paper presented at the International Congress of the Latin American Studies Association, Lima, Peru, April 30, 2017.

Soto, Sandra K. 2005. "Where in the Transnational World Are U.S. Women of Color?" In *Women's Studies for the Future: Foundations, Interrogations, Politics*, edited by Elizabeth Lapovsky Kennedy and Agatha Beins, 111–24. New Brunswick, NJ: Rutgers University Press.

Soundararajan, Thenmozhi, and Sinthujan Varatharajah. 2015. "Caste Privilege 101: A Primer for the Privileged." *Aerogram* (blog), February 10, 2015. http://theaerogram.com/caste-privilege-101-primer-privileged.

Speier, Amy. 2016. *Fertility Holidays: IVF Tourism and the Reproduction of Whiteness*. New York: New York University Press.

Spivak, Gayatri Chakravorty. 1985. "Three Women's Texts and a Critique of Imperialism." *Critical Inquiry* 12 (1): 243–61.

Spivak, Gayatri Chakravorty. 1988. "Can the Subaltern Speak?" In *Marxism and the Interpretation of Culture*, edited by Cary Nelson and Lawrence Grossberg, 271–313. London: Macmillan.

Spivak, Gayatri Chakravorty. 1999. *A Critique of Postcolonial Reason: Toward a History of the Vanishing Present*. Cambridge, MA: Harvard University Press.

Stephens, Sharon, ed. 1995. *Children and the Politics of Culture*. Princeton, NJ: Princeton University Press.

Stoler, Ann Laura. 1995. *Race and the Education of Desire: Foucault's History of Sexuality and the Colonial Order of Things*. Durham, NC: Duke University Press.

Stop Surrogacy Now. 2015. "Public Comment on Proposed Surrogacy Regulation in India." https://www.stopsurrogacynow.com/public-comment-on-proposed -surrogacy-regulation-in-india.

Subramaniam, Banu. 2019. *Holy Science: The Biopolitics of Hindu Nationalism*. Seattle: University of Washington Press.

Suchland, Jennifer. 2011. "Is Postsocialism Transnational?" *Signs: Journal of Women in Culture and Society* 36 (4): 837–62.

Sunder Rajan, Rajeswari. 2003. *The Scandal of the State: Women, Law and Citizenship in India*. New Delhi: Permanent Black.

Sutherland, Gail Hinich. 1990. "*Bīja* (Seed) and *Kṣetra* (Field): Male Surrogacy or *Niyoga* in the Mahābhārata." *Contributions to Indian Sociology* 24 (1): 77–103.

Swarr, Amanda Lock, and Richa Nagar. 2003. "Dismantling Assumptions: Interrogating 'Lesbian' Struggles for Identity and Survival in India and South Africa." *Signs: Journal of Women in Culture and Society* 29 (2): 491–516.

Swarr, Amanda Lock, and Richa Nagar, eds. 2010. *Critical Transnational Feminist Praxis*. Albany: State University of New York Press.

Tambe, Ashwini. 2010. "Contributions of Transnational Feminism: A Brief Sketch." *New Global Studies* 4 (1): article 7.

Tambe, Ashwini. 2019a. *Defining Girlhood in India: A Transnational History of Sexual Maturity Laws*. Urbana: University of Illinois Press.

Tambe, Ashwini. 2019b. "Social Geographies of Bombay's Sex Trade." In *Bombay before Mumbai: Essays in Honor of Jim Masselos*, edited by Prashant Kidambi, Manjiri Kamat, and Rachel Dwyer, 47–170. London: Hurst.

Taylor, Verta. 1989. "Social Movement Continuity: The Women's Movement in Abeyance." *American Sociological Review* 54 (5): 761–75.

Thayer, Millie. 2010a. *Making Transnational Feminism: Rural Women, NGO Activists, and Northern Donors in Brazil*. New York: Routledge.

Thayer, Millie. 2010b. "Translations and Refusals: Resignifying Meanings as Feminist Political Practice." *Feminist Studies* 36 (1): 200–230.

Thayer, Millie. 2017. "The 'Gray Zone' between Movements and Markets: Brazilian Feminists and the International Aid Chain." In *Beyond Civil Society: Activism, Participation, and Protest in Latin America*, edited by Sonia E. Alvarez, Jeffrey W. Rubin, Millie Thayer, Gianpaolo Baiocchi, and Agustín Laó-Montes, 156–76. Durham, NC: Duke University Press.

Thomason, Linda Bloodworth. 2018. "'Designing Women' Creator Goes Public with Les Moonves War: Not All Harassment Is Sexual." *Hollywood Reporter*, September 12, 2018. https://www.hollywoodreporter.com/news /designing-women-creator-les-moonves-not-all-harassment-is-sexual -1142448.

Tillett, Andrew. 2015. "Surrogacy Risks Grow as Nations Get Tough." *The West Australian*, October 19, 2015.

Tomazin, Farrah. 2016. "State Government Begins Righting a Ridiculous Wrong." *Age*, August 27, 2016. http://www.theage.com.au/comment/time -to-drag-victorias-adoption-laws-into-21st-century-20160826-gritha .html.

Tormey, Simon. 2013. *Anti-capitalism: A Beginners Guide*. London: Oneworld.

Trindade, João Carlos. 2016. "As irregularidades no processo de expulsão de Eva Anadón Moreno." WLSA Moçambique, April 1, 2016. http://www .wlsa.org.mz/as-irregularidades-no-processo-de-expulsao-de-eva-anadon -moreno.

Tvedten, Inge, Carmeliza Rosário, Sheila Faquir, and Fumo Chacuro (Swedish Institute for Public Administration [SIPU] in cooperation with Overseas Development Institute [ODI] and the Chr. Michelsen Institute [CMI]). 2015. *Evaluation of Norway's Support to Women's Rights and Gender Equality in Development Cooperation: Mozambique Case Study Report*. Oslo: Norwegian Agency for Development Cooperation.

Twine, France Winddance. 1998. *Racism in a Racial Democracy: The Maintenance of White Supremacy in Brazil*. New Brunswick, NJ: Rutgers University Press.

Twine, France Winddance. 2011. *Outsourcing the Womb: Race, Class and Gestational Surrogacy in a Global Market*. New York: Routledge

Udwin, Leslee. 2015. *India's Daughter: The Story of Jyoti Singh*. Aired on BBC *Storyville*. 62 min.

United Nations. 1989. Convention on the Rights of the Child. November 20, 1989. https://ohchr.org/en/professionalinterest/pages/crc.aspx.

United Nations Population Fund. n.d. "The Dignity Project: A Journey toward Rights and Development." International Conference on Population and Development. Accessed January 29, 2021, https://www.unfpa .org/icpd.

University of Minnesota. 2021. "About." Gender, Women & Sexuality Studies. https://cla.umn.edu/gwss/about.

Valentine, David. 2007. *Imagining Transgender: An Ethnography of a Category*. Durham, NC: Duke University Press.

Vásquez, Elizabeth. 2008. "Familias alternativas." *Diario El Telégrafo*, June 22, 2008. http://paralegalidades.blogspot.com/2010/10/familias-alternativas -editorial-diario.html.

Vaughn, Richard. 2013. "Australian Surrogacy Laws." International Fertility Law Group, March 12, 2013. https://www.iflg.net/australian-surrogacy-laws.

Volkman, Toby Alice. 2005. "Introduction: New Geographies of Kinship." In *Cultures of Transnational Adoption*, edited by Toby Alice Volkman, 1–24. Durham, NC: Duke University Press.

V.Z. n.d. "Sissi brilla na terra sem preconceito no campo." *O Estado de São Paulo*.

Wade, Bex. 2018. "This New Feminist Antifa Group Is Taking on the Far-Right." *Vice*, October 15, 2018. https://www.vice.com/en_us/article/neg58q/feminist -antifascism-assembly-protest-london.

Wald, Gayle. 2009. "Rosetta Tharpe and Feminist 'Un-forgetting.'" *Journal of Women's History* 21 (4): 157–60.

Walsh, Catherine. 2009. "The Plurinational and Intercultural State: Decolonization and State Re-founding in Ecuador." *Kult*, no. 6, 65–74.

Weinbaum, Alys E. *The Modern Girl around the World: Consumption, Modernity, and Globalization*. Durham, NC: Duke University Press, 2008.

Weitzman, Lenore J., and Diane Rizzo. 1974. *Biased Textbooks: Action Steps You Can Take*. Washington, DC: Resource Center on Sex Roles in Education.

Whittaker, Andrea. 2009. "Global Technologies and Transnational Reproduction in Thailand." *Asian Studies Review* 33 (3): 319–32.

Whittaker, Andrea, and Amy Speier. 2010. "'Cycling Overseas': Care, Commodification, and Stratification in Cross-Border Reproductive Travel." *Medical Anthropology* 29 (4): 363–83.

Wiegman, Robyn. 2012. *Object Lessons*. Durham, NC: Duke University Press.

Williams, Patricia J. 1991. *The Alchemy of Race and Rights: Diary of a Law Professor*. Cambridge, MA: Harvard University Press.

WLSA Moçambique (Women and Law in Southern Africa Research and Education Trust). 2016. "Who's Afraid of Children's Rights? Police Repression against Street Action That Was Pushing for an End to Violence against the Girl in School." WLSA, http://www.wlsa.org.mz/whos-afraid-of-childrens -rights.

Women on Words and Images. 1972. *Dick and Jane as Victims: Sex Stereotyping in Children's Readers*. Princeton, NJ: Women on Words and Images.

Wood, Josh. 2020. "She Should Be with Us: Louisville Protestors Remember Breonna Taylor." *Guardian*, June 6, 2020. https://www.theguardian.com/us -news/2020/jun/06/breonna-taylor-louisville-protest-george-floyd.

Wotipka, Christine Min, and Francisco O. Ramirez. 2008. "Women's Studies as a Global Innovation." In *The Worldwide Transformation of Higher Education*, edited by David P. Baker and Alexander W. Wiseman, 89–110. Bradford, UK: Emerald Group.

Wright, Melissa. 2006. *Disposable Women and Other Myths of Global Capitalism*. New York: Routledge.

Yanagisako, Sylvia Junko. 2002. *Producing Culture and Capital: Family Firms in Italy*. Princeton, NJ: Princeton University Press.

Yashar, Deborah J. 2005. *Contesting Citizenship in Latin America: The Rise of Indigenous Movements and the Postliberal Challenge*. Cambridge: Cambridge University Press.

Yegenoglu, Meyda. 1998. *Colonial Fantasies: Towards a Feminist Reading of Orientalism*. Cambridge: Cambridge University Press.

Yuval-Davis, Nira. 1997. *Gender and Nation*. London: Sage.

Yuval-Davis, Nira. 1999. "What Is Transversal Politics?" *Soundings*, no. 12, 94–98.

Zambeze University. 2017. "Statement to Staff, Faculty, and Students." Directorate for Community Affairs, March 28, 2017.

Zamosc, Leon. 2007. "The Indian Movement and Political Democracy in Ecuador." *Latin American Politics and Society* 49 (3): 1–34.

Editors

ASHWINI TAMBE is professor of Women, Gender, and Sexuality Studies at the University of Maryland, College Park. In the fall of 2021, she will be the director of Women's, Gender, and Sexuality Studies and professor of history at George Washington University. Her research interests are transnational feminist theory, sexual regulation in South Asia, and global political economy. She is also the editorial director of *Feminist Studies* (http://www.feministstudies.org/home.html), the oldest journal of interdisciplinary feminist scholarship in the United States. She is the author of *Defining Girlhood in India: A Transnational History of Sexual Maturity Laws* (2019), which examines the legal paradoxes in age standards for sexual consent in India. Her first monograph, *Codes of Misconduct: Regulating Prostitution in Late Colonial Bombay* (2009), traces the history of Bombay's red-light zone and the moral panics it incited. She also coedited (with Harald Fischer-Tiné) *The Limits of British Colonial Control in South Asia* (2008), which foregrounds social disorder in port cities in the Indian Ocean. Her journal articles span topics such as age as a category of analysis (*American Historical Review*, 2020), nationalism and reproduction (*South Asia*, 2019), street harassment and class politics in India (*Interventions*, 2013), climatology in scientific racism (*Theory, Culture and Society*, 2011), interdisciplinary approaches to feminist state theory (*Comparative Studies of South Asia, Africa and the Middle East*, 2010), and the long record of transnational approaches in feminist scholarship (*New Global Studies*, 2010).

MILLIE THAYER is associate professor of sociology at the University of Massachusetts Amherst and is affiliated with the Center for Latin American, Caribbean and Latino Studies and the Department of Women, Gender, and Sexuality Studies. She was a member of the *Feminist Studies* editorial collective in 2005–7 and 2010–17. Her book *Making Transnational Feminism: Rural Women, NGO Activists, and Northern Donors in Brazil* (2010) is an ethnography of cross-border feminist relationships. She is a coeditor of and contributor to *Beyond Civil Society: Activism, Participation, and Protest in Latin America* (Duke University Press, 2017), *Translocalities/ Translocalidades: Feminist Politics of Translation in the Latin/a Américas* (Duke University Press, 2014), and *Global Ethnography: Forces, Connections, and Imaginations in a Postmodern World* (2000). Her articles have addressed topics including the travels and translation of feminist discourses across national borders and social contexts, as well as the fraught relationships between activists and donors in the international aid chain. Her most recent project, based on case studies in Brazil and Mozambique, concerns the challenges of economic and political sustainability for feminist movements in the Global South.

Authors

MARY BERNSTEIN is professor of sociology at the University of Connecticut. She publishes broadly in the fields of social movements, politics, race, sexualities, gender, and law. She is winner of the American Sociological Association's 2017 Simon and Gagnon Lifetime Achievement Award for the Sociology of Sexualities and the Outstanding Article Award from the American Sociological Association Section on Collective Behavior and Social Movements (2009) for "Culture, Power, and Institutions: A Multi-institutional Politics Approach to Social Movements" (coauthored with Elizabeth Armstrong). Her research appears in a wide range of journals including the *American Sociological Review*, *American Journal of Sociology*, *Sociological Perspectives*, *Feminist Studies*, *Gender and Society*, *Social Politics*, and the NYU *Review of Law and Social Change*. She is coeditor of three books: *Queer Families, Queer Politics* (2001); *Queer Mobilizations: LGBT Activists Confront the Law* (2009); and *The Marrying Kind? Debating Same-Sex Marriage within the Lesbian and Gay Movement* (2013). Her current research examines gun violence prevention activism.

ISABEL MARIA CORTESÃO CASIMIRO is assistant professor of sociology and researcher at the Centro de Estudos Africanos, Universidade Eduardo Mondlane, Maputo, Mozambique. Her research interests include women's and human rights, feminist movements, development issues, and participatory democracy. She is coauthor of "A epidemia de HIV/Aids e a ação do Estado: Diferenças entre Brasil, África do Sul e Moçambique" (*Revista Katálysis*, 2014).

RAFAEL DE LA DEHESA is associate professor in the Department of Sociology and Anthropology at the College of Staten Island and with the Sociology Program at the Graduate Center of the City University of New York. His research interests include gender and sexuality, political sociology, social movements, social theory, and Latin American studies. He is the author of *Queering the Public Sphere in*

Mexico and Brazil: Sexual Rights Movements in Emerging Democracies (Duke University Press, 2010).

CARMEN L. DÍAZ ALBA is professor at ITESO, The Jesuit University of Guadalajara, Mexico, where she teaches history and politics in Latin America and feminist studies, and collaborates with the peace and human rights master's program. Her research interests are transnational feminist movements, Latin American politics, gender, and social movements. She is the author of "Feministas en movimiento: La red #YoVoy8deMarzo," in *México en movimientos: Resistencias y alternativas,* edited by Geoffrey Pleyers and Manuel Garza Zepeda (2017).

INDERPAL GREWAL is professor emerita in the Program in Women's, Gender, and Sexuality Studies at Yale University. Her current research interests include theorizations of patriarchy and security transnationally; essays on gender, violence, and counterinsurgency in India; and a book project on masculinity and bureaucracy in postcolonial India. Her most recent book is an examination of American exceptionalism and white sovereignty after neoliberalism, *Saving the Security State: Exceptional Citizens in Twenty-First-Century America* (Duke University Press, 2017).

CHRISTINE "CRICKET" KEATING is associate professor in the Gender, Women, and Sexuality Studies Department at the University of Washington and a codirector of the Escuela Popular Norteña. Her research is in the areas of feminist political theory, decolonial politics, popular education, coalition building, and transnational feminist theory. She is the author of *Decolonizing Democracy: Transforming the Social Contract in India* (2011) and a coeditor of LGBTQ *Politics: A Critical Reader* (2017).

AMY LIND is the Taft Research Center director and faculty chair as well as the Mary Ellen Heintz Professor of the Department of Women's, Gender, and Sexuality Studies at the University of Cincinnati. Her areas of scholarship and teaching include critical development studies, global political economy, postcolonial studies, queer theory, transnational feminisms, social movements, and studies of neoliberal governance. She is the author of *Gendered Paradoxes: Women's Movements, State Restructuring, and Global Development in Ecuador* (2005), a coeditor of *Feminist (Im)Mobilities in Fortress(ing) North America: Rights, Citizenships and Identities in Transnational Perspective* (2013), and editor of *Development, Sexual Rights and Global Governance* (2010).

LAURA L. LOVETT is associate professor of history at the University of Pittsburgh. Her scholarship concentrates on twentieth-century US women's history with special focus on the histories of childhood, youth movements, and the family. She is the author of *Conceiving the Future: Pronatalism, Reproduction, and the Family in the United States, 1890–1930* (2007) and coeditor of *When We Were Free to Be: Looking Back at a Children's Classic and the Difference It Made* (2012). Her biography of activist Dorothy Pitman Hughes, *With Her Fist Raised: Dorothy Pitman Hughes and the Transformative Power of Community Activism*, is forthcoming in 2021.

KATHRYN MOELLER is assistant professor of educational policy studies at the University of Wisconsin–Madison. Her scholarship examines the gendered, sexualized, and racialized nature of corporate power. She is the author of *The Gender Effect: Capitalism, Feminism, and the Corporate Politics of Development* (2018).

NANCY A. NAPLES is the Board of Trustees Distinguished Professor of Sociology and Women's, Gender, and Sexuality Studies at the University of Connecticut. Her research interest is in how social actors are implicated by and resist controlling and oppressive extralocal economic and political structures and policies such as welfare, immigration, and austerity policies. She is the editor of *The Companion to Women's and Gender Studies* (2020), *The Companion to Sexuality Studies* (2020), and *The Companion to Feminist Studies* (2021).

JENNIFER C. NASH is Jean Fox O'Barr Professor of Gender, Sexuality, and Feminist Studies at Duke University. Her research centers on Black feminist theories, Black sexual politics, and the intersection of race, gender, law, and visual culture. She is the author of *The Black Body in Ecstasy: Reading Race, Reading Pornography* (Duke University Press, 2014) and *Black Feminism Reimagined: After Intersectionality* (Duke University Press, 2019).

AMRITA PANDE is associate professor of sociology at the University of Cape Town, South Africa. Her research focuses on globalization, reproductive labor, and new reproductive technologies. She is the author of *Wombs in Labor: Transnational Commercial Surrogacy in India* (2014). She is also an educator-performer and tours the world with a performance lecture series, *Made in India: Notes from a Baby Farm*, based on her ethnographic work on surrogacy. She is currently writing a monograph on the "global fertility flows" of eggs, sperms, embryos, and wombs connecting the world in unexpected ways.

SRILA ROY is associate professor of sociology and chair of development studies at the University of the Witwatersrand, South Africa. She is the author of *Remembering Revolution: Gender, Violence and Subjectivity in India's Naxalbari Movement* (2012), editor of *New South Asian Feminisms* (2012), and coeditor of *New Subaltern Politics: Reconceptualizing Hegemony and Resistance in Contemporary India* (2015). She is currently writing a monograph on queer feminist politics in liberalized India and coediting a volume of essays on #MeToo in India and South Africa.

CARA K. SNYDER is assistant professor of women's, gender, and sexuality studies at the University of Louisville. Her research and teaching interests include transnational feminisms, LGBT+ studies, physical culture/sport, Latin American studies, and digital studies. She has published articles on the whitening of Brazilian women's soccer (*Women's Studies Quarterly*, 2018), the role of digital media in transnational feminist protest (*Ada: A Journal of Gender, New Media, and Technology*, 2018), and feminist mobilization amid Brazil's current political crisis (*Journal of International Women's Studies*, 2019). Snyder is currently writing a book on the activism of women and LGBT+ footballers in contemporary Brazil.

CATARINA CASIMIRO TRINDADE is a Mozambican feminist and an independent gender consultant with a recent PhD in social sciences from the Universidade Estadual de Campinas in Brazil, where she researched the field around women's rights and gender equality in Mozambique, focusing on generations of feminists who are part of it. She worked in one of the first women's rights associations in Mozambique, as a program officer and also as a gender technician, giving gender training around the country. Her research interests include gender, feminism, women's movements, and women's endogenous savings practices.